This book offers new thinking about the processes of political and cultural change in the early Middle Ages. The main focus is on relations between the centre and periphery of the Carolingian empire, in particular on the development of Brittany as a territorial principality in the ninth and tenth centuries.

A major theme is the interaction of Carolingian imperial policies, Frankish aristocratic feuding, and local Breton communities. Other issues discussed include economy and society in Brittany and Neustria, the impact of Carolingian imperialism on local Breton communities, changes in the political, ecclesiastical, and social structures arising from Carolingian overlordship of Brittany, the interaction of Celtic and Carolingian culture, and the construction of an early medieval ethnic identity. The book shows how regional autonomy and self-regulating villages were as integral to the Carolingian world as court politics, cultural imperialism and frontier strife, and it argues that, in order to understand both the establishment and the collapse of the Carolingian empire, politics at the periphery demand as much attention as politics at the centre.

Cambridge studies in medieval life and thought

PROVINCE AND EMPIRE

Cambridge studies in medieval life and thought
Fourth series

General Editor:

D. E. LUSCOMBE

Professor of Medieval History, University of Sheffield

Advisory Editors:

R. B. DOBSON

Professor of Medieval History, University of Cambridge, and Fellow of Christ's College

ROSAMOND MCKITTERICK

*Reader in Early Medieval European History, University of Cambridge,
and Fellow of Newnham College*

The series Cambridge Studies in Medieval Life and Thought was inaugurated by G. G. Coulton in 1920. Professor D. E. Luscombe now acts as General Editor of the Fourth Series, with Professor R. B. Dobson and Dr Rosamond McKitterick as Advisory Editors. The series brings together outstanding work by medieval scholars over a wide range of human endeavour extending from political economy to the history of ideas.

For a list of titles in the series, see end of book.

PROVINCE AND EMPIRE

Brittany and the Carolingians

JULIA M. H. SMITH

Associate Professor of History, Trinity College, Hartford

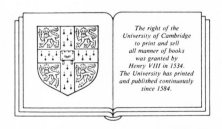

The right of the
University of Cambridge
to print and sell
all manner of books
was granted by
Henry VIII in 1534.
The University has printed
and published continuously
since 1584.

CAMBRIDGE UNIVERSITY PRESS

CAMBRIDGE

NEW YORK   PORT CHESTER

MELBOURNE   SYDNEY

Published by the Press Syndicate of the University of Cambridge
The Pitt Building, Trumpington Street, Cambridge CB2 1RP
40 West 20th Street, New York, NY 10011-4211, USA
10 Stamford Road, Oakleigh, Melbourne 3166, Australia

First published 1992

Printed in Great Britain at the University Press, Cambridge

A cataloguing record for this book is available from the British Library

Library of Congress cataloguing in publication data
Smith, Julia M. H.
Province and empire: Brittany and the Carolingians / Julia M. H.
Smith.
p.   cm. – (Cambridge studies in medieval life and thought:
4th ser., 18)
Includes index.
ISBN 0 521 38285 8
1. Brittany (France) – History.   2. France – History – To 987.
3. Carolingians.   I. Title.   II. Series.
DC611.B856S65   1992
944'.1–dc20   91-14286 CIP

ISBN 0 521 38285 8 hardback

UP

For my parents,
who took me to Brittany
for the first time in 1962

CONTENTS

ILLUSTRATIONS

ACKNOWLEDGEMENTS

The seeds of this book were sown when I began postgraduate study in 1978. That they bore fruit at all, first in my 1985 Oxford DPhil. thesis, and now in these pages, is due to the nurturing of many friends and scholars. A decade as a gipsy scholar, always with an unfinished thesis or book manuscript in my luggage, retarded the harvest but provided nutrients vital for germination. I have been particularly lucky to benefit from so many undergraduate audiences and so many colleagues, in the UK in Oxford, Sheffield, St Andrews, Manchester, and Cambridge and in the US in Hartford. I know that I owe debts to many unrecorded conversations and letters.

Especial gratitude needs to be expressed, however, to those whose sustained influence has helped me at every step of the way. In the first place are two now departed teachers. As my undergraduate Director of Studies at Newnham College, Kathleen Hughes fostered my historical interests. Despite her untimely death in 1977, her work on early medieval Ireland has always been a model for me of the benefits of viewing Celtic cultures in a broad perspective, and an inspiration in its lucid and elegant presentation of obscure and difficult material. I was therefore particularly honoured to be awarded the Kathleen Hughes Memorial Research Fellowship by Newnham College, which enabled me to write much of the final version of this book in Cambridge in 1988–9. To my thesis supervisor, the late Michael Wallace-Hadrill, I owe the initial suggestion that I consider working on the Bretons. His own inimitably high standards inspired me as a postgraduate, and his patient supervision taught me to keep my attention focussed on the larger issues. Neither can be replaced.

Foremost amongst those who have helped me more recently is Rosamond McKitterick. As undergraduate supervisor at Cambridge, mentor, and latterly editor, her friendship and critical comments have always been crucial. Wendy Davies and Janet Nelson have both given me generous access to their own work before publication, as well as frequent advice, encouragement, and inspiration. All three have saved me from a multitude of errors. In examining my DPhil. thesis, Michael Jones and Karl Leyser provided valuable comments which initiated the transformation from dissertation to book. I am also grateful to John Contreni, Robert Deshman, Sarah Foot, and Huw Pryce for sharing articles in the course of publication with me, to Jean-Pierre Brunterc'h for giving me permission to read his Ecole des Chartes thesis, and to Karl-Ferdinand Werner for giving me access to the typescript of the chapter on Brittany in his unpublished 1961 Heidelberg Habilitationsschrift. I inflicted a draft of the entire book on Michael Bentley, Kathleen Kete, Rosamond McKitterick, and Janet Nelson, and of individual chapters or sections on Simon Coupland, Wendy Davies, David Ganz, Oliver Padel, and Ian Wood. All have done much to improve it. All these and many other friends on both sides of the Atlantic have provided the encouragement and support which can never be footnoted.

To the librarians of all the places where I have studied and taught I am grateful for their help in gathering material, most particularly to Pat Bunker and Linda McKinney of Trinity College, whose interest and efficiency have made it possible for me to go on writing at Hartford. In the final stages of completion, Lesley Abrams and Sarah Foot have been my lifeline, responding to frantic e-mail messages by checking references or sending xeroxes across the Atlantic.

I am happy to acknowledge financial help from the American Council of Learned Societies who awarded me a grant-in-aid in 1988, and from Trinity College for generous help at all stages of preparation of the manuscript.

ABBREVIATIONS

AASS	*Acta Sanctorum quotquot toto orbe coluntur*, ed. J. Bollandus *et al.* (Antwerp and Brussels, 1643–present)
AASS OSB	*Acta Sanctorum Ordinis Sancti Benedicti*, ed. J. Mabillon, 9 vols. (Paris 1668–1701)
AB	*Annales de Saint-Bertin*, ed. F. Grat, J. Viellard, and S. Clémencet (Paris, 1964)
AF	*Annales Fuldenses*, ed. F. Kurze, MGH SSRG (Hanover, 1891)
ARF	*Annales Regni Francorum*, ed. F. Kurze, MGH SSRG (Hanover, 1895)
BL	British Library, London
BM	Bibliothèque Municipale
BN	Bibliothèque Nationale, Paris
Charlemagne's Heir	*Charlemagne's Heir: New Perspectives on the Reign of Louis the Pious (814–840)*, ed. P. Godman and R. Collins (Oxford, 1990)
Charles the Bald	*Charles the Bald: Court and Kingdom*, ed. M. T. Gibson and J. L. Nelson (2nd revised edn, Aldershot, 1990)
CR	*Cartulaire de l'Abbaye de Redon en Bretagne*, ed. A. de Courson, Documents Inédits sur l'Histoire de France (Paris, 1863) (charters cited by editor's numbering)
CR A	*Cartulaire de Redon*, Appendix
DA	*Deutsches Archiv für die Erforschung des Mittelalters*
EC	*Etudes Celtiques*
GSR	*The Monks of Redon: Gesta Sanctorum Rotonensium and Vita Conwoionis*, ed. C. Brett, Studies in Celtic History 10 (Woodbridge, 1989)

Abbreviations

Karl der Grosse	*Karl der Grosse: Lebenswerk und Nachleben*, ed. K. Braunfels, 4 vols. (Düsseldorf, 1965)
MGH	Monumenta Germaniae Historica
AA	Auctores Antiquissimi
Capit.	Capitularia Regum Francorum, Legum Section II
Conc.	Concilia, Legum Sectio III
D.Ger.	Diplomata Regum Germaniae ex stirpe Karolinorum
D.Kar.	Diplomata Karolinorum
Epp.	Epistolae
Form.	Formulae Merowingici et Karolini Aevi, Legum Section V
Poet.	Poetae Latini Aevi Carolini
SS	Scriptores, in folio
SSRG	Scriptores Rerum Germanicarum in usum scholarum separatim editi
SSRM	Scriptores Rerum Merovingicarum
Morice, *Preuves*	H. Morice, *Mémoires pour servir de Preuves à l'Histoire Ecclésiastique et Civile de Bretagne*, 3 vols. (Paris, 1742–6)
MSHAB	*Mémoires de la Société d'Histoire et d'Archéologie de Bretagne*
PL	Patrologiae Cursus Completus, Series Latina, ed. J.-P. Migne, 221 vols. (Paris, 1844–64)
Settimane	*Settimane di Studio del Centro Italiano di Studi sull'Alto Medioevo*

NOTE ON NOMENCLATURE

In the face of natural scribal variability of spelling, compounded with the problem of poor editions of late manuscripts of early medieval texts, I have found it impossible to adopt any consistent orthography for Old Breton names. Rather than striving for a normalised, hypothetical philological exactitude, I have preferred name forms which will enable the reader to locate the characters easily in the sources and to identify them under the guise of different spellings in other scholars' work. Hence, for Breton names known only through the Latinised form used by a Frankish writer, I have followed that spelling (e.g. Gurhamius), but have preferred the spelling of Breton sources to Frankish ones where possible (Erispoe, not Herispogius, Respogius as in the Annals of Saint-Bertin). Where there are name forms in common English usage for both Frankish and Breton names, I have used those (Charles, Lambert, Winwaloe) and have throughout avoided French forms (Noménoé, Guénolé, Melaine). When saints' names have become modern place-names or the names of churches, I have referred to the place or the church by its commonly known name (Saint-Pol, Saint-Maixent).

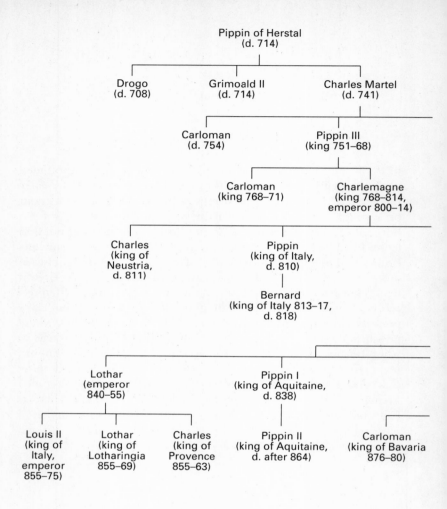

Figure 1   Carolingian kings and emperors

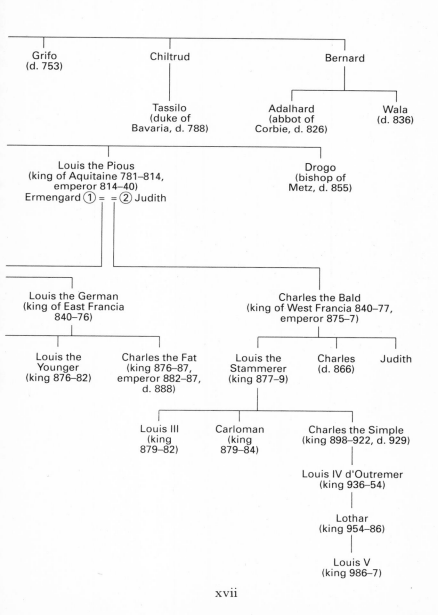

Grifo
(d. 753)

Chiltrud

Bernard

Tassilo
(duke of
Bavaria, d. 788)

Adalhard
(abbot of
Corbie, d. 826)

Wala
(d. 836)

Louis the Pious
(king of Aquitaine 781–814,
emperor 814–40)
Ermengard ① = = ② Judith

Drogo
(bishop of
Metz, d. 855)

Louis the German
(king of East Francia
840–76)

Charles the Bald
(king of West Francia 840–77,
emperor 875–7)

Louis the
Younger
(king 876–82)

Charles the Fat
(king 876–87,
emperor 882–87,
d. 888)

Louis the
Stammerer
(king 877–9)

Charles
(d. 866)

Judith

Louis III
(king
879–82)

Carloman
(king
879–84)

Charles the Simple
(king 898–922, d. 929)

Louis IV d'Outremer
(king 936–54)

Lothar
(king 954–86)

Louis V
(king 986–7)

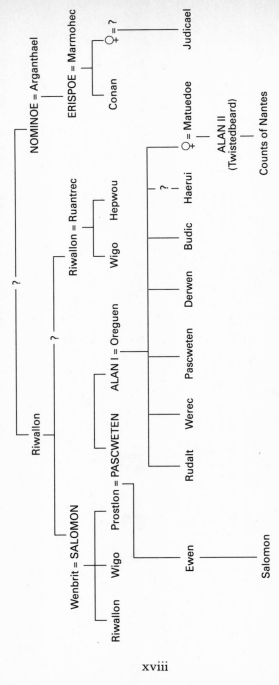

Figure 2   The rulers of Carolingian Brittany

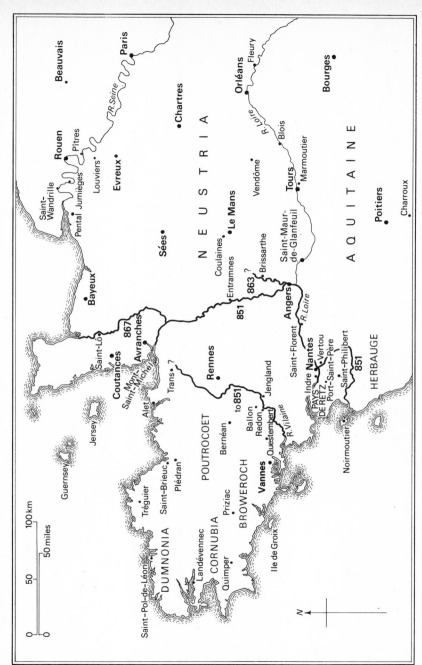

Map 1 Neustria, Brittany, and northern Aquitaine

Beauvais
Paris
Chartres
Bourges
Rouen
Pîtres
Louviers
Evreux
Orléans
Fleury
Saint-Wandrille
Pental Jumièges
Blois
R. Seine
N E U S T R I A
Le Mans
Vendôme
Tours
Marmoutier
R. Loire
Bayeux
Sées
Coulaines
Brissarthe
Saint-Maur-de-Glanfeuil
Poitiers
Charroux
A Q U I T A I N E
Saint-Lô
Entramnes
863 ?
851
Angers
R. Loire
867
Avranches
Coutances
Saint-Mont-Michel
Rennes
Saint-Florent
Nantes
Vertou
Port-Saint-Père
Saint-Philibert
851
HERBAUGE
Jersey
Alet
Trans ?
POUTROCOET
to 851
Jengland
Indre
PAYS DE RETZ
Saint-Brieuc
Plédran
Bernéan
Ballon
Redon
Questembert
R. Vilaine
Noirmoutier
Tréguier
Priziac
BROWEROCH
Vannes
Guernsey
Saint-Pol-de-Léon
Landévennec
CORNUBIA
DUMNONIA
Quimper
Ile de Groix

100 km
50 miles
50
N

xix

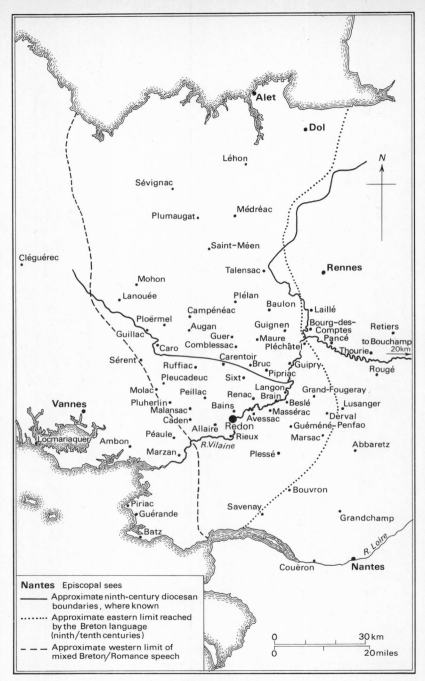

Map 2   Redon and environs

xx

INTRODUCTION

This book is about the fundamental political and social changes that often occur on the periphery of dynamic and rapidly evolving societies. This familiar theme in European history recurs from the time of Graeco-Roman expansion into the western Mediterranean and its hinterland in the sixth century BC onwards, to colonisation of the Americas and Africa starting in the fifteenth century AD. In the ancient world and the Middle Ages, historians can all too rarely study this process from the point of view of both the aggressor and the periphery, for their problem is most frequently that of literate aggressor and non-literate periphery.[1] Only where one literate culture enlarged its frontiers at the expense of another has it been possible to examine in any detail the new societies which evolved in the wake of aggression and conquest. For the Middle Ages, this has enabled studies to be undertaken of the socio-political structures which emerged around the Mediterranean as Latin Christendom expanded at the expense of Islam in the eleventh and twelfth centuries. Long before the Reconquista or the Crusades, however, north-western Europe had evolved a militant, expansionist society with its own moral identity and religious justification: Charlemagne's imperial coronation on Christmas Day, 800, was the consummation of all the Franks' aggressive and ideological inclinations. Just as militarised Germanic tribes with permanent, hierarchical power structures had earlier developed in response to the trans-Rhenine attacks of Rome's imperial armies, so new political entities emerged around the rim of the Carolingian empire.[2] In response

---

[1] As, for example, C. R. Whittaker, 'Trade and frontiers of the Roman empire', in *Trade and Famine in Classical Antiquity*, ed. P. Garnsey and C. R. Whittaker, Proceedings of the Cambridge Philological Society Supplement 8 (Cambridge, 1983), pp. 110–27; B. Cunliffe, *Greeks, Romans and Barbarians: Spheres of Interaction* (London, 1988).

[2] The changes in Germanic society that resulted from Roman pressure are most recently analysed by L. Hedeager, 'Empire, frontier and the barbarian hinterland: Rome and

to Frankish pressure, loose confederations of tribes were consolidated into new Christian kingdoms in Scandinavia and in the Slav lands of central Europe. Both these regions typify the historian's dilemma, for literacy was only introduced there when Christianity was propagated by the empire. Amongst Scandinavians as amongst Slavs, the early stages of political and social response to Carolingian and subsequently Ottonian pressure can only be studied obliquely, through the archaeological record or through the comments (often hostile) of observers within the aggressor society.

There is one region of early medieval Europe where this constraint does not apply. Brittany was the victim of Carolingian attack; it was also a literate society. We have here a unique opportunity to study the way in which the powerful, relatively cohesive Carolingian state affected a peripheral region from the vantage points of both aggressor and subject people. Thanks to the Bretons' own record-making traditions, the profound changes which came in the wake of Carolingian expansion can be documented from the perspective of the local communities of small-holders who found themselves caught up willy-nilly in the turbulent politics of the Carolingian world. In Brittany, more clearly than anywhere else in the early Middle Ages, we can understand how the margin of a powerful state might be the crucible for the formation of a new political entity.

Despite my preoccupation with what happened at the outer edge of the Carolingian world, I have deliberately eschewed characterising Brittany as a 'frontier society'. This is for several reasons. In the first place, frontier studies of both the ancient and the modern worlds are often preoccupied with the frontier as a distinctive economic and/or military system occupying the zone between two societies enjoying very different forms of political and economic structure.[3] However, of economic interchange between Franks and Bretons, very little that is precise can be said. As will emerge, in many ways the two societies were similar in

northern Europe from AD 1–400', in *Centre and Periphery in the Ancient World*, ed. M. Rowlands, M. Larsen, and K. Kristiansen (Cambridge, 1987), pp. 125–40.

[3] A convenient introduction for medievalists to frontier studies and to the historiographical legacy of Frederick Jackson Turner is provided by R. I. Burns, 'The significance of the frontier in the Middle Ages', in *Medieval Frontier Societies*, ed. R. Bartlett and A. MacKay (Oxford, 1989), pp. 307–30. For an attempt to apply notions of the 'frontier' to the ninth century, see T. F. X. Noble, 'Louis the Pious and the frontiers of the Frankish realm', in *Charlemagne's Heir*, pp. 333–47.

the fundamental nature of their social and political forms. Secondly, in the classic Turnerian sense, colonisation is a salient feature of a frontier society, whereas the Franks never colonised Brittany. In the third place, a frontier implies that something lies beyond it: yet the westernmost *département* of Brittany is aptly named Finistère, 'land's end'. From a Frankish perspective, the Bretons lived 'at the farthest edge of Gaul', with only the sea beyond.[4]

Moreover, the very term 'frontier' is highly ambiguous. It often carries connotations of political, economic, or cultural difference, but need not necessarily do so. These overtones may obscure the way that boundaries or frontiers can themselves create these very differences.[5] In studying early medieval Brittany, we may indeed observe something of how ethnic identity was constructed. We can also see the Carolingian rhetoric of ethnic difference for what it was: a highly subjective perception exploited to justify political behaviour and hegemonic attitudes. To talk of Brittany as a frontier is to prejudge the issue.

Instead, lordship is the guiding theme which I have chosen to pursue through this study of the dynamics and impact of early medieval imperialism. I am concerned with lordship on all social levels and in all spatial contexts: at the centre of the Carolingian world, in regional society, on the periphery. My emphasis is on lordship over people at least as much as on lordship over land. Above all I am interested in the interaction of different forms of lordship: imperial patronage and local communities; secular power and ecclesiastical hierarchy; obligations of loyalty and economic exploitation; the ideology of imperial hegemony and the practicalities of control.

The changes induced by the Carolingians in Brittany are most evident in patterns of lordship. It is possible to trace in considerable detail the ways in which great resources of wealth and jurisdiction were gathered together into the hands of a single lordly dynasty and the concomitant formation of a new polity. Until the ninth century, several petty tribal kingships divided the Breton peninsula; after a century of Carolingian pressure, a greatly enlarged, unified, and enduring duchy had been created that was sufficiently powerful to retain a high degree of independence to

---

[4] *ARF*, a. 786, revised text, p. 72.
[5] Compare P. Sahlins, *Boundaries: The Making of France and Spain in the Pyrenees* (Berkeley, 1989).

the end of the Middle Ages. The questions I ask are all directed towards understanding this change. In the first two chapters, I explore the differing post-Roman histories of the two regions which came to make up the Breton principality: the one Breton-speaking with a strong cultural orientation towards the British Isles, the other linguistically, culturally, and politically (until the middle of the ninth century) part of Francia. The next two chapters examine the extent of Carolingian control of and direct influence in Brittany in the reigns of Louis the Pious and then of Charles the Bald. I discuss their concern with Brittany within the much broader context of traditions of imperial hegemony, and with reference to the tensions which kept Carolingian political activity focussed on members of the ruling dynasty, the *stirps regia* itself. In these chapters, the dynamics of the Carolingian state, and the balance of centripetal and centrifugal forces within it, are traced all the way from the centre to the periphery. In chapter 5, on the anatomy of power, I assemble the evidence for the profound changes in the scope and uses of power within Brittany itself, and consider to what extent Carolingian pressure provoked them. The sixth chapter, on learning and ecclesiastical lordship, explores the tension between Carolingian norms of ecclesiastical order and Breton particularism, and demonstrates how Carolingian cultural influence and Breton ecclesiastical recalcitrance went hand in hand. In all these sections, the focus constantly shifts back and forth from the Carolingian and imperial to the Breton and local – between the 'macroscopic' and the 'molecular'.[6] Finally, I trace the breakdown of the Carolingian political process in the tenth century, and with that the contraction of horizons from the empire as a whole down to regional arenas of activity. The book concludes by noting the emergence of a new pattern of political life and new ways of exercising power in the eleventh century.

Through these chapters, I consider how and why Brittany emerged as a territorial principality. But there is also a strong Carolingian sub-theme running through them, for here at the periphery the strengths and weaknesses of the Carolingian state are most sharply etched. The importance of personal bonds of loyalty, the crucial role of Frankish aristocrats as mediators of royal power, the significance of the church as an instrument of lordship and as the purveyor of cultural and political norms are all

---

[6] I have borrowed the terms from Sahlins, *Boundaries*, p. xv.

4

evident. By means such as these political power was conveyed from the royal court to the farthest edges of the Carolingian empire. At the periphery, we also see clearly how Carolingian political life was articulated by ritual gestures of deeply Christian significance, and expressed in an ideology which equated political opposition with moral depravity. But here, far from the immediate authority of the royal presence, we can examine the rapidity with which ordered structures of lordship could break down in times of conflict, the ineffectiveness of the moral authority of the church when faced with intransigence and a differing political ethic, and the ease with which the Carolingian military machine could be stopped in its tracks.

Brittany has rarely fallen within the purview of Carolingian historiography. Scholarly investigation has been more concerned either with politics at the centre of the Carolingian empire, or with regional history *per se* (of either the French Annales school or the German Landesgeschichte variety), as applied to provinces fully within the Carolingian empire. Brittany has tended to be left to the Breton historians with their own patriotic agendas, or to Celtic philologists more concerned with establishing the universality of 'Celtic' society than with acknowledging how very localised all early medieval societies were. There is no need to rehearse here the main outlines of these two historiographical traditions; suffice it to say that in neither one have studies of the interactions of Franks and Bretons ever been prominent. In taking as my point of perspective the zone where direct rule gave way to assertions of overlordship, I have tried to write for two audiences who rarely have much to do with each other, Celticists on the one hand and students of the Carolingian world on the other. In order to do this, much has had to be taken for granted that would deserve a fuller discussion in a study of either just medieval Brittany or just the Carolingian empire.

In particular, I am aware that my understanding of the dynamics of Carolingian politics may seem unfamiliar and unorthodox to anyone schooled in French or German historiography. In keeping with a recent resurgence of interest in the political creativity of Charlemagne's successors, I am more interested in change than in decadence in the later ninth and tenth centuries. Seeking to understand the transformation of Carolingian society, I have not paused to dissect in any detail the predominant interpretive frameworks within which historians of

the early Middle Ages frequently work. I am acutely aware that
the current generation of scholars is effectively challenging many
of the common presuppositions upon which medievalists have
relied until recently. Especially in the UK, a structural understanding of the early Middle Ages is being superseded by a broad
perspective indebted to anthropologists for fresh paradigms.

On the other side of the coin, I am also aware that I have
probably been cavalier in my treatment of substantive issues and
problems in the history of Celtic-speaking regions, especially
some of the sharp philological debates which bear on the problem
of the origins of Breton society. After much reflection, I have also
concluded that my own understanding of early Breton society is
not enhanced by a hunt for points of comparison in early
medieval Wales, let alone Ireland. Linguistic affinities need not
generate closely related forms of social organisation, especially in
regions with such differing pasts. I have confined myself to
pointing out the evidence for cultural contact, wherever it exists,
and I have left untouched many of the thorny questions of mutual
influence or parallel evolution which would arise in a fuller
consideration of Brittany vis-à-vis the Brittonic regions of the
British Isles.

Whether pondering the debates about Carolingian or Celtic
societies in the early Middle Ages, my premise throughout has
been that all early medieval communities had much in common
with each other, but that all were intensely local and distinctive
in their particular complexion. Part of the singular nature of any
region lies simply in its extant sources. For Brittany, these are a
range of wildly disparate texts. I have spent many years puzzling
out how to juxtapose them in order to ask fruitful questions from
seemingly unrelated types of evidence, mostly consisting of
Breton charters and saints' lives, Frankish chronicles and papal
correspondence. Taken in its totality, this material in no way
provides an even, let alone exhaustive, coverage of early medieval
Breton history. Much of what follows tacitly acknowledges this,
and this book's contours are essentially those of the surviving
evidence. The narrative sections are fuller where the evidence
permits, sketchy where the sources are scanty. Much of the
discussion is conducted with reference to the local society of
south-eastern Brittany, because that is the area for which rich
charter evidence survives. Of communities elsewhere in Brittany,
we know nothing. Fruitful comparisons with other frontiers of

the Carolingian empire are only possible within the terms of the information provided by and attitudes expressed in Carolingian chronicles; in its local source material, Brittany is quite unparalleled. It is this anomalous provision of riches which makes this book at all possible.

Chapter 1

SETTLEMENT AND SOCIETY IN DARK AGE BRITTANY

Western Christendom in the early Middle Ages was a mosaic of local, small-scale societies. Each part of a mosaic has its own colours and patterns and dynamic; one portion may shade imperceptibly into the next, or be separated from it by clear boundaries and discontinuities of theme. And yet each individual piece is part of a whole in which meanings, rhythms, and techniques are common throughout. Thus it was in the early Middle Ages. Kingdoms, even empires, comprised provinces each with its own history, traditions, culture, social structure. Some regions had much in common with their neighbours; elsewhere formidable natural barriers and conflicting loyalties served to set communities apart. Nevertheless, throughout Europe, all societies derived almost all their wealth from an overwhelmingly agricultural economy, and did so in the face of high human mortality and low crop yields. Most, though not all, of Latin Christendom shared too a common, Roman past; everywhere the Christian church propagated a common morality and literary culture, and everywhere that culture found its own local and idiosyncratic expression.

Early medieval societies were also highly stratified: plunder, tribute, taxation, and other forms of surplus extraction sustained the power and status of a small elite. With rare exception, that stratification took for granted monarchy as the only appropriate form of government, whether or not the ruler's formal title was that of 'king'. Yet at the same time, communications were so rudimentary as to permit of no forms of government other than highly devolved ones: political power was diffused and frag-mented, shared in many different ways among many different groups. Any control over people or over land was a form of political power; only gradually did the authority of the state come to circumscribe it. From the most powerful of rulers – Charlemagne, Otto, or Cnut – through to the most petty chieftain or castellan, the essence of power was rooted in familial and domestic structures. Government took place in and through the household. The farmstead of a free peasant and the royal palace alike tessellated into the early medieval mosaic of households. And the mortar which held the tesserae together was always paternalistic authority and lordship: of father over family and household, of lord over warriors, of abbot over monastery, of king over retinue, of Christ over king. This intensely personal bond of mutual obligation and trust lay at the heart of early medieval society.[1]

Nowhere is this more evident than in the Carolingian world. Charlemagne's achievement was to create one huge and ramshackle empire out of many different provinces and small face-to-face communities. His lordship was founded on the martial prowess and willingness to share in governing of a warrior aristocracy; it was justified by reference to divine grace and the Christian ethics of the day. This vision of a Christian society, and the techniques of government and rhetoric of power developed by Charlemagne and his immediate successors Louis the Pious and Charles the Bald were to be of enduring influence, even in areas where Charlemagne himself never ruled.

I am writing about the place of one province within that Carolingian world. In Brittany, Carolingian influence was indeed of the utmost long-term significance. Yet here the Carolingians' claim to lordship was always insecure and the distinctive character of early medieval communities is immediately apparent. Hence, two main themes run throughout the chapters which follow. The first concerns the ways in which the Carolingians exercised their lordship over this people on the periphery of their empire. The second traces Carolingian influence within the region, and assesses

---

[1] For details of some of these points, see variously F. L. Cheyette, *Lordship and Community in Medieval Europe* (New York, 1968); R. Deshman, '*Christus Rex et magi reges*: kingship and Christology in Ottonian and Anglo-Saxon art', *Frühmittelalterliche Studien*, 10 (1976), 374–405; J. Fried, 'Der karolingische Herrschaftsverband im 9. Jh. zwischen "Kirche" und "Königshaus"', *Historische Zeitschrift*, 235 (1982), 1–43; R. Kottje, 'Einheit und Vielfalt des kirchlichen Lebens in der Karolingerzeit', *Zeitschrift für Kirchengeschichte*, 76 (1965), 323–42; T. Reuter, 'Plunder and tribute in the Carolingian empire', *Transactions of the Royal Historical Society*, 5th ser., 35 (1985), 75–94; S. Reynolds, *Kingdoms and Communities in Western Europe, 900–1300* (Oxford, 1984). See also R. Van Caenegem, 'Government, law and society', and J. L. Nelson, 'Kingship and empire', both in *The Cambridge History of Medieval Political Thought c. 350–c. 1450*, ed. J. H. Burns (Cambridge, 1988), pp. 174–210, 211–51.

how the local communities of Brittany responded. This book examines what the tensions between the centre and the periphery of an early medieval state meant in practice.

FROM ARMORICA TO BRITTANY

It is the purpose of this introductory chapter to sketch, as far as the meagre evidence allows, an outline of the Breton society with which the Carolingians came into conflict and which they so profoundly affected, to note some of the ways in which Brittany was like any other early medieval society, and to point up its more distinctive features. Most immediately striking is the fact that, alone of all the peoples on the European continent in the post-Roman world, the Bretons spoke (and some still do speak) a Celtic language. To account for this takes us to the heart of the traditions which differentiated Brittany from adjacent parts of Francia.

We have to begin in antiquity, when the region was but a part of the Roman *Tractus Armoricanus*, before something had happened to change its name to *Britannia*.[2] Jutting out from mainland Gaul across the southern approaches to the English Channel, the Armorican peninsula is a region which has always looked to the sea for its living as much as to the land. From prehistoric times onwards, trade routes linked the communities of the long, heavily indented Armorican coastal plain with the Atlantic coasts of the Iberian peninsula and with the south-eastern parts of the British Isles. Indeed, artefact distribution maps suggest that on the eve of the Caesarian conquest of Gaul, cross-channel affinities were stronger than those with the rest of central-northern Gaul.[3] Five hundred years of Roman rule did not shatter these cross-channel ties, but did integrate into the economy, administrative organisation, and defensive provisions of the rest of central and northern Gaul. Economic integration seems, however, to have been accompanied by a less fully Romanised way of life than that in neighbouring provinces.[4] In the western part of the

---

[2] The term *Armorica* referred to much of central Gaul; in the fourth century the *Tractus Armoricanus et Nervicanus* was defined as the provinces of *Aquitania* I and II and *Lugdunesis* II, III, and IV. *Notitia Dignitatum*, 37, ed. O. Seeck (Berlin, 1876), p. 206.

[3] P. R. Giot, J. L'Helgouach, and J. Briard, *Brittany*, Ancient Places and Peoples 13 (London, 1960); B. Cunliffe, 'Britain, the Veneti and beyond', *Oxford Journal of Archaeology*, 1 (1982), 39–68.

[4] P. Galliou, *L'Armorique Romaine* (Braspars, 1984), esp. pp. 232–5.

traditions made frequent reference to the passage of monks, frequently in the company of companions and relations, from south Wales, Cornwall, and sometimes Ireland across to Brittany.[16]

Nor is it possible to estimate the extent of any cross-channel migration that may have taken place. It is significant, however, that although the Bretons had their own name for themselves, *Letavii*, Frankish writers did not bother to differentiate between Bretons and Britons; to them, both alike were *Brittones*.[17] Throughout the Middle Ages, there remained an awareness of close affiliation between the Bretons on the one side of the Channel and the Cornish and Welsh on the other: at Llandaff, men remembered in the eleventh or twelfth century that the Welsh and Bretons 'were of one language and one people, although geographically separate'.[18]

Language certainly provides the best clue to the affinity between Bretons and Britons. Over the last hundred years there has been much fervent debate as to whether the Breton language was derived in essence from insular Brittonic or from the closely related continental Gaulish language.[19] Whatever the origins of the Breton language, three points clearly affirm the closeness of the linguistic tie to the British Isles: first, that Old Breton and Cornish, and in some important respects also Welsh, continued to evolve in parallel until the tenth or eleventh centuries.[20] In the second place, until the eleventh century, Old Breton shared a common orthography with Old Cornish and Welsh, which is

---

[16] Compare E. G. Bowen, *Saints, Seaways and Settlements in the Celtic Lands* (Cardiff, 1969), pp. 160–90; but note too the cautions of W. N. Yates, 'The "Age of Saints" in Carmarthenshire: a study of church dedications', *The Carmarthenshire Antiquary*, 9 (1973), 53–81.

[17] On *Letavii, Letavia*, see Fleuriot, *Origines*, pp. 53–4. This name may be insular in origin, and occurs in vernacular form in the tenth-century Old Welsh poem, *Armes Prydein*, lines 153, 174. *Armes Prydein. The Prophecy of Britain*, ed. I. Williams; English version by R. Bromwich, Medieval and Modern Welsh Studies 6 (Dublin, 1972), pp. 12, 14.

[18] *The Text of the Book of Llan Dâv*, ed. J. G. Evans and J. Rhys (Oxford, 1893), p. 181.

[19] The major contributions to the debate are J. Loth, *L'Emigration Bretonne du 5ᵉ au 7ᵉ siècle de notre ère* (Rennes, 1883); K. H. Jackson, *Language and History in Early Britain* (Edinburgh, 1953); F. Falc'hun, *L'Histoire de la Langue Bretonne d'après la Géographie Linguistique*, 2 vols. (2nd edn., Paris, 1963); Fleuriot, *Origines*.

[20] Jackson, *Language and History*, pp. 19–24; B. L. Olson and O. J. Padel, 'A tenth-century list of Cornish parochial saints', *Cambridge Medieval Celtic Studies*, 12 (1986), 33–71, at pp. 38–40; E. P. Hamp, 'Morphological correspondences in Cornish and Breton', *The Journal of Celtic Studies*, 2 (1953–8), 5–24.

presumed to be of insular British origin.[21] Third, the earliest extant Breton manuscripts are written in insular script, and those later Breton manuscripts written in Caroline minuscule continue to exhibit palaeographical features otherwise characteristic of early Welsh manuscripts.[22] In effect, in its earliest written form, in glosses of the late eighth and ninth centuries, Old Breton is thoroughly insular in appearance, and is almost indistinguishable from Old Welsh of the same date.

Thus, as in the pre-Roman period, close cross-channel contacts gave early medieval Brittany a cultural orientation towards the British Isles, and also contributed to the separate political evolution of the region in the Middle Ages. British settlement in Armorica was nevertheless part of the much wider pattern of social disruption and movement of people which affected both Gaul and the British Isles during and after the collapse of Roman rule. Although some Britons found new homes elsewhere on the Atlantic seaboard of mainland Europe in places as far apart as north-western Spain and Flanders,[23] only in the Armorican peninsula were language, social identity, and political structures profoundly and permanently affected.

The area thus transformed can be ascertained very approximately by mapping the area of Breton place-names from when they first appear in written form in the ninth century. It is, in effect, the area west of an S-shaped line from Mont-Saint-Michel to the head of the estuary of the Loire near Donges, a line which leaves Rennes and Nantes well to its east.[24] Despite traces of Romance-speaking enclaves in place-names west of this line,[25] Gallo-Romans and Brittonic settlers must have fairly rapidly coalesced into a people with a single, Breton, identity: all early medieval texts, Frankish and Breton, present the Bretons as a single people, a *gens* whose origin-legend looked back to the British Isles.

Although the Armorican peninsula was never as deeply

---

[21] Jackson, *Language and History*, pp. 67–75; Olson and Padel, 'Cornish parochial saints', p. 38. [22] For further details see below, pp. 167–8.

[23] Fleuriot, *Origines*, pp. 149–56; P. David, *Etudes Historiques sur la Galice et le Portugal du VIᵉ au XIIᵉ siècle* (Lisbon, 1947), pp. 57–63, with comments of E. A. Thompson, 'Britonia', in *Christianity in Britain, 300–700*, ed. M. W. Barley and R. P. C. Hanson (Leicester, 1968), pp. 201–5.

[24] The place-name evidence is usefully surveyed and bibliographical guidance provided by Chédeville and Guillotel, *Bretagne*, pp. 89–112.

[25] L. Fleuriot, 'Recherches sur les enclaves romanes anciennes en territoire bretonnant', *EC*, 8 (1958), 164–78.

Romanised as the rest of central Gaul, early medieval Breton society nevertheless evolved within a sub-Roman context. Roman roads criss-crossed the peninsula and influenced the evolving medieval settlement pattern; Roman habitation sites abounded and were quarried for building stone, built over or re-used, especially for churches. Bishoprics of late Roman foundation laid the basis for the medieval ecclesiastical organisation of the eastern half of the peninsula. The survival as bishops' sees of Rennes, Nantes, Vannes, and probably also Alet ensured some continuing occupation of these urban sites; the late Roman administrative boundaries which separated these dioceses from each other persisted, as they did in most other parts of Gaul.[26] However, it is far from certain whether there was ever a significant late Roman Christian presence in the fifth and westernmost *civitas*, that of the *Osismii*, and Roman boundaries did not survive into the Middle Ages in western Brittany.[27]

The remaining bishoprics in the region may all have been Breton foundations. Dol was first attested as a monastery in the eighth century, then as a bishopric in the second quarter of the ninth century; Quimper and Saint-Pol are both first mentioned in the middle of the ninth century; monastic foundations in origin, Saint-Brieuc and Tréguier were probably bishops' seats from the late tenth century.[28] Each of these hails a Breton saint as its founder. Circumstantial evidence suggests that the christianisation of Brittany took place in the context of close links with the British Isles. Of the plethora of very obscure saints whose names are compounded into Breton place-names, or who are recorded as the

---

[26] D. Aupest-Conduché, 'Quelques réflexions sur les débuts du Christianisme dans les diocèses de Rennes, Vannes et Nantes', *Annales de Bretagne*, 79 (1972), 135–47; L. Langouët, 'L'origine gallo-romaine de l'evêché d'Alet à la lumière des fouilles récentes', *Bulletin de la Société d'Histoire et d'Archéologie de l'Arrondissement de Saint-Malo* (1974), 95–107; L. Pietri and J. Biarne, *Topographie Chrétienne des Cités de la Gaule des origines au milieu du VIIIe siècle. V: Province Ecclésiastique de Tours (Lugdunensis Tertia)* (Paris, 1987). [27] Pape, *Osismes*, pp. 36–42, 228–9.

[28] The early history of the see of Dol is particularly obscure, and is bound up with controversies over the dating of the earliest life of its founder, Samson. The *Vita Samsonis* aside, the earliest references to Dol are as a monastery in the *Martyrologium Hieronymianum* of 722, AASS Nov. ii.i, 97, and as the seat of a bishop called John who presided at the translation of the relics of St Leutfred at La-Croix-Saint-Leufroi in the second quarter of the ninth century. *Vita et Miracula Leutfredi Abbatis Madriacensis*, 25, MGH SSRM vii.i, 16. For full bibliography on the first life of Samson, see M. Lapidge and R. Sharpe, *A Bibliography of Celtic-Latin Literature, 400–1200* (Dublin, 1985), no. 950, p. 261. On the foundation of Saint-Brieuc and Tréguier, see A. Chédeville and N.-Y. Tonnerre, *La Bretagne Féodale, XIe–XIIIe siècle* (Rennes, 1987), pp. 31–2.

patrons of churches, many recur in Wales, Cornwall, or both.[29] Furthermore, Brittany shares with Wales and Cornwall a toponymy which is overwhelmingly religious in character, and in which certain generic elements are again common to all three regions.[30] Although no clear chronology of Breton place-name formation can be established, the names themselves are strongly suggestive of close ecclesiastical contacts with Britain. Another pointer in this direction is the diffusion of texts and ideas. In particular, the sphere of influence of Gildas and his writings indicates that, especially in the sixth century, churches in Brittany, as well as in Cornwall and Ireland, were indebted to Wales for spiritual guidance.[31] Subsequent ecclesiastical traditions were influenced by these contacts.

Language and culture oriented post-Roman Brittany firmly towards south-west Britain. Not until the ninth century did the cultural influence of the neighbouring Frankish church begin to make itself felt; in the sixth and seventh centuries, few Merovingian churchmen bothered themselves with the Bretons.[32] Isolated from the adjacent regions of Gaul by language and social identity, Breton society evolved its own characteristic social forms. That there also developed a tradition of resistance to Merovingian efforts to extend Frankish overlordship over the Bretons is clear from the work of the one Merovingian writer who was concerned about the Bretons, Gregory, bishop of Tours. Gregory provides our earliest evidence that the Armorican peninsula was under the political control of the Bretons.

[29] J. Loth, *Les Noms des Saints Bretons* (Paris, 1910); Olson and Padel, 'Cornish parochial saints'.
[30] B. Tanguy, 'L'hagio-onomastique bretonne: problématique et methodologie', *107ᵉ Congrès National des Sociétés Savantes, Brest, 1982. Philologie et Histoire jusqu'à 1610. II: Questions d'Histoire de Bretagne* (Paris, 1984), pp. 323–40. For a comparative discussion see O. J. Padel, *Cornish Place-Name Elements*, English Place-Name Society 56–7 (Nottingham, 1985), s.v. *lann, *lok, plu, tre*; O. J. Padel, 'Cornish names of parish churches', *Cornish Studies*, 4–5 (1976–7), 15–27; O. J. Padel, 'Cornish plu, "parish"', *Cornish Studies*, 2 (1974), 75–8. In certain important respects, however, Breton toponymy is distinctive.
[31] R. Sharpe, 'Gildas as a father of the church', in *Gildas: New Approaches*, ed. M. Lapidge and D. Dumville, Studies in Celtic History 5 (Woodbridge, 1984), pp. 191–205.
[32] Merovingian ecclesiastics active in the area immediately east of Brittany were apparently oblivious to the existence of the Bretons, who are not mentioned in any of the following lives: Donatus, *Vita Ermenlandi Abbatis Antrensis*, MGH SSRM v.674–710; *Vita Antiquissima Sancti Martini Vertavensis*, AASS Oct. x.802–5; *Vita Melanii Episcopi Redonici*, MGH SSRM iii.370–6; Venantius Fortunatus, *Vita Sancti Albini* and *Vita Sancti Paterni*, MGH AA iv.ii, 27–33, 33–7.

WEALTH AND WARFARE IN EARLY MEDIEVAL BRITTANY

The Armorican peninsula fell under the metropolitan jurisdiction of the bishop of Tours, and Gregory was not the first incumbent of the see to take note of the Bretons' disruptive effect on the organisation of the ecclesiastical province.[33] He was also worried by the effect that conflict between Bretons and Franks had on the political stability of the area. His *Histories* were to provide the Carolingians with their main source of information about the Bretons, and about Frankish claims to lordship over them; they also offer us a powerful image of the condition of Breton society in Gregory's day. In exploring those concerns to which the bishop of Tours addressed himself, it must be borne in mind that Gregory's knowledge was limited to affairs in south-eastern Brittany in the second half of the sixth century. Of the Bretons to the north and west of Vannes he knew nothing, and indeed, with the exception of a few ninth-century saints' lives, these regions are effectively undocumented throughout the early Middle Ages. Like most Frankish writers, Merovingian and Carolingian, Gregory betrays no knowledge of nor any interest in the Bretons, except when clashes occurred between Franks and those Bretons immediately west of the border.

The keynote of Gregory's comments on the Bretons is conflict: conflict between Bretons and Franks, and amongst the Bretons themselves. This theme is reinforced by Gregory's interest in occasions when the Bretons were drawn into the Merovingians' own internecine rivalries.[34] In essence, the Bretons, like the Franks, were a people whose political organisation thrived on the raiding and plundering necessary to generate the wealth needed to sustain a warrior leader's armed retinue.

One putative reason for Gregory's insistence on the strained relations between Bretons and Franks is that the county of

---

[33] See above, n. 12 for the letter to Lovocat and Catihern to which Licinius of Tours was a signatory. In 567, the council of Tours legislated against the ordination of Bretons or Romans taking place without the permission of the metropolitan or other bishops of the province. *Concilia Galliae A. 511–A.695*, ed. C. Munier, Corpus Christianorum Series Latina 148a (Turnholt, 1963), p. 179.

[34] Gregory comments on the ways in which the Bretons were drawn into the revolt of Chramn against his father Chlothar I in 560, and into the manoeuvrings of Queen Fredegund against Duke Beppolen in 590. *Libri Historiarum Decem*, IV.20, X.9, 11, ed. B. Krusch and W. Levison, MGH SSRM I.i (2nd edn., 1951), pp. 152–4, 491–4, 495. On Chramn's alliance with the Bretons against Chlothar see also Marius of Avenches, *Chronica*, a. 560, MGH AA XI.237.

Vannes, in central-southern Brittany, was possibly only passing under effective Breton control during Gregory's lifetime.[35] A better-documented reason, however, was the eagerness of Merovingian rulers to extract tribute from the Bretons and to number them amongst the subject peoples who acknowledged Frankish rule. Like all successful early medieval dynasties, the early Merovingians were aggressively hegemonic, and the Bretons were a convenient victim.

Despite Gregory's passing assertion that the Bretons had been subject to Frankish overlordship since the time of Clovis,[36] the first Merovingian ruler whose efforts to subjugate the Bretons are documented was Chilperic I (561–84). In 578, he sent against Waroch, ruler of Vannes, a large army which marched up to the river Vilaine, whose lower reaches formed the traditional boundary between the *civitates* of Nantes and Vannes. After three days of fighting, Waroch came to terms with the king's envoys, handing over his son as a hostage, swearing fidelity to Chilperic, and agreeing to rule the city of Vannes in the king's name in return for annual payments of tribute to Chilperic. In subsequently breaking these promises, Waroch set a pattern of refusal to comply with the demands of Frankish kings which was to characterise relations between Bretons and Franks throughout the early Middle Ages.[37] According to the panegyric of Venantius Fortunatus, the Bretons were only one of many peoples who trembled under Chilperic's domination: Goths, Gascons, Danes, Jutes, and Saxons all felt his power.[38] Chilperic's attack on the Bretons was but one instance of a powerful Merovingian king securing his position through warfare and the exaction of tribute, a hegemony better documented in the regions to the north and east of the Merovingian realms.[39]

Gregory also tells us that in 587 Chilperic's successor Guntramn (561–92) renewed the claim to overlordship over Waroch. The Breton, however, promptly broke his oath to Guntramn and

---

[35] This is suggested by the fact that the Vannetais took its Breton name, Broweroch, from the leader Waroch whose exploits in the 570s Gregory documents.

[36] In the course of describing the conflict between the two Breton brothers Chanao and Macliau, Gregory lets slip the claim that 'nam semper Brittani sub Francorum potestatem post obitum regis Chlodovechi fuerunt, et comites, non regis appellati sunt'. *Lib. Hist.*, IV.4, pp. 137–8.

[37] Gregory of Tours, *Lib. Hist.*, V.26, pp. 232–3.

[38] *Carmina*, IX.1, MGH AA IV.i, 203.

[39] I. N. Wood, *The Merovingian North Sea* (Alingsås, 1983).

reneged both on the written undertaking he had made and on the promise to pay 1,000 *solidi* in compensation for his raids on the county of Nantes. In the course of a Frankish campaign into the Vannetais two years later, Waroch gave his nephew as a hostage and token of good faith, and again promptly broke his word.[40] The last Merovingian on record as being powerful enough to demand the submission of a Breton ruler was Dagobert I (629–38). He perhaps campaigned into Brittany, for *Brittani* were amongst the many captives in his court whom Eligius, royal goldsmith and bishop of Noyon, ransomed.[41] What is certain is that in 635 Dagobert summoned the Breton king, Judicael, to his court under threat of invasion and exacted a promise of submission, which Judicael immediately flouted by refusing to eat at the royal table.[42]

Like the Merovingian kings, Breton leaders relied on warfare and plunder to secure their power. For them, the Frankish-controlled lands of easternmost Armorica were the only areas within reach, and Gregory records repeated raids into the counties of Rennes and Nantes during the second half of the sixth century. In the course of these, the Bretons frequently carried off booty and captives.[43] The Breton rulers were evidently sufficiently powerful that their attacks were a major irritation to the Franks, and the Franks may frequently have found themselves on the defensive against the Bretons.[44]

From ninth-century Frankish sources, we learn that the Bretons were the more feared because their military tactics confused the Franks and put them at a disadvantage. Two reasons explain this. In the first place, as Gregory of Tours had already noted, the Bretons were able to take advantage of their knowledge of the marshy terrain of the Vilaine valley to ambush the Franks, and to attack them as they struggled across the river.[45] And secondly, the Bretons had a reputation by the ninth century for the agility of their horsemen, who made a habit of attacking, wheeling away to

---

[40] Gregory of Tours, *Lib. Hist.*, IX.18, X.9, pp. 431–2, 491–4.

[41] *Vita Eligii Episcopi Noviomagensis*, I.10, MGH SSRM IV.678.

[42] *Chronicle of Fredegar*, IV.78, *The Fourth Book of the Chronicle of Fredegar with its Continuations*, ed. J. M. Wallace-Hadrill (London, 1960), p. 66; *Vita Eligii*, I.13, p. 680.

[43] Gregory of Tours, *Lib. Hist.*, V.29, 31; IX.18, 24; X.9, pp. 234–5, 236, 431–2, 444, 491–4.   [44] On the Frankish march, see below, pp. 45–6.

[45] Gregory of Tours, *Lib. Hist.*, X.9, pp. 491–4; cf. *Chronicon Fontanellense*, a. 846 (*recte* 845), in *Les Premières Annales de Fontanelle*, ed. J. Laporte, Société de l'Histoire de Normandie, Mélanges, 15th ser. (Rouen, 1951), p. 79.

regroup and then attacking again, while unleashing volleys of throwing-spears. The more heavily armed Frankish cavalry were trained to engage with their enemy at close quarters and found themselves quite unable to respond to Breton assaults.[46] Writing in the early tenth century, Regino of Prüm could aptly compare the dreaded Hungarians to the Bretons, the only difference being that they used arrows where the Bretons preferred darts.[47] In the words of a tenth-century Welsh poet, the Bretons were 'warriors on war-horses': such was their reputation far and wide.[48]

In addition to his concern with military conflict, Gregory is also our earliest and only firm pre-Carolingian guide to Breton social and political organisation.[49] He indicates that the Breton peninsula

[46] Writing in the region of Louis the Pious, Ermold the Black commented on the Bretons' use of throwing-spears. *Carmen in Honorem Hludowici Pii*, III.241, 376, 451–6, MGH Poet. II.48, 51, 54. The most detailed description of Breton tactics is that of Regino of Prüm: 'Carolus cum magno exercitu Brittanniam intravit. Pugna committitur, Saxones, qui conducti fuerant, ad excipiendos velocium equorum anfractuosos recursus in prima fronte ponuntur, sed primo impetu spiculis Brittonum territi in acie se recondunt. Brittones more solito huc illucque cum equis ad huiuscemodi conflictum exercitatis discursantes modo consertam Francorum aciem impetunt ac totis viribus in medio spicula torquent, nunc fugam simulantes insequentium nihilominus pectoribus spicula figunt. Franci, qui comminus strictis gladiis pugnare consueverant, attoniti stabant, novitate ante inexperti discriminis perculsi, nec ad insequendum idonei nec in unum conglobati tuti.' *Chronicon*, a. 860 (*recte* 851), ed. F. Kurze, MGH SSRG (Hanover, 1890), pp. 78–9. Regino has heightened the tone of this account by discreet allusions to the Parthians' victory at Magnesia, as told by Justin. M. Manitius, 'Regino und Justin', *Neues Archiv der Gesellschaft für ältere deutsche Geschichtskunde*, 25 (1899), 192–201.
[47] Regino, *Chronicon*, a. 889, p. 133.　　　[48] *Armes Prydein*, line 154, p. 12.
[49] There is, however, a great deal of potential information on social and political structures of the sixth to eighth centuries in Brittany and/or the most immediately adjacent area of Gaul in the collection of legal prescriptions entitled *Excerpta de Libris Romanorum et Francorum* (published as *Canones Wallici* by L. Bieler, *The Irish Penitentials*, Scriptores Latini Hiberniae 5 (Dublin, 1975), pp. 136–59). Whilst there is good circumstantial evidence for the Breton origin of this text, together with firm proof that it was copied and used in ninth- and tenth-century Brittany (five out of the six manuscripts are Breton, and one had Old Breton glosses of the mid-ninth century), it has not yet been dated more closely than to the period stretching from the early sixth century to the end of the eighth century. Its textual interdependence with both the *Lex Salica* and the *Collectio Canonum Hibernensis* suggests that not all its provisions may be actual reflections of the social practices of the place in which it was compiled. It is also quite probable that it reflects social arrangements of various times and degrees of archaism. Until these textual problems are capable of greater resolution, it is not appropriate to use the *Excerpta* to reconstruct early Breton social or political organisation. See further L. Fleuriot, 'Un fragment en latin des très anciennes lois bretonnes armoricaines du VIᵉ siècle', *Annales de Bretagne*, 78 (1971), 601–60; D. N. Dumville, 'On the dating of the early Breton lawcodes', *EC*, 21 (1984), 207–21; W. Davies, 'Suretyship in the *Cartulaire de Redon*', in *Lawyers and Laymen*, ed. T. M. Charles-Edwards, M. E. Owen, and D. B. Walters (Cardiff, 1986), pp. 72–91, at p. 90 n. 42.

was politically fragmented into several *regna*. Not surprisingly, the various rulers were quick to prey on each other's kingdoms, just as they did on the Frankish lands to the east. Like the Merovingians, they also feuded within their own families. From the tale of one such conflict – that of Macliau with his brother, the ruler Chanao, in which Macliau escaped death by hiding in a burial mound and was then consecrated bishop of Vannes, which post he filled until his brother had died – we may guess that at least this ruler turned to the church to consolidate his power.[50] And the Merovingian name, Theuderic, borne by the son of another Breton ruler, Bodic, suggests that this man may have strengthened his own position by resorting to a Frankish marriage alliance.[51] Despite the feuding, there is a clear expectation of succession within the family behind Gregory's accounts. Indeed, his picture of regional, hereditary rulers is echoed elsewhere, for later genealogies preserve a tradition of hereditary rulership, and Carolingian sources confirm that the region was politically fragmented until the early ninth century.[52]

The Breton rulers with whom the Merovingians came into contact were evidently powerful men. They must have been effective lords: effective to gather together the raiding parties which so irritated the Franks, effective also to raise the tribute payments demanded by the Merovingians, for in 588 Waroch promised to pay a compensation of 1,000 gold *solidi* to Guntramn and Chlothar and in 635, Judicael went laden with gifts to Dagobert's palace at Clichy.[53] Their residences – rural stockades in easily defended sites – must have been centres of wealth, of consumption and at least rudimentary administration.[54]

---

[50] Gregory of Tours, *Lib. Hist.*, IV.4, pp. 137–8.
[51] Gregory of Tours, *Lib. Hist.*, V.16, p. 214.
[52] L. Fleuriot, 'Old Breton genealogies and early British traditions', *Bulletin of the Board of Celtic Studies*, 26 (1974), 1–6; A. Oheix, 'L'histoire de Cournouaille d'après un livre récent', *Bulletin de la Société Archéologique du Finistère*, 39 (1912), 3–24, at pp. 13–21. For Carolingian comments on Breton political structures, see below, p. 73.
[53] Gregory of Tours, *Lib. Hist.*, IX.18, p. 432; *Chronicle of Fredegar*, IV.78, p. 66; *Vita Eligii*, I.13, p. 680.
[54] These residences are only known from ninth-century evidence. Ermold the Black, who had joined one of Louis the Pious' campaigns into Brittany, described the stronghold of the ruler Morman as defended by hedges, ditches, and marshes. *In Honorem Hludowici*, III.93–4, p. 44. An annalist writing at Charlemagne's court described how the Frankish army campaigning against the Bretons stormed 'firmitates eorum locis palustribus'. *ARF*, a. 786, p. 72. No such pre-Carolingian 'high status' site has yet been identified archaeologically. All known fortified sites are of tenth-century or later date. L. Langouët, 'Les fortifications de terre et les mottes castrales', in *Artistes,*

Province and empire

The other main centres in which wealth was accumulated were the major churches and monasteries of the region. Indeed, such tiny fragments of information as do pertain to landed wealth all refer to ecclesiastical lordship. In particular, Gregory's contemporary, Bertramn, bishop of Le Mans, is known to have had lands in central-northern Brittany, as well as his huge scatter of properties throughout much of Gaul.[55] Additionally, in the ninth century several Breton churches recorded traditions of early landed endowments, notably the cathedrals of Saint-Pol and Alet.[56] There is just enough evidence to suggest that landed resources, and the lordship they implied, sustained a powerful clerical elite in at least some parts of the region.

As seen through Gregory of Tours' eyes, sixth-century Brittany bears certain resemblances to the Gallo-Frankish world within which the bishop of Tours was himself at home. Both societies were sustained by plunder and warfare; neither had a clear military predominance over the other. Among the Bretons as among the Franks, a ruling elite comprising both lay rulers and leading ecclesiastics based its power on substantial accumulations of wealth. Violent rivalries amongst the Bretons' hereditary ruling families hint at similar familial and patrimonial attitudes to those that prevailed amongst the Franks. From Gregory's point of view, a major difference was that the Franks made repeated demands that the Bretons recognise their lordship. Two centuries after Gregory's death, the Carolingians' insistent revival of this Merovingian claim to hegemony would bring the two societies into much closer contact than hitherto. The result was of enduring consequence for both Bretons and Franks.

Artisans et Production Artistique en Bretagne au Moyen Age, ed. X. Barral i Altet, G. de Carne, A. Chédeville *et al.* (Rennes, 1983), pp. 187–92.

[55] Bertramn of Le Mans owned the *villa Celonica* which lay near Tréguier, *in territorio Tricurino*. *Actus Pontificum Cenomannis in Urbe Degentium*, ed. G. Buson and A. Ledru, Archives Historiques du Maine 2 (Le Mans, 1901), p. 104.

[56] Symptomatic of these early endowments is the use of 'Celtic' charter terminology in the *vitae* of Paul Aurelian, reputed founder of Saint-Pol, and of Malo of Alet. See W. Davies, 'The Latin charter-tradition in western Britain, Brittany and Ireland in the early medieval period', in *Ireland in Europe in the Early Middle Ages*, ed. D. Whitelock, R. McKitterick, and D. N. Dumville (Cambridge, 1982), pp. 258–80, at pp. 272–3. Also, the monastery of Saint-Méen certainly had a pre-Carolingian endowment: its title-deeds were lost in a fire during Charlemagne's reign. Morice, *Preuves*, I.225–6.

Settlement and society in dark age Brittany

LOCAL COMMUNITIES IN SOUTH-EASTERN BRITTANY

Like any other medieval society, Breton society was highly stratified, with great disparities of wealth, with legal boundaries setting apart the unfree from the free, and with a much greater concentration of political power in the hands of some than of others. But unlike most other early medieval societies, it is possible to examine in considerable detail its lower echelons, to assess the relationship of land and power within village communities, and to understand some of the ways in which groups of small-time farmers regulated their own affairs. That this is possible is due to the preservation of the huge early medieval archive from the Breton monastery of Redon. Three hundred and forty-five extant private charters dating from between 801 and 924 survive, mostly in the mid-eleventh-century cartulary of Redon. They enable rural society to be analysed in minute detail in the small region of south-eastern Brittany where the abbey's early landholdings were concentrated.[57]

As with any cartulary, the perspective offered by this archive is ultimately a seigneurial one, reflecting the monks' lordship over land and people. The charters have another interest for the historian, however, because they record a great mass of information on the physical and human environment within which the monks operated. Their interest is all the greater because the nature of the charter collection and of the charters themselves is such that it is possible to exploit them as a lens through which to view social conventions operating unaffected by monastic property interests.[58] The lens reveals clearly a landscape dominated by small-holders, where large concentrations of lands in the hands of individuals were the exception not the norm, and where political power was not a simple correlative of landed wealth.

Redon was founded in 832 at the confluence of the rivers Oust

---

[57] This microscopic investigation has recently been completed by W. Davies, *Small Worlds: The Village Community in Early Medieval Brittany* (London, 1988), to which I am greatly indebted.

[58] For detailed analysis of the cartulary itself and of its contents, see W. Davies, 'The composition of the Redon cartulary', *Francia*, 17.i (1990), 69–90; W. Davies, 'Forgery in the Cartulaire de Redon', *Fälschungen im Mittelalter*, MGH Schriften 33, 6 vols. (Munich, 1988–9), IV.265–74; H. Guillotel, 'Les cartulaires de l'abbaye de Redon', *MSHAB*, 63 (1986), 27–48.

and Vilaine, right on the eastern boundary of the county of Vannes. The landed endowment which it very rapidly accumulated was heavily concentrated in the Vannetais within 40 km of the abbey church, but with outlying properties as far afield to the north-west as the central hills of the Breton peninsula. In the south and east the monastery's lands extended further than the area where Breton was spoken into regions which, at the time of the monastery's foundation, were under Frankish control. These properties, in the south of the county of Rennes and scattered across the county of Nantes as far as the city's hinterland, reveal a rather different world from that of the Breton lands north and west of Redon and will be discussed further in the following chapter.

The Redon archive presents an interesting combination of social continuity and of change. Changes in rural life in the course of the ninth century in the area around Redon resulted from the rapid expansion of the monastery's landlordship together with the consequences of the changing political interactions of Bretons and Franks. Yet these pressures by no means eroded the fundamental organisation of Breton farmers in largely self-regulating communities, or the predominance amongst them of small-time freeholders. In these respects, Breton social structures were clearly of pre-Carolingian origin. Unfortunately, lack of comparative evidence makes it impossible to discern either the origins of the more distinctive features of Breton society or to assess to what extent communities elsewhere in Brittany resembled those in the eastern Vannetais.

Nevertheless, the documents themselves provide hints that village life here had evolved within the context of late Roman conventions and with some degree of contact with the neighbouring lands in the post-Roman period. In particular, of the charter forms in common use in the Redon area in the ninth century, several used formulas almost identical to those in the seventh-century Formulary of Angers and the eighth-century formulary from Tours, but which were outmoded in these places by the ninth century.[59] Furthermore, it has been suggested that the regularity with which transactions amongst small-scale

---

[59] Davies, *Small Worlds*, pp. 136–7; P. Gasnault, 'Les actes privés de l'abbaye de Saint-Martin de Tours du VIIIe au XIIe siècle', *Bibliothèque de l'Ecole des Chartes*, 112 (1954), 26–66, at p. 30.

proprietors as well as large landowners were committed to writing by local clerical notaries may have derived from late Roman procedures for registering transactions in municipal archives.[60] Other customs to which the charters are witness are also explicable in terms of the late Roman heritage. The widespread use of sureties in the Redon area, enlisted to guarantee transactions concerning landed property, makes most sense as a local development of late Roman legal provisions.[61] Finally, the terminology used for the obligations of tenant to landlord is again characteristic of the late and post-Roman west, and may be a clue that seigneurial exactions had devolved from Roman fiscal obligations.[62]

The damp Atlantic climate and relatively poor soils of western Brittany do not permit the cultivation of wheat: in the 1070s, William of Poitiers commented on the overwhelmingly pastoral nature of the Breton economy.[63] By contrast, the south-eastern part of Brittany where Redon held its lands enjoys a more moderate and warmer climate. Here, where charters listing renders payable in both livestock and cereals reveal a mixed arable and pastoral economy, the ninth-century landscape was in general well-peopled and heavily exploited. Beyond the cluster of buildings round the main church of a community, stood scattered houses for proprietors or their serfs, usually adjacent to the main part of each unit of ownership, and set in a landscape of enclosed cultivated fields, interspersed with meadows, orchards, woodland, and heath.[64]

Everywhere, the basic unit of property was the small-holding (Old Breton *ran*, Latin *pars*). Varying in size from approximately 5 to 60 hectares, and fetching prices ranging from about 8 to 30 *solidi* when sold to another local proprietor or to Redon, they gave the countryside a characteristically broken, patchwork appearance.[65] There is no evidence that large, compact lordships interrupted this pattern. Even the benefactions to Redon of the ruling elite were similar, being collections of several such small

---

[60] Davies, *Small Worlds*, pp. 137–8.   [61] Davies, 'Suretyship', esp. pp. 84–7.
[62] Davies, *Small Worlds*, pp. 50–1.
[63] William of Poitiers, *History of William the Conqueror*, I.44: 'Uberrimo lacte, parcissimo pane, sese transigunt. Pinguia pabula gignunt pecoribus loca vasta et ferme nescia segetum.' *Histoire de Guillaume le Conquérant*, ed. R. Foreville, Les Classiques de l'Histoire de France au Moyen Age 23 (Paris, 1952), pp. 108–10.
[64] Davies, *Small Worlds*, pp. 29–40.   [65] Davies, *Small Worlds*, pp. 41–7.

properties.[66] By the end of the ninth century, Redon's lands consisted of hundreds of such farmsteads, some adjacent to others, some widely scattered. The ubiquity of these small-holdings is the key to understanding the social structure of the region.

Only a small proportion of the men whose names are known ever took part in property transactions. As for the majority, either they possessed no resources to spare beyond the land which supported themselves and their immediate family, or they effectively moved in circles untouched by Redon's interests. Of those who did buy, sell, or donate land, or who raised cash loans by pawning their lands to their richer neighbours, a general stratification has been established. Most can only be associated with a single *ran*, but about one third of known property owners owned up to four or five small-holdings, which might be scattered over two or three villages. These they might work with the assistance of one or two servile families, or by letting out land to tenants.[67] In general, these small-holdings were passed on down from one generation to the next within the same family, and close kin often had an interest in their relatives' land. But land was also fairly easily alienable by both the sons and the daughters who had inherited it, and property acquired by purchase, exchange, or donation might be re-sold, or transmitted within the family.[68] Quite apart from the impact which Redon's acquisitiveness had on local property holding, it is clear that among the more substantial proprietors, land changed hands easily and frequently. The monastery's foundations may even have heated up the already active property market.

The interests of one Arthuiu illustrate many of these points. In 835, a man called Moenken was in need of cash and raised 4 *solidi* by pledging his plot of land, Ranriculf, to Arthuiu, one of the more substantial landowners in the immediate vicinity of Redon. As with most of the pledges documented in the Redon cartulary, the term of this one was seven years, twice renewable up to a final total of twenty-one years. Moenken found two men to stand surety for the deal; they and a further sixteen men witnessed the

---

[66] For example, CR A13, a grant made by the ruler Nominoe in 842 consisting of eight named plots, one with serfs attached. The penalty for breaking this donation was a fine of 300 *solidi*; since monetary sanctions were normally twice the value of the land, this charter conveyed lands worth a total of about 150 *solidi*.

[67] See Davies, *Small Worlds*, pp. 86–104 for a much more detailed analysis.

[68] Davies, *Small Worlds*, pp. 71–6 on inheritance and property within the family.

transaction, which was concluded in the church at Bains.[69] Evidently Moenken was unable to redeem his land, for some years later, Arthuiu sold Ranriculf, together with another plot, Ranbudhoiarn, to his own wife, for a total of 30 *solidi* and 12 *denarii*. She subsequently gave the land to Redon, but reserved the use of it for herself for the remainder of her lifetime.[70] Another series of Arthuiu's transactions also ultimately benefited Redon. Their object was the hermitage of Wokamoe. In 833, Arthuiu purchased half of it from Cleroc. At the same time he was party to two pledges, in which he received its other half as security for cash lent to Ricun and his son Iarcun and to Ricun's nephew Omnis. None of the members of this family redeemed the lands, and Redon eventually acquired Wokamoe as a gift from Arthuiu.[71] Arthuiu's dealings well illustrate the types of property transactions and their consequences that were common in south-eastern Brittany at the time of Redon's foundation.

Despite the presence of several substantial property owners like Arthuiu, it remains evident that only a few people could afford to buy or sell land. These men and women formed a relatively prosperous stratum in what was in many ways a 'peasant' society of families who were characterised by narrow geographical horizons and were immediately dependent upon the land they worked for their livelihood. Their world was essentially that of the *plebs*. Roughly equivalent in size to a later parish in the region, the ninth-century *plebs* was a group of people together with the area inhabited by them, and it formed both a religious community and the only unit of secular regulation smaller than a county. The fundamental importance of this unit of association is suggested by the large number of Breton place-names whose first element is *plou-*, from *plebem*.[72] Most people lived, worked, and worshipped within the community of the *plebs*. Only those proprietors with a scatter of holdings, or who were actively involved in the running of local affairs, can be traced beyond their own *plebs*.[73]

---

[69] CR 199. This charter was subsequently interpolated by Redon. See Davies, 'Forgery', p. 271.

[70] CR 186. Neither of these two subsequent transactions is precisely datable.

[71] CR 181, 182, 183.

[72] There has been much debate on the origins of this unusual form of organisation; see the trenchant remarks of W. Davies, 'Priests and rural communities in east Brittany in the ninth century', *EC*, 20 (1983), 177–97, at pp. 177–80. For place-names, see B. Tanguy, 'Les paroisses primitives en plou- et leurs saints éponymes', *Bulletin de la Société Archéologique du Finistère*, 109 (1981), pp. 121–55.

[73] Davies, *Small Worlds*, pp. 105–33, 155–9.

At the upper level of these rural communities, that of the substantial free proprietor with interests spanning several *plebes* and with property to spare for the church, are found men with the power to terrorise their neighbours, or with the status to exercise certain regulatory and jurisdictional functions within the *plebs*. The former were local thugs, whom we meet most typically when they threatened violence against the monks and their lands.[74] The latter (who sometimes also terrorised the local communities and the monks) were men described in Latin as *tyranni*, or in Latinised Breton as *tiarni*, *machtierni*. *Machtiern* is a Brittonic word with strong connotations of rulership. The machtierns' position as men of standing within the community was reinforced by their close association with the residences or courts (Old Breton *lis*, translated into Latin as *aula*) where transactions were often completed and witnessed. Apparently, they were men whose primary responsibilities were overseeing, validating, and regulating property transactions and presiding over the courts which settled disputes over past transactions.[75] They are unlikely to have fulfilled these tasks altruistically, and there is evidence that they may have been in receipt of certain dues and payments from within the *plebes* within which they functioned.[76] Their prominence in the charters means that we know far more of the mechanisms for regulating and assuring property transfers among Breton villagers than in almost any other part of early medieval Europe.

A particularly well-documented example of a machtiern and his family is Riwalt son of Iarnwocon. Riwalt appears as machtiern between 835 and 844 in the *plebes* of Guillac, Campénéac, Ploërmel, and Augan, an unusually large number for one machtiern.[77] He also owned property in Augan and Campénéac, and was associated with a *lis* in each place.[78] It was quite common for several members of the same family to be machtierns; of Riwalt's two sons, Frawal and Deurhoiarn, the latter was machtiern in Ploërmel, and possibly also Augan and

---

[74] For example, *GSR*, 1.5–7, pp. 121–31.

[75] M. Planiol, *Histoire des Institutions de la Bretagne*, 5 vols. (Mayenne, 1981–4), II.63–96; J. T. Sheringham, 'Les machtierns. Quelques témoignages gallois et corniques', *MSHAB*, 58 (1981), 61–72; Davies, *Small Worlds*, pp. 138–42, 175–83.

[76] The evidence is discussed by Davies, *Small Worlds*, pp. 139–40, who suggests that the payments were made to machtierns in a seigneurial capacity; unlike Professor Davies, I am inclined to believe that it does indicate that dues were paid to machtierns *qua* machtierns. [77] CR 116, 194, A7. [78] CR 6, 107, 122, 194.

Caro in the 840s and 850s.[79] Deurhoiarn also owned land in Augan and Plélan, and is known to have died and been buried in Redon's dependent church of Saint-Maixent in Plélan in January 876; his wife Roiantken was very soon thereafter laid to rest beside him.[80] Roiantken was a wealthy woman in her own right whose own property transactions spanned half a century. In 821, she purchased a *ran* with one attached family of serfs for 15 *solidi* from her brother Catweten, which she retained after her brother had taken her to the court of the machtiern Iarnhitin to try to recover the land; in 867 she bought land from Maenwobri which he had previously bought from one Haelwicon, and in 869 she donated it to Redon; finally, shortly before she died, she gave the monastery the property she had received from her father-in-law Riwalt as a morning-gift at her marriage.[81] Yet another donation to Redon, made in conjunction with her husband and their son Iarnwocon, is not closely datable.[82] After both Deurhoiarn and Roiantken had died, Iarnwocon gave further land in Augan and Plélan to Saint-Maixent and in their memory gave his own son, Sulwoion, as an oblate at the same time.[83] In their capacity as machtierns, Riwalt and Deurhoiarn are encountered as witnesses to grants to Redon (particularly to ones made by members of their own family), to a transaction in Guillac where a priest demanded a horse from another machtiern and paid him in land, and to a pledge when a priest in Caro lent money to a man and wife.[84]

No clear economic or legal distinction seems to have separated the machtierns from the even more powerful *optimates* who constituted the retinues of the ninth-century Breton rulers. Of these very powerful men, who may have formed a regional nobility, the Redon evidence reveals much less; most must have had interests in the undocumented areas beyond Redon's restricted horizons, and only when they gave lands or jurisdictional rights to Redon, as did Pascweten, count of Vannes, or when they infringed the abbey's interests do we get hints of their property holdings and powers of lordship.[85]

Both before and during the Carolingian period, the rulers'

[79] CR 24, 122, 175, 193.   [80] CR 79, 236.
[81] CR 146, 147, 172–4, 236.   [82] CR 175.   [83] CR 79, 236.
[84] CR 24, 116, 175, 193, 194.
[85] *Optimates* is the word used by a late ninth-century Redon writer for the men who made up the Breton leader's retinue. *GSR*, I.10, p. 139. For the charter evidence as to who these men may have been, see Davies, *Small Worlds*, pp. 163–75.

retinues were also warbands. In the late ninth century, and presumably also before then, the most powerful of these leading Bretons had their own military followings; one of them, Wrhwant, could muster 200 men for a fight against the Vikings.[86] As to how such forces were levied, there is no direct evidence. However, if a late ninth-century miracle story is to be believed, powerful men had available in their retinues highly trained young horsemen, *pueri*, whose skill at riding war-horses, *caballi*, could be put to the test.[87] And judging by the importance of horses, sometimes specifically war-horses, and the high prices which they commanded in land transactions between the local landowners around Redon, the cavalry which so terrorised the Franks may have been recruited from amongst the wealthier local proprietors.[88]

The most striking aspect of early ninth-century Breton society as revealed in the Redon charters is the absence of firm links between war leaders and small-holders. Officials called *maiores* may have been tax collectors, but we do not know on whose account they worked.[89] No evidence reveals whether machtierns were elected or appointed, or who selected them. We also lack information as to how warbands were formed. The dominant impression left by the extant sources is one of the lack of a clear hierarchy of lordship. In many medieval societies, the tension between lordship and community provided the dynamic for political and social change: yet in early ninth-century Brittany, it is remarkably hard to identify that stress.

Rather, fragmented and incoherent patterns of power marked out south-eastern Brittany. Machtierns regulated local affairs

---

[86] Regino, *Chronicon*, a. 874, pp. 108–9.

[87] In his life of Winwaloe, Wrdisten described how Fracan and Riwal, ruler of Dumnonia, settled a dispute about whose horse was the faster by racing their 'caballi' whose jockeys were 'levissimi...pueri...artificiosissime ad cursum bene edocti'. *Vita Winwaloei*, 1.18, '*Vita S. Winwaloei primi abbatis landevenecensis auctore Wurdestino*', ed. C. de Smedt, *Analecta Bollandiana*, 7 (1888), 167–264, at p. 203.

[88] CR 116: sale of an *equus valde bonus* by a priest to a machtiern in return for land; CR 136: part of the purchase price of land bought by a priest includes two *equi*; CR 138: price of land in a sale between two laymen includes a *caballus* worth 9 *solidi*; CR 171: another sale of land between two individuals in which a *caballus* and a dog (called *Couuiranus*) contributed the equivalent of 20 *solidi* towards the total price of 30 *solidi*. For purchase of a church for gold, silver, and *caballi optimi* by a relative of one of the late ninth-century rulers of Brittany, see *Cartulaire de l'Abbaye de Landévennec*, ed. R. Le Men and E. Ernault, Documents Inédits sur l'Histoire de France, Mélanges 5 (Paris, 1886), pp. 533–600, no. 24, at p. 561.

[89] Davies, *Small Worlds*, pp. 142–6.

within the *plebs* rather than within the propertied accumulation of powerful men (although the growth of Redon's lordship gradually changed this in *plebes* in the immediate vicinity of the abbey church[90]). There were alienable rights of superior lordship over *plebes*, quite possibly of a fiscal nature, for we find donations of whole *plebes* being made to churches, and yet there is no instance of a machtiern ever making such a grant.[91] We must suppose that the pre-Carolingian rulers of the Bretons were the wealthiest men in their own regions, just as their ninth-century successors were, and yet there is every sign that the local communities were quite capable of organising many of their own affairs without appreciable control or intervention from the ultimate rulers both before and during the ninth century. In this respect at least, Brittany must have been much like Carolingian Francia, where, 'in the county itself, or out in the villas of the countryside, local power in the ninth century operated with little demonstrable intrusion from outside or above'.[92]

So often our understanding of early medieval society is an exclusively top-downwards one, the impression which the drafters of royal lawcodes or huge aristocratic land grants wished to convey. From those charters in the Redon cartulary directly concerning the monastery's property and rights and claims, we can certainly derive a reasonably clear picture of the growth of the abbey's lordship. But where we see ninth-century Breton society unaffected by Redon's interests, we perhaps get a more realistic glimpse of the complexities of an early medieval society. In this world powers of regulation and authority were so thoroughly diffused and dispersed that modern (and Roman-law) distinctions between public or private rights and powers are meaningless.[93] Instead, we see how structures of lordship rooted in land-ownership by no means coincided with structures of jurisdiction, with the processes for regulating community affairs, or with any clear system of military recruitment. In short, it was a world in which the village communities which were the main forum for the regulation of land transactions might nevertheless sustain regional rulers and their mounted retinues.

[90] On Redon's seigneurial interests, see Davies, *Small Worlds*, pp. 188–200.
[91] See further pp. 134–5 below.
[92] J. L. Nelson, 'Dispute settlement in Carolingian West Francia', in *The Settlement of Disputes in Early Medieval Europe*, ed. W. Davies and P. Fouracre (Cambridge, 1986), pp. 45–64, at p. 62.
[93] Compare Van Caenegem, 'Government, law and society', pp. 178–9.

The half-millennium from the decay of the Roman state in the early years of the fifth century until the opening of the ninth century is a period of Breton history effectively irrecoverable in all but the scantiest outline. Although the process which created close affinities with the culture of south-west Britain remains open to discussion, it is nevertheless clear that, by the early Carolingian period, Breton society had developed its own well-established rhythms and conventions within the framework of its late Roman legacy. It was a society with its own predatory warrior elite; yet it so happens that we know more of the peasants than of the warriors. The characteristics of early Breton society are all the more evident when contrasted with the neighbouring Frankish lands. To these we now turn.

Chapter 2

NEUSTRIA AND THE BRETON MARCH

Of all the kingdoms which emerged from the wreckage of the western Roman empire, that of the Franks was the most successful and the most enduring. However, neither Merovingians nor Carolingians ruled a homogeneous society. The heart of their kingdom was the Roman province of Gaul, where centuries of Roman rule had established administrative conventions and provided the environment within which Christian worship had spread, above all in urban areas. This large and rich province was unevenly Romanised, and everywhere ancient traditions of agricultural exploitation were adjusted to the local climate and relief. The collapse of the *pax Romana* induced dislocations in trade, settlement patterns, and land use, and the uneven distribution of immigrants of various Germanic peoples strengthened the regional diversities of early medieval Gaul and helped forge new ethnic identities within it.[1]

Over this rich and variegated kingdom, Merovingian rule ebbed and flowed. Dynastic infighting, the competence or incompetence of individual kings, the lure of resources to be won beyond the frontiers all played their part in shaping the ever-fluid geography of power and authority. The sea-bed over which this tide washed was at some times accepting, at others resistant. Entrenched regional interests – churches, cities, aristocratic families – set up eddies, but more often grew by accretion than decayed through attrition. Relics of Roman administrative machinery gradually corroded and crumbled in this changed environment. And as the strong and ultimately irresistible current of Arnulfing power began to run from the Rhineland into Gaul from the late seventh century, the sands shifted still more. In some places, the change of ruling dynasty happened slowly and quietly,

---

[1] See the synthesis of E. James, *The Origins of France: From Clovis to the Capetians, 500–1000* (London, 1982), pp. 13–41.

as the new tide trickled round old obstacles through freshly scoured channels of power. Elsewhere, crashing waves of repeated military assault bore down on and finally crushed opposition to the new regime. In the three centuries from Childeric to Charlemagne, Gaul underwent a sea-change from Roman province to early medieval patrimony.

From the Ebro to the Elbe and from Bavaria to Brittany, the Carolingian empire acquired its cohesion from the loyalty which the *stirps regia* attracted. Cultural, ethnic, and economic disparities had multiplied as the kingdom expanded; new regional and provincial identities were created. Nevertheless, however much royal power fluctuated, however the tensions inherent in political life manifested themselves, the essential fabric of early medieval society remained the same: small communities knit together into local or regional groupings. Any one part of the Carolingian world can, then, be studied from many different angles. The characteristics of village society demand consideration as much as the exigencies of provincial lordship. Expressions of ethnic or regional identity are as important as the impact of royal power. The translation of local rifts into the politics of the royal court are as significant as the effect on the localities of rivalries within the royal retinue. Evidence permitting, we may grasp the complexities and occasionally the nuances of the many disparate societies which constituted Charlemagne's empire.

One region of Gaul holds our close attention. 'The land between the Seine and the Loire', known as Neustria from the seventh century,[2] marched with Brittany at one extreme and at the other abutted the Carolingian dynasty's Rhineland base. Carolingian interest in Brittany was mediated through this area, and parts of western Neustria were integral to the transformation which Brittany itself underwent in the ninth and early tenth centuries. This chapter is not a comprehensive analysis of early medieval Neustria. Rather, it focusses on the forms of lordship which structured western Neustrian society, on the ebb and flow of royal power here and on the economic exchanges and patterns of property ownership which linked western Neustria to the

---

[2] E. Ewig, 'Die fränkischen Teilungen und Teilreiche (511–613)', *Akademie der Wissenschaften und der Literatur Mainz. Abhandlungen der geistes- und sozialwissenschaftlichen Klasse*, 9 (1953), 651–715, at pp. 693–700 (reprinted in E. Ewig, *Spätantikes und fränkisches Gallien. Gesammelte Schriften (1952–1973)*, ed. H. Atsma, 2 vols., Beihefte der Francia 3 (Munich 1976–9), I.114–71).

wider world. Through such themes we can more readily understand how the Carolingian tide surged into Brittany, and what some of the obstacles it encountered were.

LOCAL COMMUNITIES AND REGIONAL ECONOMY

In geological terms, all the land as far east as Angers is part of the Armorican massif. The Vilaine valley transects this land mass across the neck of the peninsular region: in the early Middle Ages, the river's middle and lower reaches formed a traditional line of political demarcation. This marshy ground, however, was no great barrier, crossed as it was in several places by Roman roads.[3] The valley certainly did not correspond to any firm social or linguistic division. To its west, ninth-century charter writers used the distinctive terminology for local administrative units characteristic of the lower Loire basin;[4] to its east, Breton place-names and personal names occurred. In particular, heavy Breton settlement in the Guérande peninsula between the mouths of the Loire and the Vilaine was well established by the time it was first documented in the ninth century. Further north, Frankish writers often applied the label *Britannia* to the area around Mont-Saint-Michel and Rennes, although the Breton presence here was not strong enough to have left any permanent imprint on the toponymy.[5] Off the coast of the Cotentin peninsula, the Channel Islands were in Breton hands; Charlemagne had occasion to have dealings with these people.[6] This north-eastern corner of the Armorican peninsula was an area where interpreters were to be found, and speakers of Breton and speakers of 'proto-Romance'

[3] N.-Y. Tonnerre, 'Les pays de la basse Vilaine au haut moyen âge', *MSHAB*, 63 (1986), 29–72.

[4] In particular, the word *condita* was used as a synonym of *plebs* for describing some communities in the Vannetais. It is otherwise only found in the counties of Rennes, Nantes, Anjou, Maine, Touraine, the Blésois, and Poitou. Its meaning is quite unclear; one suggestion is that it is a relic of late Roman or very early Merovingian fiscal arrangements throughout the *Tractus Armoricanus*. F. Lot, 'La conquête du pays d'entre Seine-et-Loire par les Francs: la ligue armoricaine et les destinées du duché du Maine', *Revue Historique*, 155 (1930), 241–53, at p. 250; M. Rouche, *L'Aquitaine des Wisigothes aux Arabes (418–781)* (Paris, 1979), p. 152.

[5] Venantius Fortunatus, *Vita Paterni*, 10, p. 36; *Annales Mettenses Priores*, a. 830 (ed. B. de Simson, MGH SSRG, Hanover, 1905), pp. 95–6; *Itinerarium Bernardi, monachi franci*, 21, 23, ed. T. Tobler, *Descriptiones Terrae Sanctae ex saeculo VIII, IX, XII et XV* (Leipzig, 1874), pp. 97–9. *AB*, a.830, p. 1, should also be read as referring to this area.

[6] *Miracula Sancti Wandregiseli*, 7, MGH SS xv.i, 407; *Vita Sancti Marculphi Abbatis*, 2, AASS Mai. I.73–4.

must have intermingled here.[7] Across the neck of the Armorican peninsula, Britannia shaded off into Francia.

In spite of this, settlement patterns and methods of exploitation on the eastern fringe of the Armorican peninsula do appear to have been different from those found further west. The handful of charters in the Redon archive for lands in the county of Rennes, together with a somewhat larger number from Nantes, indicate something of the ninth-century economy of the area immediately to the east of the Vilaine. These charters immediately reveal a less dispersed settlement pattern and a much wider range of size and value of property than is found in Breton-speaking regions. Two transactions in Lusanger each conveyed modest plots for only 6 *solidi*, but at Grandchamp, near Nantes, a church with its attached *mansus* changed hands in October 808 for 200 *solidi*.[8] Property prices tended to be significantly higher in these Frankish areas: all sales of land recorded in the Redon charters where the price was 40 *solidi* or more were of land in the Nantais or Rennais.[9] Furthermore, some of the largest estates in the region had substantial serf populations. For example, the transfer of an estate at Thourie in the county of Rennes to Redon on 12 August 845 included five serf families, five female serfs with their offspring, and one solitary male, all of whose names were carefully recorded.[10] There is little in common here with the small-holdings of the eastern Vannetais.

Where details of the properties are given, they suggest a mixed arable economy in which viticulture was also important.[11] Most charters simply mention vines amongst the pertinent features of the land being sold, but in January 837/8, a vineyard with its

---

[7] For a casual reference to boys speaking to the king through an interpreter, see *Vita Maglorii Episcopi*, 22, AASS Oct. x.789.

[8] CR 217, 231 (Lusanger), 33 (Grandchamp).

[9] Davies, *Small Worlds*, pp. 58–60, tabulates property prices in the Redon cartulary. The following charters (following the chronological order of listing in this table) come from the Frankish areas of Nantes and Rennes: CR 33, 227, 226, 228, 229, 230, 43, 181, 210, 209, 217, 125, 244.   [10] CR 41.

[11] For example CR 43, a *mansus* in Grandchamp worth 120 *solidi* had attached buildings, dwellings, vines, land, and orchards; a *mansus* in Lusanger (CR 229) was sold for only 10 *solidi* with its buildings, a piece of land, and meadow belonging to it (*petiola de terra mea et de prato meo ad ipsum alodum pertinentes*) and another field (*campus*) with the meadow (*pratus*) which belonged to it. The mixed economy is reflected in the dues payable on a *villa* in Fougeray: 3 pigs, 3 wethers, 3 lambs, 23 *modii* of oats, 18 *modii* of wheat and 9 *modii* of rye (CR 262). On the various words used to describe these properties, see P. Flatrès, 'Les anciennes structures rurales de Bretagne d'après le cartulaire de Redon', *Etudes Rurales*, 41 (1971), 87–93, at pp. 88–9.

attached land in Grandchamp was sold for the large sum of 150 *solidi*.[12] Vineyards were doubtless a major source of wealth in the hinterland of Nantes, for Breton raids into this area sometimes specifically targeted them.[13] There are hints too that the farming economy may have been supplemented by mineral extraction. Property at Laillé just south of Rennes was located at a place called *ad illa minaria*; at the tin mines at Abbaretz in the county of Nantes have been found pieces of two Merovingian gold *tremisses* and a bronze Byzantine coin of *c.* 585, which may indicate sixth-century mining there, although there is no indication how much longer the mines remained in use.[14]

In one place, the economy was certainly not primarily agricultural. Described in a text from Angers as 'densely populated, on account of the very great salt industry',[15] the coast of the Guérande peninsula was, and still is, a centre for salt panning, and until the nineteenth century was a Breton-speaking area. Although we know nothing about the trading of Guérande salt, charter evidence nevertheless makes it clear that salt was extracted on a commercial scale and that new salt workings were being created in the ninth century.[16]

There are also hints of complex tenurial and financial relationships in this particular industry. Some saltpans were associated with large agricultural estates located on the ridge of land immediately overlooking the saltpans.[17] Others were attached to Redon's paupers' hospice.[18] Transactions concerning three saltpans were concluded by a man and his lord in a way that suggests the man had held them from his lord.[19] It is striking that there are no records of the sale of salt workings, yet on many occasions Redon made a loan of cash against a pledge of a saltpan.[20] These pledges suggest a particular need for cash, but also that there may have been other, undocumented, tenurial or financial customs which affected the ways in which property transactions in the area were conducted.[21]

---

[12] CR 210.   [13] Gregory of Tours, *Lib. Hist.*, IX.18, 24, pp. 431–2, 444.
[14] C. Champaud, 'L'exploitation ancienne de cassitérite d'Abbaretz-Nozay', *Annales de Bretagne*, 64 (1957), 46–96, at pp. 68, 72.
[15] *Miracula Sancti Albini Episcopi Andegavensis*, 3, AASS. Mar. I.62.
[16] Davies, *Small Worlds*, p. 53. CR 22, A39 are grants of sites on which *salinae* are to be made.   [17] CR 23, 26.   [18] CR 234.
[19] CR 86, 169, 170.
[20] CR 60, 73, 86, 95, 104, 169, 170, 234. These represent two-thirds of all pledge transactions in which Redon was involved.
[21] Cf. Davies, *Small Worlds*, pp. 57–60, 135.

The salt-based economy of Breton-speaking Guérande contrasts with the tenurial and social relations of the Frankish agricultural communities of Grandchamp, due east of Guérande beyond the marshes of the Grande Brière, and of Lusanger, about 75 km to the north-east. The Lusanger records offer an exceptionally detailed window into familial life and property dealings at local level in ninth-century western Neustria, and for this reason are worth detailed analysis. They tell us of one family in particular. Austroberta had two husbands, first Agenhart and then Uandefred. By her first marriage, she had a son Agon (or Agonild); by her second two sons, Onger and Gerwis.[22] Austroberta's lands in Lusanger lay in three places, the *villa Faito*, the *villa Botcatman* and the *villa Isartius*. With her first husband, Agenhart, she owned land in the *villa Faito*, and on 4 April 819, they purchased for 40 *solidi* an allod which was surrounded on three of its four sides by land which they already owned.[23] Three years later, their son Agon had purchased land in the same place from his aunt Acfrud and uncle Arluin, land which his aunt had inherited from her own father, another Agon, and which was adjacent on one side to other land of Acfrud. This must have been a substantial allod, for it sold for 100 *solidi*.[24] Austroberta's property interests with her second husband, Uandefred, lay in the *villa Botcatman*, and here the holdings seem to have been smaller. In March 830, they bought from one Aicus a *mansus* with the buildings where Aicus' father had lived together with more land which Aicus had inherited from his father, all for only 20 *solidi*.[25] The following year, their son Onger bought more land from Aicus' paternal inheritance, again for only 10 *solidi*.[26] In June 833, Agon sold land which he had inherited from his mother in the *villa Isartius* to his half-brothers Onger and Gerwis.[27] Austroberta seems also to have had other land in *villa Isartius*, which for the time being she retained.[28]

The charters which detail these transactions have survived because Redon subsequently acquired some or all of Austroberta's lands. A small plot in the *villa Botcatman* she sold to the abbey at

---

[22] CR 231 has an appended note describing Austroberta's two families; the context makes it highly likely that the donor of this charter, Agonild, is the same man as the son Agon by her first husband. The rest of the genealogical information is supplied in passing references in other charters.   [23] CR 226.

[24] CR 227, of 26 May 816.   [25] CR 229.   [26] CR 230.

[27] CR 231.   [28] Cf. CR 225.

an unknown date, but on 29 July 864 she and Uandefred gave a large donation of land to Redon. These lands are specified as being in *Botcatman* and *Fait*, but it may have been on the same occasion that the monastery acquired her lands in *Isartius* as well.[29] By 868, the lands obtained from her in all three places had fallen into the hands of Hirdran, who restored them to the abbey in that year but was granted their usufruct for the rest of his life.[30]

These Lusanger charters underscore the inseparability of family and land. Austroberta's family profited at the expense of Aicus' family holdings, but property was also redistributed within her own family, passing from one generation to the next by sale as well as by inheritance. The documents hint at the care taken to expand and consolidate each member's holdings, but properly witnessed and documented sales between close relatives were perhaps also concluded in an effort to limit the potential for disputes over inheritances. All these charters include a sanction of a double fine to be levied on anyone including *ullus de coheredibus vel propinquis* who might dispute the transactions, and the threat from heirs and relatives must have been very real. Moreover, the dealings of Austroberta's family are important evidence of the significance of women in the transmission of property, not only Austroberta herself, but also the other women of Lusanger who appear alongside their husbands as vendors, purchasers, and witnesses.[31]

The families of Austroberta and Aicus were part of the most humble property-owning stratum of Frankish society to which the historical record gives access. Although property prices suggest that at least some of their plots of land were considerably larger than those which characterised the Vannetais, these Frankish families nevertheless had much in common with their Breton counterparts. The frequent redistribution of land within individual families both east and west of the Vilaine hints at the complexity and fluidity of landholding patterns at village level. In neither region was it the arrival of a big corporate investor such as Redon which created the land market. Furthermore, in the local society of both the Vannetais and the Nantais, women often played a crucial role in the accumulation and redistribution of a family's landed property. As determiners of ownership and heirship, women had much to lose from Redon's growth.

[29] CR 217, 57.   [30] CR 225.   [31] CR 226, 227, 228.

Although the charters from nearby Grandchamp suggest an essentially similar pattern of acquisition and redistribution of land,[32] it is unfortunately impossible to see the broader social milieu into which these families fitted. We have no sense of whether the men and women of Lusanger had property interests further afield, how their wealth compared with that of other families in the area, or how they compared with families to the east. Nevertheless, we may suspect that they were the early medieval equivalent of the local squirearchy of western Neustria. Their activities appear to have been geographically restricted. Sales or donations of land to Redon of course established bonds and contacts with the monastic community there. We know too that some of the inhabitants of Grandchamp, and also those of Savenay a little to the west, had occasional contact with the nearby city of Nantes, named in the *actum* clause of two charters, one for each place.[33] More surprising is the mention of Angers in the equivalent clause of another Grandchamp document.[34] But beyond this, no other evidence delimits the social or geographical horizons of the local communities of the ninth-century Nantais. On the other hand, there is nothing reminiscent of the wealth and range of activity of the Merovingian aristocracy of the region, men such as Felix, bishop of Nantes (549–82), who came from an aristocratic Aquitainian episcopal dynasty; or his contemporary, Victurius, bishop of Rennes, probably of a noble family of Le Mans; or Bertramn, bishop of Le Mans, whose will of 616 lists estates stretching from Paris to Bordeaux and westwards into central-northern Brittany.[35] And beside the magnates whom the Carolingians were to introduce into the Nantais, Austroberta's kin are small fry indeed. Insofar as they are documented in the Redon cartulary, early ninth-century landowners in the hinterland of Nantes may have owned somewhat larger landholdings than their Breton counterparts, but beyond their own immediate vicinity they seem to have lacked status or significance.

This is not to say, however, that these Frankish communities were isolated, secluded from social or economic pressures and

---

[32] CR 33, 42, 43, 210, 211, 214.   [33] CR 209, 33.   [34] CR 214.
[35] On Felix: K. F. Stroheker, *Der senatorische Adel im spätantiken Gallien* (Tübingen, 1948), no. 148, pp. 172–3; M. Heinzelmann, *Bischofsherrschaft in Gallien: Zur Kontinuität römischer Führungsschichten vom 4. zum 7. Jahrhundert. Soziale, prosopographische und bildungsgeschichtliche Aspekte,* Beihefte der Francia 5 (Munich, 1976), pp. 214–15; on Victurius: Chédeville and Guillotel, *Bretagne,* p. 160; for Bertramn of Le Mans: *Actus Pontificum Cenomannis,* pp. 101–141, and above, p. 22.

contacts. Archaeological and numismatic evidence supplements the sparse written record, and hints at commercial contacts which linked the Nantais to more distant regions. Nantes itself had been a large and rich Merovingian city, and although strategically and doubtless also economically important in the ninth century, it was probably past its heyday by the time it came under Carolingian control.[36] The city's trading contacts were extensive in the sixth century: into Aquitaine, up the Loire valley and also to the north of the river, across the English Channel to Britain and Ireland and as far north as the Low Countries.[37] Proximity to such a rich entrepot must have affected the hinterland of the city; one reflection of this is perhaps the striking of Merovingian gold *tremisses* on local initiative at several mints in the counties of Nantes, Rennes, and Vannes.[38] By the early eighth century, however, the northwards shift of trade routes towards the Rhineland was having an effect on the lands round the mouth of the Loire, and trade from southern Aquitaine up the Atlantic coast of Gaul was diminishing. The composition of the coin hoard from Bais (Ille-et-Vilaine) illustrates this shift. Deposited probably in about 740, this hoard of silver deniers, ingots, and bracelets from south-east of Rennes is composed in very large part of coins from Neustria and Poitou, with outliers from the Rhône valley and the Auvergne and 29 sceattas from England and the Rhineland.[39] By

[36] Rouche, *Aquitaine*, pp. 293–5, discusses the wealth and topography of the sixth-century city.

[37] Trading contacts with Ireland are discussed by E. James, 'Ireland and western Gaul in the Merovingian period', in *Ireland in Early Medieval Europe*, ed. D. Whitelock, R. McKitterick, and D. Dumville (Cambridge, 1982), pp. 362–86. For finds of Aquitainian sarcophagi, pottery, and decorated terracotta bricks found at Nantes see E. James, *The Merovingian Archaeology of South-West Gaul*, 2 vols., British Archaeological Reports S-25 (Oxford, 1977), pp. 89, 91, 243, 287–9. Onomastic evidence which hints at Irish settlement near Nantes is provided by J.-P. Brunterc'h, 'L'extension du ressort politique et religieux du Nantais au sud de la Loire: essai sur les origines de la dislocation du pagus d'Herbauge (IXe s.–987)' (thesis, Université de Paris IV, 1981), p. 66. (There is a published summary of this thesis in *Positions des Thèses de l'Ecole des Chartes* (Paris, 1981), pp. 39–49.) Findspots in Neustria and the Rhineland of coins from the Nantes mint are given by J. Lafaurie, 'Monnaies mérovingiennes de Nantes du VIe siècle', *Bulletin de la Société Française de Numismatique*, 28 (1973), 391–4.

[38] P. Grierson and M. Blackburn, *Medieval European Coinage with a Catalogue of the Coins in the Fitzwilliam Museum, Cambridge. I. The Early Middle Ages (5th–10th Centuries)* (Cambridge, 1986), pp. 90–100; M. Prou, *Les Monnaies Mérovingiennes de la Bibliothèque Nationale* (Paris, 1892), pp. 114–18, 124–9.

[39] J. Lafaurie, *Catalogue des Deniers Mérovingiens de la Trouvaille de Bais (Ille-et-Vilaine) rédigé par Maurice Prou et Etienne Bougenot. Edition de 1907 avec de nouveaux commentaires et attributions par Jean Lafaurie* (Paris, 1981); Chédeville and Guillotel, *Bretagne*, p. 182.

the ninth century, Nantes was no longer in as close economic association with Aquitaine as earlier. Evidence to estimate the city's significance as a Carolingian trading centre is hard to find, and by the middle of the ninth century, such trade as did still move from northern Aquitaine to Neustria and the Rhineland may have bypassed the city altogether. Although the mint was active until at least the reign of Charles the Bald, few Carolingian coins from Nantes are known, far fewer than from Rennes. In place of links with Aquitaine and beyond, later ninth-century Rennes and Nantes were centres of the regional Neustrian trade network, which oriented them to Le Mans, Angers, Tours, and Orléans and the Loire valley hinterland.[40]

Some trading contacts must have extended westwards from Nantes and Rennes into the area of Breton settlement. After the sporadic minting of *tremisses* in the county of Vannes had ceased, no coins were minted again west of the Vilaine in the early Middle Ages. The Carolingian monetary system was certainly recognised by the Bretons, for the *solidus* and *denarius* were used as units of value in the Redon charters, and payments are twice explicitly described in terms of *solidi karolici*.[41] Although prices were always expressed in monetary terms, it is debatable how far the use of coin affected local communities, and cash may have been hard to obtain in the villages around Redon.[42] Just enough Carolingian coins do exist from findspots within Brittany to confirm that *solidi karolici* did indeed penetrate the region, but given the lack of full analysis of those hoards and Carolingian coins which have been found there, it is impossible even to begin to assess the extent to which Carolingian coinage circulated west of the Vilaine.[43] Isolated coins have, however, been found in

---

[40] J. Lafaurie, 'Deux trésors monétaires carolingiens: Saumeray (Eure-et-Loire), Rennes (Ille-et-Vilaine)', *Revue Numismatique*, 6th ser., 7 (1965), 262–305; D. M. Metcalf, 'A sketch of the currency in the time of Charles the Bald', in *Charles the Bald*, pp. 65–97; M. Van Rey, 'Die Münzprägung Karls des Kahlen und die westfränkische Königslandschaft', in *Die Stadt in der europäischen Geschichte. Festschrift Edith Ennen*, ed. W. Besch, K. Fehn, D. Höroldt, F. Irsigler, and M. Zender (Bonn, 1972), pp. 153–84; three *denarii* of Charles the Bald's pre-864 coinage from the mint at Melle in Poitou, found at Plessé, north-east of Nantes, are reported in *Bulletin de Numismatique*, 7 (1900), 29.   [41] CR 86, 118.

[42] Davies, *Small Worlds*, pp. 58–60, 98–9. Even in the wealthier villages of the Nantais, charters sometimes are explicit that prices are payable in a mixture of cash and kind. CR 210, 227, 228.

[43] Nineteenth-century reports of a hoard of 2,000 Carolingian coins from Priziac (Davies, *Small Worlds*, p. 56) have never been substantiated; the hoards from Questembert and Saint-Brieuc have never been studied in detail. J. Duplessy, *Les*

aristocracy.[75] Although Charles had secured his half-brothers' recognition of his rule over the West Frankish kingdom in 843, he was nevertheless faced with repeated challenges to his authority from his half-brothers Lothar and Louis the German and also from his nephew Pippin II in Aquitaine. Neustria was left without a subking of its own until 856, when Charles installed his own son Louis the Stammerer as its ruler. This intrusion of a child of ten, old enough to represent his father's power but young enough to be easily manipulated by resentful magnates, upset the delicate balance of lordship and patronage. This was the last attempt to establish a focus of royal control at Le Mans.

For the aristocracy in the ninth century, politics concerned the tension between the claims of royal lordship, of family, and of property interests.[76] Self-interest could set brother against brother among the aristocracy, just as it did within the royal household itself. For this reason it is too simple to construe Carolingian politics in terms of competing clan-based interest groups, as has often been done.[77] Nevertheless, a preliminary step in understanding the political turmoil in ninth-century Neustria is the tentative identification, where possible, of significant blood relationships among the aristocracy and in particular of the heritable claims to property and office which such relationships might convey. To use such fragmentary evidence as exists to establish familial ties does have its risks, not least among them the danger of taking biological relationships too readily for the basis of common political identity.[78] But since matters of family and property were among the mainsprings of political action, the

---

[75] K. Brunner, *Oppositionelle Gruppen im Karolingerreich*, Veröffentlichungen des Instituts für österreichische Geschichtsforschung 25 (Vienna, 1979), pp. 96–119; P. Classen, 'Die Verträge von Verdun und von Coulaines, 843, als politische Grundlagen des westfränkischen Reiches', *Historische Zeitschrift*, 196 (1963), 1–35; S. R. Airlie, 'The political behaviour of the secular magnates in Francia, 829–879' (DPhil, Oxford, 1985), pp. 67–77.

[76] Airlie, 'Political behaviour', pp. 1–12; J. Martindale, 'The French aristocracy in the early Middle Ages. A reappraisal', *Past and Present*, 75 (1977), 5–45; J. L. Nelson, 'Public *Histories* and private history in the work of Nithard', *Speculum*, 60 (1985), 251–93, and bibliography there cited (reprinted in *Politics and Ritual*, pp. 196–237).

[77] See most recently Brunner, *Oppositionelle Gruppen*, also Dhondt, *Naissance*.

[78] See the cautions to this effect of D. A. Bullough, '*Europae pater*: Charlemagne and his achievement in the light of modern scholarship', *English Historical Review*, 85 (1970), 59–105, at p. 80; C. B. Bouchard, 'The origins of the French nobility: a reassessment', *American Historical Review*, 86 (1981), 501–32. The methodological problems of studying the early medieval nobility and surrounding historiographical controversies are discussed more fully than is possible here by J. B. Freed, 'Reflections on the medieval German nobility', *American Historical Review*, 91 (1986), 553–75.

attempt is necessary for a fuller understanding of Neustrian politics.

Hand in hand with the establishment of the Carolingian empire went the emergence of an aristocracy with empire-wide interests in lands and offices.[79] Particularly notable for their far-flung activities were members of the so-called 'Widonid' kin-group. This group of relatives was characterised by the recurrence of the names Wido, Warnar, and Lambert. The concentration of property which this family owned in the Vosges suggests that their origins lay in that region, and members of the family were prominent as counts and monastic patrons in the central Rhineland where they can be traced from the middle of the eighth century onwards. One branch of this family acquired lands in Italy in the early ninth century and achieved fame as dukes of Spoleto in the tenth century; another member was active on the south-eastern frontier of the Carolingian empire in Charlemagne's reign.[80] It is almost certain that the men with the names Wido and Lambert who held countships in the Breton marcher area in the first half of the ninth century were related to this family. In 799 the commander of the Breton march was one Wido, and it is possible that he was the same person as his contemporary, the Wido who in 796 made a donation to the family's monastery of Hornbach, and who, with his brothers Hrodold and Warnar, had claims to the monastery of Mettlach rejected in about 782.[81] Léon Levillain has suggested that the Frankish count Frodald mentioned in a charter from the Vannetais of 29 September 801 may, under the variant spelling, be Wido's brother Hrodold.[82] Whatever his association with this kin-group, Wido held a prominent position in western Neustria in Charlemagne's reign. Which county he administered is unknown, but in addition to being in command of the Breton march, he was a royal *missus* in Tours in 802.[83] He

[79] K.-F. Werner, 'Bedeutende Adelsfamilien im Reich Karls des Grossen', in *Karl der Grosse*, I.83–142.

[80] W. Metz, 'Miszellen zur Geschichte der Widonen und der Salier, vornehmlich in Deutschland', *Historisches Jahrbuch*, 85 (1965), 1–27; M. Mitterauer, *Karolingische Markgrafen im Sudosten. Fränkische Reichsaristokratie und bayerischer Stammesadel im österreichischen Raum*, Archiv für österreichischen Geschichte 123 (Vienna, 1963), pp. 64–72.

[81] Metz, 'Miszellen'; M. Chaume, *Les Origines du Duché du Bourgogne*, 2 vols. in 4 (Dijon, 1925–37), I.534; MGH D.Kar. I.200–2, no. 148.

[82] CR 191. L. Levillain, 'La marche de Bretagne, ses marquis et ses comtes', *Annales de Bretagne*, 58 (1951), 89–117, at p. 115.

[83] Alcuin, *Epistolae*, 249, MGH Epp. IV.404.

was also the correspondent for whom Alcuin wrote his *Liber de Virtutibus et Vitiis*.[84]

Members of this family in western Neustria can be traced from the early eighth century right through to the tenth century.[85] Those who feature prominently in the following pages include a Wido who is described as count of Vannes in charters from the last few years of Charlemagne's reign until January 830.[86] Whether he was the same Wido who commanded the Breton march in 799, his son, or some other relative remains unclear.[87] Another possible member was Lambert, count of Nantes and commander of the Breton march in 818, posts which he held until 834. The Wido who was associated with Hornbach in Charlemagne's reign had a son called Lambert, mentioned in a diploma of Louis the Pious; Maurice Chaume's suggestion that Lambert of Nantes was the son of Wido, commander of the Breton march, has been widely accepted.[88] In the 840s another Lambert was struggling to get hold of Nantes; in all probability he was the son of the earlier Count Lambert. Both this second Lambert and his brother Warnar were closely involved with the Bretons, whose assistance they exploited in their struggles against Charles the Bald. There is also evidence of this family's interest in Neustrian churches and their property, for the second Lambert was lay abbot of Saint-Aubin at Angers for a while and his sister Duoda was abbess of Craon in western Anjou. And if name-elements are to be trusted, several bishops may also have been relations of this sprawling family: Wernar, the bishop of Rennes who attended the council of Germigny (843), Landramn I, archbishop of Tours between 816 and 835, his successor Landramn II (archbishop 847–c. 850) and Landramn, bishop of Nantes c. 886–897.[89]

As well as Wido and his relatives, members of the family of Rorigo were closely associated with the Breton marcher area. The frequent use of names commencing with *Gauz-* in this family, together with their long association with Le Mans, make it

---

[84] Alcuin, *Epistolae*, 305, p. 464.

[85] K.-F. Werner, 'Untersuchungen zur Frühzeit des französichen Fürstentums', *Die Welt als Geschichte*, 18 (1958), 256–89, 19 (1959), 146–93, 20 (1960), 87–119, at 18 (1958), 269–70; Brunterc'h, 'Le duché du Maine', p. 46 and n. 95.

[86] See below, p. 74.

[87] Dhondt, *Naissance*, p. 319; cf. Levillain, 'La marche de Bretagne', p. 116; J. Boussard, 'Les destinées de la Neustrie du IXe au XIe siècle', *Cahiers de Civilisation Médiévale*, 11 (1968), 15–28.

[88] Chaume, *Bourgogne*, I.354; Chédeville and Guillotel, *Bretagne*, pp. 203–4.

[89] Duchesne, *Fastes Episcopaux*, II.307, 342, 367.

possible that they were in some way related to the Gauciolenus who ruled Le Mans as bishop for much of the eighth century.[90] They were certainly related to the many *Hervei* and *Rainaldi* of ninth-century Neustria and Aquitaine. Rorigo himself first appears at Charlemagne's court, the lover of Charlemagne's daughter Rotrud, and by her the father of Louis, abbot of Saint-Denis and arch-chancellor to Charles the Bald. Rorigo was also a patron and restorer of his family's monastery of Saint-Maur, at Glanfeuil near Angers. He and his sons by his wife Bilichild – Gauzfrid, Rorigo, and Gauzlin – were prominent in Neustrian and Aquitainian affairs for most of the ninth century and were landowners in Maine, Anjou, and Poitou.[91] The wide-ranging claims to office and influence of members of this family make it impossible to treat Neustrian politics in isolation from those of Aquitaine and beyond.

Neustrian politics in the first half of the ninth century were dominated by these two kin-groups, the relatives of Wido and of Rorigo, and by rivalries between some of their members. Both families clearly regarded the Breton peninsula as within their particular sphere of interest. The consequences of this for the Bretons will become evident in the following chapters.

Quarrelling between representatives of these two families was given a further twist by the presence of other magnates appointed to offices to counterbalance their influence. For example, in 841 Nantes was given to Rainald, a member of a family which was related to Rorigo and which had property and ecclesiastical interests in northern Aquitaine and Anjou.[92] Later still, another family of Rhineland origin, that of Robert the Strong (ancestor of the Capetian kings), established a foothold in Neustria at Tours and Angers during the reign of Charles the Bald. Robert's family

---

[90] Opinions differ as to whether Gauciolenus and his father Chrotgarius were members of the local Neustrian aristocracy, or were Carolingian supporters brought into the region by Charles Martel. H. Ebling, *Prosopographie der Amtsträger des Merowingerreiches von Chlothar II (613) bis Karl Martell (741)*, Beihefte der Francia 2 (Munich, 1974), nos. 131–2, pp. 117–19; cf. Werner, 'Bedeutende Adelsfamilien', at pp. 103–4, 137–42.

[91] O. G. Oexle, 'Bischof Ebroin von Poitiers und seine Verwandten', *Frühmittelalterliche Studien*, 3 (1969), 138–210; K.—F. Werner, 'Gauzlin von Saint-Denis und die westfränkische Reichsteilung von Amiens (März 880)', *DA*, 35 (1979), 395–462, at pp. 404–10.

[92] Brunterc'h, 'L'extension du ressort politique et religieux du Nantais', pp. 80–5, 115–16; Dhondt, *Naissance*, pp. 322–3; Werner, 'Untersuchungen', 19 (1959), p. 180; R. M. Hogan, 'The *Rainaldi* of Angers: "New Men" or descendants of Carolingian *nobiles*?', *Medieval Prosopography*, 2 (1981), 35–62, at pp. 39–41.

and followers aggressively expanded their influence throughout western Neustria in the second half of the ninth century.[93] The web of ties which Robert the Strong created even spilled over into areas of Breton interest and influence. One of his vassals, Cadilo, owned land in the county of Nantes which he gave to Redon, and in the early tenth century one of Robert's son's vassals, Viscount Fulk of Angers, was vying with the Breton ruler for control of Nantes.[94]

By the time Fulk was asserting his claim to Nantes, all the Frankish kingdoms were fragmenting into dynastic principalities as effective power passed more and more into the hands of many different aristocratic families.[95] In Neustria, where Carolingian lordship had only been established late in the eighth century, royal authority was under almost continuous challenge from 830 onwards, and the tensions which sundered the unity of the Carolingian state became evident at an early date. Here, in the core of what from 843 was the West Frankish kingdom, magnates jostled for influence, for access to the resources of ancient abbeys and for freedom from close royal supervision. Neustria with the Breton march has been described as the 'merry-go-round' on which the Carolingian aristocracy played.[96] Magnate rivalries, a distant king, the periodic appearance of a young prince in the apanage of Maine: these formed the matrix within which the Carolingians had to deal with the Bretons and the threat they posed.

[93] Dhondt, *Naissance*, pp. 93–7, 130–45, 323–4; Werner, 'Untersuchungen', 19 (1959), pp. 150–69.

[94] On Cadilo, see CR 59, 69, and Werner, 'Untersuchungen', 19 (1959), p. 179. The identification of Cadilo, beneficiary of Redon with Robert the Strong's vassal of the same name is assured by the fact that Cadilo's charter for Redon is witnessed by Robert's close associate Odo and by one Uuaningo, a name known to recur in the family of Robert's vassal Cadilo. On Fulk of Angers, see Werner, 'Untersuchungen', 18 (1958), pp. 266–9, and below, p. 195.

[95] Dhondt, *Naissance*; K.-F. Werner, 'Kingdom and principality in twelfth-century France', in *The Medieval Nobility*, ed. T. Reuter (Amsterdam, 1979), pp. 243–90; K.-F. Werner, 'La genèse des duchés en France et en Allemagne', *Settimane*, 27 (1979), 175–207; H.-W. Goetz, '*Dux*' und '*Ducatus*'. *Begriffs- und verfassungsgeschichtliche Untersuchungen zur Entstehung des sogenannten 'jüngeren' Stammesherzogtums an der Wende vom neunten zum zehnten Jahrhundert* (Bochum, 1977).

[96] Brunner, *Oppositionelle Gruppen*, p. 125: 'Drehscheibe des Spieles der Mächtigen war immer noch Neustrien mit der bretonischen Mark.'

FRANKISH CHURCHES AND THE CONQUEST OF BRITTANY

There remains one more important element in the tenurial and political landscape of western Neustria: ecclesiastical landholding. We know almost nothing at all of the property interests of local churches,[97] but enough can be said about monastic landowning to demonstrate the web of tenurial obligations which criss-crossed the region and created links with more distant places. These links led directly from the western fringes of the Breton march to the spiritual heart of the Carolingian empire and helped prompt the Carolingians to take action against the Bretons.

Ecclesiastical property relations can be documented from the late seventh century onwards. Ermenland's monastery of Indre, for example, was endowed with lands in the dioceses of Poitou and Coutances as well as with more local properties near Nantes, and after the founder's death, the monastery and its lands were administered by its mother house, Saint-Wandrille in the diocese of Rouen.[98] In a judgement issued between 657 and 673, Chlothar III confirmed Saint-Denis in possession of lands in Maine, Anjou, Touraine, and the county of Rennes.[99] The see of Reims, like Saint-Denis a church exceptionally closely associated with both Merovingian and Carolingian rulers, also possessed lands in the Rennais, which were covered by the terms of a privilege of immunity granted by Dagobert III (711–15).[100] Another monastery owning lands in the marcher region was Prüm in the Ardennes, founded by Charlemagne's great-grandmother in 720 and refounded by Pippin III in 752. Among these lands were fifteen estates in the *pagus* of Rennes granted in 765 by one Egidius.[101]

Carolingian kings added – albeit meagrely – to the ecclesi-

---

[97] The plot of land attached to the church in the *vicus* of Grandchamp has already been mentioned above, p. 36; presumably other local churches were similarly provided for. As for episcopal endowments, an idea of their extent is only possible from the middle of the tenth century. Brunterc'h, 'Puissance temporelle'.

[98] Donatus, *Vita Ermenlandi*, 9–12, 14, pp. 696–8, 700; *Vita Ansberti*, 10, MGH SSRM v.625–6; Chédeville and Guillotel, *Bretagne*, p. 170.

[99] For detailed discussion and identification of the estates, see Brunterc'h, 'Géographie historique et hagiographie', pp. 45–7.

[100] Flodoard, *Historia Remensis Ecclesiae*, II.11, MGH SS XIII.459.

[101] H. Beyer, *Urkundenbuch zur Geschichte der, jetzt die preussischen Regierungsbezirke Coblenz und Trier bildenden mittelrheinischen Territorien. I (bis zum 1169)* (Koblenz, 1860), no. 19, pp. 23–4; for identifications, Brunterc'h, 'Géographie historique et hagiographie', pp. 48–50.

astical endowments in the west of Neustria, and it is these grants which form the best record of the extension of Carolingian lordship into the marcher region. Saint-Médard at Soissons benefited from a grant of Charlemagne's, made some time before 800, of a monastery near Nantes.[102] In 807, Prüm acquired from Charlemagne lands in Anjou and the Rennais confiscated from one Godebertus for crimes which included incest.[103] Between 814 and 818, Louis the Pious gave land on the border to an otherwise unknown Abbot Witchar.[104]

A significant pattern emerges from these land grants. The monasteries of Saint-Denis, Saint-Médard, and Saint-Wandrille and the see of Reims all enjoyed close royal favour and great prestige under both Merovingians and Carolingians; Prüm, a less ancient foundation, was one of the Carolingians' family monasteries. Many of the Neustrian estates given to these churches lay in the heavily forested and sparsely populated districts of the Breton marcher zone. It would seem that the Carolingians were relying upon these trusted churches to thrust Frankish influence into the border region and to represent royal authority there.[105] Here as in other militarily and politically sensitive spots, ecclesiastical landholdings provided a means of holding down frontier regions and advancing Carolingian lordship.[106]

This impelled the churches concerned to take note of Breton affairs, particularly when the security of their landholding might be at stake. It so happens that the churches endowed with lands in this sensitive region were all major centres for the writing of history: much of what we know about Frankish attitudes towards and dealing with the Bretons comes from works written by

---

[102] *Annales Ordinis Sancti Benedicti*, ed. J. Mabillon, 6 vols. (Paris, 1703–39), II.840–1.
[103] MGH D.Kar. I.274–5, no. 205.
[104] Ermoldus Nigellus, *In Honorem Hludovici*, III.91–2, p. 44.
[105] Brunterc'h, 'Géographie historique et hagiographie', p. 54.
[106] Compare Geberding, *The Rise of the Carolingians*, pp. 127–8 on Süstern; A. Dierkens, *Abbayes et Chapitres entre Sambre et Meuse (VIIᵉ–XIᵉ siècles). Contribution à l'Histoire Religieuse des Campagnes du haut Moyen Age*, Beihefte der Francia 14 (Sigmaringen, 1985), p. 326 on Lobbes, Nivelles, and Stavelot as representatives of Arnulfing power along the Neustrian/Austrasian border; P. Geary, *Aristocracy in Provence. The Rhône Basin at the Dawn of the Carolingian Age*, Monographien zur Geschichte des Mittelalters 31 (Stuttgart, 1985), p. 125 on the importance of Novalesa in securing the alpine passes into Lombardy for the Carolingians; R. Hodges, J. Moreland, and H. Patterson, 'San Vincenzo al Volturno, the kingdom of Benevento and the Carolingians', in *Papers in Italian Archaeology*, ed. C. Malone and S. Stoddart, 4 vols., British Archaeological Reports, International Series 243–6 (Oxford, 1985), IV.261–85 on Carolingian patronage and iconography in the Beneventan borderlands.

members of these communities. Without the *Annales Mettenses Priores*, propaganda for the Carolingian cause compiled at either Saint-Denis or Chelles in 805, without the Chronicle of Saint-Wandrille, without the annalistic tradition of Reims – Hincmar's contribution to the Annals of Saint-Bertin and the Annals of the tenth-century cathedral canon Flodoard – or without the chronicle written between 906 and 915 by Regino, abbot of Prüm, it would be impossible to write large sections of this book. Even Saint-Médard, although not a source of information about Breton affairs, deserves a mention in this context, for someone there at the end of the ninth century had a taste for Breton etymologies.[107] Our knowledge of the strife between Bretons and Franks in the early Middle Ages comes from those with vested interests in the border area.

Although there is no explicit evidence of Breton raids into Frankish lands in the middle of the eighth century, nevertheless the organisation of the march by 778 under a single *praefectus*, Roland of epic fame, suggests that the region was not tranquil, even though in that particular year the prefect could absent himself to campaign on another frontier of Charlemagne's realms.[108] The need for churches to protect their property may have contributed to the intensification of military activity in the area. Powerful ecclesiastical voices perhaps urged Charlemagne to take firm action and may have reminded him of his Merovingian predecessors' claims to overlordship over the Bretons. At any event, it was an easy move from the indirect assertion of Carolingian power in the border region to aggressive campaigning against the Bretons.

In contrast with Aquitaine and Saxony, the Bretons were subjected easily and swiftly. Pippin III had campaigned against Vannes on the eve of his elevation to the throne in 751, as part of his effort to secure Neustria.[109] Not until 786 was another expedition against the Bretons launched, this time led by Charlemagne's seneschal, Audulf.[110] A more impressive victory was won a few years later by Count Wido, the commander of the Breton march. After his army had marched the length and

---

[107] F. Lot, 'Un faiseur d'étymologies bretonnes au IXe siècle', *Mélanges Bretons et Celtiques offerts à J. Loth* (Rennes, 1927), pp. 381–5.

[108] Einhard, *Vita Karoli Magni*, 9, ed. O. Holder-Egger, MGH SSRG (Hanover, 1911), p. 12.

[109] For a defence of this suggestion instead of the usual date of 753 for Pippin's sack of Vannes, see Smith, 'The sack of Vannes'.   [110] *ARF*, a. 786, p. 72.

breadth of the peninsula in 799, all the Bretons surrendered. This victory marked a decisive change in the military balance between Franks and Bretons: the Carolingian court chronicle frankly admitted that for the first time ever, the whole of the land of the Bretons was subject to the Franks.[111]

The region which Charlemagne's armies conquered in 799 had a long tradition of hostility towards the Franks. The extension of Carolingian lordship over the Bretons was the logical continuation of the spread of royal power, ecclesiastical landholding, and aristocratic influence into Neustria. From Charlemagne's perspective, the Bretons were important not only because he inherited a claim to hegemony over them from the Merovingians, but also because they affected the security of royal interests in western Neustria. The marcher area itself was one where Carolingian authority was fragile because only tardily established: a history of freedom from royal direct intervention shaped the politics of this region until the middle of the ninth century. Here too Breton raiding was potentially most destructive, and through the magnates of this region the allegiance of the Bretons might be secured or lost. But it was for Louis the Pious, rather than for Charlemagne, that Neustria and the Breton march was to prove a political minefield.

[111] *ARF*, a. 799, p. 108; *Annales Mettenses Priores*, a. 800, p. 85.

Chapter 3

THE BRETONS IN THE CHRISTIAN EMPIRE OF LOUIS THE PIOUS

Charlemagne died in 814. By accident, not design, he passed on his empire to a single heir, his only surviving son Louis the Pious. Louis had had a thorough training for rulership: as subking of Aquitaine since childhood, and as a participant on campaigns against the Avars, Saxons, and Beneventans. On his accession, he brought with him to Aachen new men and new ideas, and, above all, a renewed commitment to promoting Christian values and beliefs. Where Charlemagne had been hailed as David, Louis the Pious was Solomon; to his father's Constantine he was Theodosius.[1] From Louis' own close family to the distant frontiers of his empire, everyone was to be touched by his vision of Christian peace and concord: 'You are the peace of the world', declared Amalarius of Metz.[2] A great programme of reforming legislation in the opening years of his reign set out the goals and the ways to achieve them. The keystone was the *Ordinatio Imperii* of 817, in which, having crowned his eldest son Lothar as co-emperor, and made provisions for the succession which would establish his younger sons Louis and Pippin in subordinate kingships, he regulated the conduct of the three brothers towards each other, and established an ideal of fraternal co-operation, Christian charity, and peace for all people.[3]

The British Isles apart, Louis' empire was coterminous with Latin Christendom. The *Ordinatio Imperii* defined the Christian community of the Carolingian state in a way which included all

---

[1] K.-F. Werner, '*Hludovicus Augustus*: gouverner l'empire chrétien – idées et réalités', in *Charlemagne's Heir*, pp. 3–123, at pp. 56–60.

[2] Amalarius of Metz, *De Ecclesiasticis Officiis*, preface, PL cv.988, cited by Werner, '*Hludovicus Augustus*', p. 58 n. 202.

[3] T. Schieffer, 'Die Krise des karolingische Imperiums', in *Aus Mittelalter und Neuzeit: Festschrift für G. Kallen*, ed. J. Engel and H. M. Klinkenburg (Bonn, 1957), pp. 1–15; J. Semmler, 'Reichsidee und kirchliche Gesetzgebung', *Zeitschrift für Kirchengeschichte*, 71 (1960), 37–65; T. F. X. Noble, 'The monastic ideal as the model for reform: the case of Louis the Pious', *Revue Bénédictine*, 86 (1976), 235–50.

those peripheral peoples over whom the Franks claimed hegemony. To the subkingdom of Aquitaine intended for Pippin were attached Gascony and the Spanish march; with Louis' Bavarian kingdom were included the Carinthians, Bohemians, Avars, and Slavs.[4] All other regions and their marches were to be left under the care of the emperor himself. In effect, Louis' realm was not only defined by political frontiers, but was also delimited by a 'moral barrier' that marked the gulf between his Christian subjects and those outside the empire.[5] Even where Louis' rule shaded off into lordship over non-Christian peoples at its remotest northern and eastern rim, the emperor did his best to further Christianity by supporting missionary activity to Scandinavia and sponsoring the baptism of Danish chiefs.

Within this profoundly Christian empire, the Bretons and Gascons were in an anomalous position. Of those peripheral peoples over whom the Merovingians had claimed lordship, only they were not firmly reconquered and brought to accept Carolingian rule.[6] A Carolingian propagandist writing in 805 claimed that the Bretons had been brought back under Frankish rule just as had the Saxons, Frisians, Alemannians, Bavarians, Aquitainians, and Gascons.[7] But the reality was rather different. Alemannians, Bavarians, Saxons, and Aquitainians all came to acquiesce in, or were forced to acquiesce in, Carolingian rule during the reigns of Pippin III and Charlemagne, and thereafter were rapidly and profoundly influenced by Carolingian government and the standards of the Frankish church. By contrast, the Bretons and Gascons were the only Christian peoples over whom the Franks claimed lordship who could not be made to accept Carolingian rule.[8] They thus posed a particular challenge to Louis' mission of Christendom united and at peace under him. Of

---

[4] MGH Capit. I.271, no. 136, clauses 1, 2.

[5] The phrase is that of A. Alföldi, 'The moral barrier on Rhine and Danube', in *Congress of Roman Frontier Studies, 1949*, ed. E. Birley (Durham, 1952), pp. 1–16.

[6] The duchy of Benevento is a quite different case: never the object of Merovingian claims, it was a border zone claimed by both the Carolingian and Byzantine empires.

[7] *Annales Mettenses Priores*, a. 687, pp. 12–13. On the authorship and date of composition of these annals see H. Hoffmann, *Untersuchungen zur karolingischen Annalistik* (Bonn, 1958), pp. 9–68; I. Haselbach, *Aufstieg und Herrschaft der Karlinger in der Darstellung der sogennanten Annales Mettenses Priores*, Historische Studien 412 (Lübeck, 1970), and also the review by J. M. Wallace-Hadrill, *English Historical Review*, 86 (1971), 154–6; Bullough, '*Europae pater*', p. 65.

[8] K. Reindel, 'Bayern im Karolingerreich', in *Karl der Grosse*, I.220–46; P. Wolff, 'L'Aquitaine et ses marges', in *Karl der Grosse*, I.269–306; L. Auzias, *L'Aquitaine Carolingienne*, Bibliothèque Méridionale, 2nd ser., 28 (Toulouse, 1937).

the Gascons we know too little to be able to analyse in any detail how the Carolingians regarded them.[9] By contrast, there is just enough information on Louis' involvement with the Bretons for us to establish how he regarded the problem they posed to his notion of a Christian empire, and to identify the strategies he adopted for dealing with them. In Brittany, we can watch Louis the Pious' efforts to redraw the moral barrier that marked out his empire.

Much of this effort was necessarily military and administrative. An analysis of Louis' strategies for imposing his lordship on the Bretons involves careful scrutiny of exiguous documentation in the context of the politics of his reign. Recent scholarship has done much to enhance our appreciation of the administrative sophistication and legislative developments of Louis' empire: in his dealings with Brittany we may trace his flexible and ultimately fairly successful handling of a political conundrum which did not yield a flurry of capitular, conciliar, or diplomatic evidence. Louis' interactions with the Bretons offer a case-study in Carolingian techniques of imperial propaganda and domination. They show us what imperial peace meant in practice.

In addition, something of the impact of Carolingian rule can be discerned. Louis' decisions were of the utmost long-term significance for the political and cultural evolution of the Bretons, for his reign presages the opening up of Brittany to sustained Frankish influence. By examining the rhetorical justification of Louis' involvement in Brittany, his techniques of governing the region, and the interaction of local and imperial politics, this chapter demonstrates how the macroscopic dissolved into the molecular at the frontiers of the Carolingian world.

IMPERIAL RHETORIC AND BRETON REVOLT

Carolingian writers rarely took a dispassionate interest in the behaviour of the emperor's subjects. Where politics and morality overlapped as totally as they did in matters of oath-taking and oath-breaking – of loyalty and rebellion – it was natural for accounts of events to be tinged with zealous righteousness or self-

[9] R. Collins, *The Basques* (Oxford, 1986), pp. 106–32; R. Collins, 'The Basques in Aquitaine and Navarre: problems of frontier government', in *War and Government in the Middle Ages. Essays in Honour of J. O. Prestwich*, ed. J. Gillingham and J. C. Holt (Woodbridge, 1984), pp. 3–17.

justification. Much of the historiography of the reign of Louis the Pious derives from men within or very close to the imperial retinue, and it is therefore little surprise that in reporting Breton affairs, early ninth-century writers show a firmly partisan stand. Chroniclers and biographers, panegyrists and polemicists alike condemn Breton recidivist behaviour in no uncertain terms. Behind the rhetoric, we may sense that Louis the Pious perceived the Bretons as a real moral problem. It is also clear that they posed a significant military threat. The Bretons were a challenge to the ideology enunciated in the *Ordinatio Imperii,* and for the first half of his reign, Louis strove to assimilate the Bretons as fully as possible into his *imperium.* Only in Brittany did Louis abandon his generally defensive frontier policy for more aggressive action.[10]

Accusations of treachery and fickleness were commonplace in Carolingian chroniclers' accounts of the Franks' efforts to subjugate non-Frankish peoples to their rule, but the charges levelled against the Bretons became much harsher under Louis the Pious than they had been in Charlemagne's reign. One writer in particular reveals the deep-seated Frankish animosities towards the Bretons. This is Ermold the Black, whose verse panegyric *In Honour of Louis the Pious* was composed between 826 and February 828 while the author was banished from Louis the Pious' court; Ermold wrote in an attempt to regain imperial favour.[11] Ermold condemned the Bretons as 'lying, proud, rebellious, lacking in goodness, Christians in name only' and in words lifted straight from Caesar's account of the Gauls, he described their purported incestuous habits.[12] He asserted that the land occupied by this 'hostile people' was Frankish land in which the Bretons, exiled from their own country, had been allowed to settle by the Franks. The Bretons repaid their hosts with warfare not tribute, rejecting rightful Frankish authority.[13] Ermold's rhetoric has obvious debts to the classical tradition of denigrating peoples opposed to imperial expansion as thereby morally corrupt.[14] In

[10] T. Reuter, 'The end of Carolingian military expansion', in *Charlemagne's Heir,* pp. 391–405.
[11] Its function and form are discussed by P. Godman, 'Louis "the Pious" and his poets', *Frühmittelalterliche Studien,* 19 (1985), 239–89.
[12] Ermoldus Nigellus, *In Honorem Hludowici,* III.43–5, p. 42.
[13] Ermoldus Nigellus, *In Honorem Hludowici,* III.73–88, 311–24, pp. 43, 50.
[14] Compare G. B. Ladner, 'On Roman attitudes towards barbarians in late antiquity', *Viator,* 7 (1976), 1–26; W. R. Jones, 'The image of the barbarian in medieval Europe', *Comparative Studies in Society and History,* 13 (1971), 376–407.

Ermold's eyes, Breton depravity was all the grater because the Bretons were Christian. Breton resistance to the Franks tarnished the image of Louis' Christian empire.

The stridency with which Ermold proclaimed Louis' rightful rule over the Bretons points up the precariousness of Frankish lordship over this people. He was expressing the irritation of a Frankish court which had discovered the hollowness of Charlemagne's claim to have subjugated the Bretons, and which had had to deal with repeated Breton unrest since 799. Nor was Ermold alone in these attitudes. Both the compiler of the Royal Frankish Annals at Louis' court, and the emperor's anonymous biographer, the 'Astronomer', betray similar prejudices. Yet it is these writers who constitute our main source of information on relations between Bretons and Franks in the reign of Louis the Pious. As we turn our attention to Louis' dealings with the Bretons, we must bear in mind that these sources all offer us a highly partial account, and that we can only see the Bretons in their terms, as in a distorting mirror.

Louis the Pious' first recorded encounter with the Bretons came in 818, as part of his efforts in the opening years of his reign to establish firm frontiers to his empire and conclude peace with surrounding peoples.[15] On reaching the imperial palace at Aachen after his father's death on 28 January 814, Louis had received envoys from all the kingdoms and peoples on his borders and from all those peoples who had been subject to Charlemagne. As reported by Thegan, the envoys inaugurated the ethics of the new regime: promises of peace and good faith were made freely to the emperor, without compulsion.[16] Thegan, however, wrote his biography of Louis the Pious almost at the end of the reign, in 837, and his account of the opening of Louis' reign is tinged with idealism. It is more likely that some of these neighbouring peoples took the opportunity presented by the accession of the new emperor to make gestures of independence from Carolingian tutelage. Thus, although in 815 Louis concluded a peace with the Danes to establish the northern frontier of his empire, at about the same time he removed the Basque leader because of his 'excessive insolence and depravity' (which must mean that the Basques had failed to recognise Louis' lordship), and in 816 campaigned into

---

[15] Cf. Ermoldus Nigellus, *In Honorem Hludowici*, III.5, p. 41.
[16] Thegan, *Vita Hludowici Imperatoris*, 9, MGH SS II.593.

Gascony to deal with the ensuing Basque revolt.[17] In the following years, Louis continued to strive for peace along the frontiers of his realm. In 816–17 he received a delegation from Abd-al-Rahman, the emir of Cordova, and reached a settlement with the Byzantines, Slavs, and Dalmatians of the south-eastern frontier of the empire.[18] All these negotiations were a preliminary to disposition of the empire in the *Ordinatio Imperii* in 817.

Having suppressed the revolt against the provisions of the *Ordinatio* mounted by his nephew, Bernard of Italy, and in so doing reaffirmed his vision of a Christian empire founded on peace both at the frontiers and at the centre,[19] Louis was free to deal with the Bretons by the spring of 818. They had certainly thrown off Frankish overlordship by 818, probably very soon after Charlemagne's death, after an earlier attempt to do so in 811.[20] According to the 'Astronomer', the Bretons were refusing to pay tribute, and in their disobedience 'had been so insolent as to dare to call one of their number, Morman, king'.[21] The Bretons' use of the word *rex* to describe Morman's status is a clear sign of their rejection of Carolingian overlordship; in Ermold's view, it was inappropriate to call Morman king, because he ruled nothing.[22] As with Frankish assertions of hegemony over the Slavs beyond the eastern frontiers of the empire, inconsistencies and discrepancies in the status or rank ascribed to the ruler of a *gens* are a hint that each side held a fundamentally different view of their relationship.[23]

Ermold describes negotiations between Louis' envoy, Abbot Witchar, and Morman, in which the Breton leader refused to submit to pious Louis' 'righteous rule': as a result, Louis invaded Brittany.[24] Unlike his father, Louis himself led the campaign against the Bretons. He summoned a very large army drawn from

[17] Thegan, *Vita Hludowici*, 14, p. 593; *ARF*, a. 816, p. 144; Collins, *The Basques*, pp. 127–8. [18] *ARF*, a. 817, p. 145.

[19] T. F. X. Noble, 'The revolt of King Bernard of Italy in 817: its causes and consequences', *Studi Medievali*, 3rd ser., 15 (1974), 315–26; Airlie, 'Political behaviour', pp. 40–3. [20] *ARF*, a. 811, p. 135.

[21] 'Astronomer', *Vita Hludowici Imperatoris*, 30, MGH SS ii.623.

[22] 'Dici si liceat rex, quia nulla regit', *In Honorem Hludowici*, iii.56, p. 42.

[23] F. Graus, 'Rex-Dux Moraviae', *Sbornik prací filosofické faculty brnenske university, Rada historicke*, 7 (1960), 181–90 (with German summary); similarly A. R. Lewis, 'The dukes in the *Regnum Francorum*, AD 550–751', *Speculum*, 51 (1976), 381–410 at n. 101. Compare Gregory of Tours' assertion that after the death of Clovis, the Bretons were under Frankish lordship and hence their rulers were called counts and not kings. *Lib. Hist.*, iv.4, pp. 137–8, quoted above, p. 18 n. 36.

[24] Morman is urged: 'Perge celer regisque pii pia suscipe jura' at iii.133, p. 45.

all provinces of his empire to assemble at Vannes, then advanced his camp westwards to Priziac on the left bank of the river Ellé (probably the western boundary of the county of Vannes) and from there launched attacks on Breton strongholds. Breton resistance collapsed immediately after Morman had been killed by one of the imperial retinue. From the Frankish point of view, it was a quick and easy campaign, and Louis returned home 'with the triumph of victory', as the Chronicle of Moissac expressed it, having imposed his will on the whole region.[25]

Louis' pacification of Brittany did not last, for trouble broke out again in 822. In the autumn of that year, the counts of the marcher region ravaged the lands of a rebel named Wihomarc.[26] Wihomarc, however, managed to offer more sustained opposition to the Franks than they had previously encountered amongst the Bretons, and several years passed before he was finally eliminated. In 824, Louis again led his army into Brittany in person to deal with another revolt led by Wihomarc.[27] In September the army assembled at Rennes, which suggests that the focus of unrest was central-northern Brittany. Split into three parts under the command of the emperor and his sons Pippin and Louis, the Frankish army spent six weeks ravaging the region before withdrawing to Rouen in November.[28] Frankish sources stress the scale of the devastation inflicted by the Carolingian army but are not at all candid about the outcome of the campaign. In effect, it was a severe setback for the Franks. When Wihomarc and other Breton leaders came to Aachen the following year, the emperor made unaccustomed concessions to them. In return for promises of future loyalty, the Bretons were forgiven and sent home laden with gifts. But they promptly retaliated by ravaging the Frankish lands of the marcher region, and the unrest was only ended when Lambert, count of Nantes, caught Wihomarc in his own home, and killed him.[29]

---

[25] *Chronicon Moissacense*, a. 818, MGH SS I.313; also *ARF*, a. 818, p. 148; 'Astronomer', *Vita Hludowici*, 30, p. 623; Thegan, *Vita Hludowici*, 25, p. 596; Ermoldus Nigellus, *In Honorem Hludowici*, III.335–502, pp. 50–5; Wrdisten, '*Vita S. Winwaloei*', II.11, pp. 226–7.

[26] *ARF*, a. 822, p. 159; 'Astronomer', *Vita Hludowici*, 35, p. 626.

[27] Wihomarc's role in the rebellion of 824 is made clear in the *ARF* a. 825, p. 167.

[28] *ARF*, a. 824, p. 165; Thegan, *Vita Hludowici*, 31, p. 597; Ermoldus Nigellus, *In Honorem Hludowici*, IV.113–46, pp. 61–2.

[29] *ARF*, a. 825, p. 167; 'Astronomer', *Vita Hludowici*, 19, pp. 628–9. The only chronicler to hint at Frankish defeat in 824 is Regino of Prüm, who attributes an unsuccessful campaign against the Bretons to Louis in 836. *Chronicon*, a. 836, p. 74. Here as

After 825, Louis' relations with the Bretons changed, and the second half of his reign was generally one of compromise and accord. But by then the damage was done, and nothing could eradicate the humiliations of Louis' early years. An indication of this is the deep impression which Breton affairs left on the Franks. In about 860 in Mainz, the defection of the Bretons and Slavs in Louis' reign was seen as partial fulfilment of prophecies of the decay of his empire which Charlemagne had received in a vision.[30] Much later, the eleventh-century *vita* of Frederick, bishop of Utrecht during Louis' reign, cast the Bretons as the avenging hand of God, whose defeat of Louis fulfilled Frederick's prophecy that if Louis married Judith (here described as his cousin, and hence the bishop's opposition to the match), nation would rise against nation.[31] Breton resistance to Louis' lordship was no series of mere frontier skirmishes; it struck at the heart of Carolingian claims to rightful rule over a Christian *imperium* of nations.

THE TOKENS OF LORDSHIP

How did Charlemagne and Louis the Pious try to control and govern this unruly people? In what manner was overlordship expressed? Typically, the provinces conquered by the Carolingians were assimilated as fully as possible into the empire with the help of trusted Frankish administrators, secular and ecclesiastical, and through the promulgation of legislation and the grants of diplomas to favoured recipients. Brittany saw virtually none of this. Nevertheless, enduring changes in the structure of Breton society itself were inaugurated in response to repeated Carolingian military aggression.

In essence, the 'conquest' of 799 and the renewed subjugations of 818 and 825 entailed rituals of submission by the Breton chiefs. The Royal Frankish Annals mention that in 799 Count Wido

elsewhere, Regino's chronology is notoriously inaccurate; K.-F. Werner, 'Zur Arbeitsweise des Regino von Prüm', *Die Welt als Geschichte*, 19 (1959), 96–116.

[30] P. Geary, 'Germanic tradition and royal ideology in the ninth century: the "Visio Karoli Magni"', *Frühmittelalterliche Studien*, 21 (1987), 274–94, with edition of the *Visio* on pp. 293–4.

[31] *Acta Frederici Episcopi et Martiris Ultrajecti in Belgio*, 3, 5, AASS Jul. iv.463, 466. Here the defeat is dated to 835 and attributed to Morman. Verbal parallels suggest that this information was derived from Regino of Prüm, as n. 29 above.

received the weapons given up by 'all' the Breton chiefs, each with its defeated owner's name inscribed on it and that he then presented the arms to Charlemagne.[32] In 786 at Worms and again in 800 at Tours the Breton leaders were brought into the king's presence, on the latter occasion making offerings to him.[33] On these occasions the submission must have involved the making of oaths and the giving of hands. Ermold recalled that Morman had often performed these rituals to Charlemagne.[34]

Attendance at the royal court, oaths and the giving of hands traditionally confirmed and symbolised the submission to an overlord, as did the exaction of tribute and of hostages. In addition to the gestures of submission performed to him, we know that Louis the Pious took hostages, and repeated references in sources from the 820s to Breton refusal to pay tribute make it likely that both Charlemagne and Louis the Pious revived Merovingian demands for tribute.[35] Louis the Pious may also have negotiated an agreed frontier between Bretons and Franks, as he did with the Slavs and Danes at the beginning of his reign.[36] In effect, Charlemagne and Louis the Pious expressed their hegemony over the Bretons by the same means as Chilperic had done in the sixth century, and Dagobert I in the seventh, and no differently from the ways in which the Merovingians and

[32] *ARF*, a. 799, p. 108.

[33] *ARF*, a. 786, p. 72; *Annales Mettenses Priores*, a. 800, p. 85.

[34] Louis has his emissary ask Morman 'Non memorat jurata fides, seu dextera Francis / Saepe data, et Carolo servitia exhibita?' *In Honorem Hludowici*, III.313–15, p. 50. It may have been on the basis of an oath taken to Louis the Pious that the machtierns Portitoe and Wruili are referred to as *vassi dominici* in a charter of 824/30. CR 196.

[35] Hostages: *ARF*, a. 818, 824, pp. 148, 165, *Chronicon Moissacense*, a. 818, p. 313, *AB*, a. 837, p. 22; hostages and hand-giving: 'Astronomer', *Vita Hludowici*, 30, p. 623; refusal to pay tribute: *ARF*, revised text a. 786, p. 73, Ermoldus Nigellus, *In Honorem Hludowici*, III.23, 77, 212–14, pp. 42, 43, 47. The only other reference to tribute payments are Hincmar's notes in the Annals of Saint-Bertin that the traditional annual tribute of fifty pounds of silver was paid in 863 and again in 864. *AB*, a. 863, 864, pp. 96, 113.

[36] When Nominoe was described raiding eastwards to Le Mans in 844, he was said to be 'fines sibi suisque antecessoribus distributos insolenter egrediens' (*AB*, a. 844, pp. 47–8); since Nominoe was in control of Brittany from 831, his 'antecessores' must have been the leaders of the 820s or even earlier. A negotiated frontier was established between Waroch and the envoys of Chlothar and Guntramn in 588 (Gregory of Tours, *Lib. Hist.*, IX.18, pp. 431–2), and in 850, Nominoe was accused of breaking formally established boundaries which dated back to the beginnings of Frankish domination over the Bretons. Lupus of Ferrières, *Correspondance*, ed. L. Levillain, 2 vols., Les Classiques de l'Histoire de France au Moyen Age 10, 16 (2nd edn, Paris, 1964), II.62, no. 81.

Carolingians treated their pagan neighbours to the north and east.[37]

These tactics were not those used to control other peripheral regions. In contrast with Aquitaine, Neustria, and Burgundy, no Austrasian Franks were appointed to rule Breton monasteries, no Breton church lands were diverted to support Frankish officials.[38] No Frankish magnates at any time became permanently established in Breton-speaking Brittany. In contrast with Alemannia, Thuringia, Bavaria, Neustria, or Provence, opposition to the spread of Carolingian power was not led by princely families of Frankish origin, resentful of the rise of one of their number to such a pre-eminent position.[39] Rather, the Franks encountered local Breton rulers who were maintaining a long tradition of defiance of Frankish claims to overlordship. Unlike every other part of the Carolingian empire (except perhaps Gascony), it is immediately striking that none of the Breton lordly families of the eleventh century either claimed descent from Carolingian officials, or can be shown to have had them among their ancestors. There is no equivalent from the reigns of either Charlemagne or Louis the Pious of the *Capitulare Aquitanicum*, issued in the wake of Pippin III's final subjection of the Aquitainians in 768, or of Charlemagne's two capitularies legislating for the government of the Saxons, the ferociously harsh *Capitulatio de partibus Saxoniae* of 785 and the more moderate *Capitulare Saxonicum* of 797.[40] Charlemagne's interest in 'national' lawcodes was confined to his Germanic subjects; there is no Breton parallel to the versions of the *Lex Saxonum*, the *Lex Thuringorum* or the *Lex Frisionum* drawn up in association with the great Aachen assembly of 802/3.[41]

The rare occasions when Charlemagne and Louis the Pious ventured beyond displays of hegemonic overlordship are

---

[37] Compare Wood, *Merovingian North Sea*; F. L. Ganshof, 'The treaties of the Carolingians', *Medieval and Renaissance Studies*, 3 (1967), 23–52, esp. 23–5; R. Ernst, 'Karolingische Nordostpolitik zur Zeit Ludwigs des Frommen', in *Östliches Europa: Spiegel der Geschichte. Festschrift für Manfred Hellmann*, ed. C. Goehrke, E. Oberländer, and D. Wojtecki, Quellen und Studien zur Geschichte des östlichen Europa 9 (Wiesbaden, 1977), pp. 81–107.

[38] J. Semmler, 'Pippin III. und die fränkischen Klöster', *Francia*, 3 (1975), 88–146.

[39] See the convenient summary of Geary, *Aristocracy in Provence*, pp. 138–9, and above, pp. 46–7 for Neustria.   [40] MGH Capit. 1.42–3, 68–72, nos. 18, 26, 27.

[41] On which see R. Buchner, *Deutschlands Geschichtsquellen im Mittelalter. Vorzeit und Karolinger. Beiheft: Die Rechtsquellen* (Weimar, 1953), pp. 39–44; C. Schott, 'Der Stand der Leges-Forschung', *Frühmittelalterliche Studien*, 13 (1979), 29–55, at pp. 41–2.

therefore particularly significant. In this respect, the county of Vannes stands apart as an area of real Carolingian influence, and merits separate treatment.[42] As far as all the rest of Brittany is concerned, extremely meagre evidence hints at an abortive attempt to extend to Brittany some of the techniques of integration employed elsewhere. On only one occasion is Charlemagne known to have extended his lordship beyond the Breton military leaders. During a revolt late in his reign, the monastery of Saint-Méen, at Gaël in north-eastern Brittany, was sacked and its treasury and archives destroyed, presumably by the Franks.[43] After the sacking, Helocar, the bishop of Alet under whose control the monastery fell, obtained from Charlemagne a *pancarta* (not extant) confirming that Saint-Méen possessed all those lands to which its title deeds had been destroyed.[44] This imperial confirmation of the abbey's landed endowments certainly implied a claim to recognition of Carolingian overlord-ship here at Saint-Méen. But it was no token of direct Carolingian administrative authority in Brittany. Rather, like the diplomas for the Beneventan monasteries of San Vincenzo and Monte Cassino which Charlemagne had issued when he campaigned south of Rome in 787, the diploma was the equivalent of planting the flag in an area under only tenuous Carolingian influence.[45]

In contrast to Charlemagne, Louis the Pious pressed home his claims to lordship over the Bretons more rigorously. Not only did he himself lead his armies against the Bretons on two occasions, he made some effort to establish direct agents of royal power in Brittany. In the wake of the victory of 818, he instituted a Frankish count in the *pagus trans silvam* (in Breton, Poutrocoet), the area west of the county of Rennes and north of the county of Vannes. This was Rorigo, a member of one of the most important Neustrian magnate families.[46] His countship is mentioned in two Breton charter dating clauses from 819/20, one of which is from Lanouée in central Brittany. At an unknown date in the reign of Louis the Pious, but before 839, he is also recorded owning land

[42] Below, pp. 74–7.
[43] Morice, *Preuves*, 1.225–6; cf. Reuter, 'Plunder and tribute'.
[44] Morice, *Preuves*, 1.225–6. Charlemagne's charter is referred to in Louis the Pious' diploma for Saint-Méen, which itself only survives incorporated into a *vidimus* of 1294.
[45] MGH D.Kar. 1.211–17, nos. 156–9; *ARF*, a. 787, p. 74; C. Wickham, *Early Medieval Italy. Central Power and Local Society, 400–1000* (London, 1981), p. 49; Hodges *et al.*, 'San Vincenzo al Volturno'.   [46] See above, pp. 53–4.

in Brittany, at Bernéan.[47] The appointment of a Frankish office-
holder to authority over the Bretons appears to have been short-
lived; perhaps it was this intrusion into local power structures of
central-northern Brittany that prompted Wihomarc's revolts of
822–5.

Louis was rather more successful in asserting his lordship over
Breton churches and did his best to bring the Bretons into his
imperial *Reichskirche*. Discussion of his efforts to realise the claims
of the metropolitan church of Tours to jurisdiction over the
Breton bishoprics is best deferred;[48] at this point, however, Louis'
legislation for Breton monasteries is enlightening.

The programme of monastic legislation inaugurated in close
association with Benedict of Aniane in 816–19 was central to
Louis' ideal of a Christian empire. The replacement of the various
religious observances which had characterised the Carolingian
empire until 814 with uniform codes of living for monks, for
nuns, and for canonesses was envisaged as a means to religious
harmony and uniformity. Concord and unity within the church
were to buttress the ideals of imperial unity and peace which
Louis was fostering.[49] He initiated this programme by calling in
all his predecessors' ecclesiastical diplomas and confirming them
himself, often adding grants of immunity and protection. This
new combination of privileges for bishoprics and monasteries
alike laid the firm legal foundations of Louis' imperial church.[50]

Saint-Méen was one of the monasteries thus affected. On 25
March 816, the diploma which Charlemagne had granted to
Helocar received Louis' confirmation, and Saint-Méen acquired

[47] CR 164; H. Guillotel, 'L'action de Charles le Chauve vis-à-vis de la Bretagne de 843
à 851', *MSHAB*, 53 (1975–6), 5–32, at p. 31 n. 124; Odo of Glanfeuil, *Historia
Translationis Sancti Mauri*, 2, MGH SS xv.i, 466 refers to Rorigo's estate in Brittany,
'Brenouuen amplissimum possessionis suae cespitem'. Its location is established by
Chédeville and Guillotel, *Bretagne*, p. 220.   [48] Below, pp. 152–3.
[49] MGH Capit. I.275–80, no. 138; MGH Conc. II.307–468, nos. 39–41; *Legislatio
Aquisgranensis*, ed. J. Semmler, *Corpus Consuetudinum Monasticarum*, i, ed. K. Hallinger
(Siegburg, 1963), pp. 433–99. On the significance of this legislation, see J. Semmler,
'Die Beschlüsse des Aachener Konzils im Jahre 816', *Zeitschrift für Kirchengeschichte*,
74 (1963), 15–82; Semmler, 'Reichsidee und kirchliche Gesetzgebung'; P. Schmitz,
'L'influence de Saint Benoît dans l'histoire de l'ordre de Saint-Benoît', *Settimane*, 4
(1957), 401–15; Noble, 'The monastic ideal as the model for reform'. For a summary
of the imperial ideas of Louis' contemporaries, see J. M. Wallace-Hadrill, *The Frankish
Church* (Oxford, 1983), pp. 226–41.
[50] Thegan, *Vita Hludowici*, 10, p. 593; J. Semmler, 'Traditio und Königsschutz. Studien
zur Geschichte der königlichen Monasteria', *Zeitschrift der Savigny-Stiftung für
Rechtsgeschichte. Kanonistische Abteilung*, 45 (1959), 1–33.

the same standing in law vis-à-vis the king as did so many Frankish churches.[51] The immunity was granted on the same standard terms as enjoyed by church lands elsewhere, namely a ban on royal officials entering church property to conduct their business or hear lawsuits there. It is highly unlikely that the tentacles of day-to-day imperial administration penetrated so deeply into Brittany: the significance of Louis' diploma for Saint-Méen is in its assertion of a claim to direct lordship and in the indirect evidence which it provides that Louis' instructions recalling his predecessors' diplomas had indeed been sent out into Brittany.

The other Breton monastery which fell within Louis' purview during the early years of his reign was Landévennec, situated at the mouth of the river Aulne, at the head of the Bay of Brest in western Brittany. Whilst encamped at Priziac in 818, Louis had received a visit from Matmonoc, abbot of Landévennec, and after learning of the 'Irish' customs and tonsure followed at this monastery, he issued a diploma ordering the monks to adopt the Roman tonsure and the Rule of St Benedict.[52] His stated aim was to bring this remote monastery into the universal church. It is a commonplace that Louis' efforts to establish general observance of the Benedictine Rule throughout his empire met with bitter and entrenched opposition in many important Frankish monasteries; by contrast, Landévennec is the only monastery where Louis' legislation can be proven to have been welcomed.[53] The introduction of Benedictine observances mitigated the harshness of the customs instituted by Landévennec's founder, Winwaloe, and was welcomed by the weaker monks who had found the scant clothing allocation allowed to them by the monastery's traditional customs to be sadly inadequate.

So far as the very fragmentary nature of the surviving evidence for the first half of the reign allows us to judge, Louis' 'righteous' rule over the Bretons was in practice largely confined to dealings with a few major churches. Although he was certainly more concerned to bring the Bretons under control than was

[51] Morice, *Preuves*, I.225–6.
[52] Wrdisten, '*Vita S. Winwaloei*', II.12–13, pp. 226–7.
[53] The evidence of opposition to the monastic reforms and for the incomplete adherence to the Rule of St Benedict is summarised by R. McKitterick, *The Frankish Kingdoms under the Carolingians, 751–987* (London, 1983), pp. 117–21. For the reaction at Landévennec, see Wrdisten, as previous note.

Charlemagne, that is not to say that his success was very much greater. Most of Brittany was lightly touched by Carolingian lordship, in distinction from the other outlying regions which Pippin III and Charlemagne had brought under their control.

Christian though it was, Brittany remained on the outer margins of the Carolingian empire. However, it was not unaffected by a generation or more of Frankish campaigning in the area. Just as military conflict between the late Roman empire and the Germanic tribes on its northern borders had encouraged the emergence of 'national' kingships in place of former loose confederacies of tribes, so too the peoples on the rim of the Carolingian state tended to respond by banding together under a single ruler. This process was furthered by Frankish arbitration amongst rival candidates, or by Frankish recognition of a single king in place of acknowledging the simultaneous rights of more than one rival. Such interventions were characteristic of Louis the Pious' negotiations with both the Danes and the Slavs. In Denmark, he promoted a single Danish kingship, recognising only the claims of Harald, and not those of Harald's rivals, the sons of the former king Godofrid; in his dealings with the Abodrite Slavs, he removed their king Sclaomir in 818 and substituted Ceadrag son of Duke Thrasco, and in 823 settled the disputed succession of the Wilzi Slavs at their own request.[54]

Brittany offers a close parallel. The transition from political fragmentation to unified principality marked one of the most fundamental changes of the ninth century. Encouraged and hastened by the Carolingians themselves, this evolution was essentially a response to the pressures and tensions between Bretons and Franks. In the reign of Charlemagne, the region settled by the Bretons remained divided between several local rulers, as it had been in the sixth century. Frankish annalists who reported Charlemagne's attacks on the Bretons and their submissions to him were consistent in describing the Breton leaders always in the plural, and always anonymously.[55] By the time of Louis' reign, Frankish sources report the names of Breton leaders, and attribute leadership of revolts to named individuals, first Morman and then Wihomarc. In neither case is the geographical extent or nature of their power known, but to one

---

[54] See the discussion of Ernst, 'Karolingische Nordostpolitik'.
[55] The terms used are *duces, primores, comites, capitanei. ARF*, a. 786, and revised version, 799, 825, 826, pp. 72, 73, 108, 167, 169; *Annales Mettenses Priores*, a. 800, p. 85.

Frankish commentator at least, 'Wihomarc seemed to have greater authority than the other Breton leaders'.[56] In the early ninth century, then, the notion of a single Breton leader was emerging.[57] The appearance of more powerful Breton rulers may explain why Louis the Pious had greater difficulty in suppressing Breton revolts than did his father. The leadership of Morman and Wihomarc may have been essentially military, born out of a widespread resentment of Frankish interference. The tension of the years between 818 and 826 had triggered concerted Breton political and military action on an apparently hitherto unprecedented scale. It will be seen that it did not take Louis the Pious long to capitalise on this.

THE COUNTY OF VANNES UNDER THE CAROLINGIANS

In one region, Frankish domination more nearly approximated direct government. This was the county of Vannes – Broweroch – the region from which the vast majority of the Redon charters derive. Pippin III had sacked Vannes itself in 751, and this fortified centre may have remained in Frankish hands thereafter. Several Frankish counts were appointed to administer the Vannetais by Charlemagne and Louis the Pious, and there are hints that they did so in accordance with common Frankish administrative practices.

The earliest surviving Breton charter, of 29 September 801, records a lawsuit heard at Langon, in the east of the county of Vannes, by two *missi*, both with Frankish names – Gautro and Hermandro – who acted on behalf of the Frankish count Frodald.[58] Dating clauses of charters from 813 to January 830 mention another Frankish count, Wido, perhaps a relative of Frodald.[59] In 836/7, Louis sent one Gonfred, possibly a relative of Rorigo, to administer the county, but he found himself thwarted by the Bretons.[60]

56 'Astronomer', *Vita Hludowici*, 39, pp. 628–9.
57 See too the comments of W. Davis, 'On the distribution of political power in Brittany in the mid-ninth century', in *Charles the Bald*, pp. 98–114, at pp. 104–5.
58 CR 191.
59 CR 133 (= 34), 135, 146, 151, 155, 212, 255. All these charters can be precisely dated to specific dates between 30 December 813 and 16 January 830; further references to Wido are in charters for which a range of dates is possible, but which could all date from before January 830: CR 131, 152, 166, 196, 212, 255.
60 GSR, I.11, p. 141. Gonfred seems to have been a member of a family local to the Le Mans–Chartres area. Brunterc'h, 'Le duché du Maine', p. 78. See also below, n. 104.

Such evidence as there is shows Frodald and Wido doing the sort of things that Frankish counts usually did, notably exercising judicial functions and regulating land transactions. The record of the judicial enquiry held at Langon in 801 is evidence of Frodald's responsibility for legal proceedings; on one occasion Wido authorised a sale of land at Peillac, and on another was present at, and presumably gave his approval for, a substantial purchase of land by a priest from his two brothers in Langon.[61] It is also a fair presumption that the counts had military responsibilities, and that they worked in co-ordination with other marcher counts in this respect.

A delicate question is whether Charlemagne's counts introduced his judicial reforms into the Breton villages of south-eastern Brittany. Several records of lawsuits have a distinctively Frankish vocabulary, notably using the word *mallus* (or *mallus publicus*) for a court session, or referring to the judgement finders as *scabini*.[62] *Scabini* were experienced men appointed to give judgement in Frankish comital courts, intended to replace the earlier, less skilled *rachimburgi*. It is generally assumed that Charlemagne instituted the panels of *scabini* in the early 770s as part of a series of judicial reforms, and that their use spread throughout the empire thereafter.[63] However, *scabini* appear in charters from many parts of the empire long before their earliest mention in royal legislation, and the specifications laid down in capitularies from 803 onwards for the appointment and service of *scabini* do not

[61] CR 212, 192. CR 192 is a lawsuit concerning the alleged sale by Agon to his brothers in which he produced witnesses who testified 'quod vidissent et audissent quando supradictus Agun donavit .C. solidos inter Uuidonem et Adalun et Ratuili et alios'. Adalun, Ratuili, and the others are not identifiable. The three brother were the heirs of the defendant of the case heard by the *missi comitis* Gautro and Hermandro.

[62] *Mallus (publicus)*: CR 47, 61, 124, 192, A20. Other expressions for a court are *placitum* (*publicum*) or the Old Breton equivalent, *lis*.
    Scabini: CR 124, 147, 180, 191, 192, A3. This evidence is discussed in detail by Planiol, *Institutions*, II.100–3. In CR 180, the *scabini* are also referred to as *boni viri*, and other charters, not confined to the Vannetais, make reference to *seniores*, *viri nobiles*, *viri idonei* who evidently performed the same function as the *scabini*. CR 106, 127, 129, 162, 271. For discussion of these men's roles in legal proceedings, see W. Davies, 'Disputes, their conduct and their settlement in the village communities of eastern Brittany in the ninth century', *History and Anthropology*, 1 (1985), 289–312; W. Davies, 'People and places in dispute in ninth-century Brittany', in *The Settlement of Disputes in Early Medieval Europe*, ed. W. Davies and P. Fouracre (Cambridge, 1986), pp. 65–84; Davies, *Small Worlds*, pp. 146–60.

[63] F. L. Ganshof, *Frankish Institutions under Charlemagne* (New York, 1968), pp. 77–8; Bullough, '*Europae Pater*', pp. 90–2.

correspond with what the charter evidence suggests actually took place, in Brittany or elsewhere.[64] The problem of the relationship of local and often widely varying judicial arrangements to the normative standards presented in royal legislation is therefore an acute one. To argue, as Wendy Davies has done, that the judicial practices of south-eastern Brittany in the ninth century are unlikely to be of Carolingian origin because they deviate from the recommendations of Charlemagne's legislation 'more than might be expected for a recent introduction'[65] is to beg the question for the whole of the empire. There is no doubt that Frankish legal terminology was indeed adopted into Breton usage. In addition, it is noteworthy that *scabini* gave judgement in the case heard by the Frankish *missi comitis* in 801, and the real possibility that in the county of Vannes judicial procedures as well as terminology had much in common with those in other parts of the empire should be borne in mind.

At an ecclesiastical level too, Carolingian lordship affected the Vannetais. The appearance of the Frankish name Raginarius amongst the otherwise Breton names of the ninth-century bishops of Vannes is suggestive; Louis may have made an appointment to the see in the early 820s.[66] It was during Raginarius' episcopate that the monastery of Redon was established in 832, and although founding members of the community met with opposition from Raginarius, they nevertheless enjoyed the friendship of two of Louis' counts, Wido of Vannes and Rorigo of Poutrocoet.[67] After initial rejection by Louis the Pious, Conwoion, founding abbot of Redon, won Carolingian patronage in 834, and thereafter Redon rapidly became established as a source of spiritual support for the Carolingian dynasty and empire, a representation amongst the Bretons of Louis' imperial ideal of peace, stability, and concord, and a centre for the dissemination of Carolingian ecclesiastical culture. Here prayers were said for the emperor and his family, here the power of the universal Catholic church was realised through the relics of the martyr pope Marcellinus, and here the

[64] B. Althoffer, *Les Scabins* (Nancy, 1938); F. N. Estey, 'The *scabini* and the local courts', *Speculum*, 26 (1951), 119–29.

[65] Davies, 'People and places in dispute', p. 83; also *Small Worlds*, pp. 209–10.

[66] Raginarius is named in firmly dated charters between 13 July 826 and 24 January 838 (CR 133; Morice, *Preuves*, I.272), but he *may* have been in office as early as 1 April 821 (CR 133). Cf. Duchesne, *Fastes Episcopaux*, II.374.

[67] *GSR*, I.1, 8, pp. 111, 113.

Benedictine rule was instituted and diffused to other Breton monasteries.[68]

The entire county of Vannes was of vital importance to the Franks. Vannes itself had formed the mustering-point for the campaign of 818; the counts and bishops whose seat was there were agents of royal authority. The Vannetais afforded the Franks a bridgehead into Brittany, and held out the prospect of closer control and of firmer integration into the Carolingian empire. In the troubled final decade of his reign, Louis was to rely upon the support he found in the Vannetais.

NEUSTRIAN POLITICS AND THE BRETON 'MISSATICUM'

In the 830s, the regime enunciated in the *Ordinatio Imperii* collapsed. Tensions within the Carolingian dynasty itself exacerbated rivalries amongst members of the aristocracy, and in the revolts which shook the empire in 830 and 833–4, the volatile allegiances of some of the magnates of western Neustria became evident. The revolts had their epicentre in the royal *ducatus Cenomannicus*. Perennial issues of succession and patronage lay at the roots of the rebellions, which triggered uncertainties far and wide. Even Breton villages were touched.

Against this background, together with the additional worry of ever more persistent Viking raids on the Atlantic coast of Francia, Louis the Pious was acutely aware of the need to maintain uncontested lordship over the Bretons, and to prevent, if possible, Frankish unrest sparking off another round of damaging Breton rebellions. The measures which he took to secure his rule over the Bretons and to quieten western Neustria were important: they influenced the subsequent political development of both Brittany and Neustria, and they also marked a new departure in Carolingian thinking about how to handle the Bretons.

Insofar as it affected Neustria and the Breton march, the narrative of the turmoil of these years is fairly clear.[69] Foremost among the dissatisfied Neustrian magnates were Lambert, count

---

[68] J. M. H. Smith, 'Culte impérial et politique frontalière dans la vallée de la Vilaine: le témoignage des diplômes carolingiens dans le cartulaire de Redon', in *Landévennec et la Monachisme Breton*, ed. Simon, pp. 129–39.

[69] The following paragraphs focus exclusively on Neustria and the Loire Valley; the only general account is L. Halphen, *Charlemagne et l'Empire Carolingien* (Paris, 1947), pp. 268–300. For a penetrating analysis of the issues involved, see Airlie, 'Political behaviour', pp. 40–110.

of Nantes, Hugh, count of Tours and Matfrid, count of Orléans. Hugh was father-in-law of Louis the Pious' eldest son Lothar; Lambert was a close associate of Lothar's brother Pippin, the subking of Aquitaine. Both Hugh and Matfrid had fallen from royal favour after being accused of ineptitude whilst leading a campaign into Spain in 828; their dismissal from their Neustrian *honores* provided an opportunity for other grievances against Matfrid's behaviour to be aired.[70] In their place, Bernard of Septimania and his family profited. Bernard's cousin Odo was given the county of Orléans, and in 829 Bernard himself was recalled from the Spanish march and made Louis' chamberlain. It was round this man's good fortunes, and the nearness he enjoyed to both Louis and his wife Judith, that noble resentments crystallised. The events of 830 saw Bernard fighting for his political life in face of the hostility of Lambert, Hugh, and Matfrid. At the same time, Louis' three eldest sons, Lothar, Louis, and Pippin, were upset by the grant of Alemannia, Rhaetia, and part of Burgundy to their young half-brother, Charles 'the Bald', a rearrangement of the succession which entailed the prospect of a reduction of their own shares in the paternal inheritance.[71] The balance of lordship and patronage between those Carolingians in the running for a crown of their own and their noble followers had been disturbed.

Encouraged by Bernard of Septimania, Louis the Pious set out with the entire Frankish army in February 830 on a campaign 'towards Breton regions'.[72] If the Bretons were indeed in revolt, the unrest was so minor as to warrant no subsequent attention; later, Louis was accused of having led out the army during the holy season of Lent, for no good reason.[73] It is quite possible that Louis and Bernard's main intention was to make a show of strength in the neighbourhood of the marcher lands of Lambert of Nantes and his relative Wido of Vannes, and indeed subsequent events were to show how unreliable was the loyalty of Lambert and his associates.[74] As the Frankish army proceeded from Nijmegen towards Rennes, Frankish magnates revolted. Urged

---

[70] *ARF*, a. 828, p. 174; 'Astronomer', *Vita Hludowici*, 41–2, pp. 630–1; Adrevald, *Miracula Sancti Benedicti*, 20, MGH SS xv.i, 487; MGH Capit. II.10, no. 188 c. 3.

[71] Thegan, *Vita Hludowici*, 35, p. 597.

[73] *AB*, a. 830, p. 1; *Annales Mettenses Priores*, a. 830, pp. 95–6.

[73] *Episcoporum de poenitentia, quam Hludowicus imperator professus est, relatio Compendiensis*, MGH Capit. II.54, no. 197 c. 3.

[74] Brunner, *Oppositionelle Gruppen*, p. 110.

on by Hugh and Matfrid, Lothar and Pippin joined in, their targets the removal of Judith and her son Charles, together with Bernard of Septimania and his relatives. Lambert was one of those to whom Pippin entrusted responsibility for bringing Judith from Laon to Verberie, where it was finally decided to send her off to a 'safe house' in the nunnery of Sainte-Croix at Poitiers for confinement.[75]

By the late summer of 830, Louis was back in control. He immediately acted to restore his authority in northern Poitou, the area where Pippin and Lambert could together effectively dominate the entire Loire valley. To demonstrate his authority and to strengthen coastal defences against the Vikings, Louis issued a diploma on 2 August 830 permitting the monks of the island of Noirmoutier, who were suffering from annual Viking attacks, to fortify their monastery, and granting them generous exemptions from public service and tax obligations.[76] Two other diplomas, both for the monastery of Charroux, south of Poitiers, were a further sign that Louis had influence in Poitou.[77] At the assembly which met at Nijmegen in October to negotiate an end to the revolt, Lambert was excluded from the gathering, and was sent back to the Breton march, where Helisachar, abbot of Saint-Riquier, was to see justice was done to him.[78] In effect, Lambert was banished from royal favour but not stripped of office. Other rebels were sent into exile or into monastic custody, but at an assembly at Ingelheim in May 831, Louis pardoned them and restored to them their property but not their *honores*.[79] Among them was Matfrid, whom Pippin had restored to Orléans for a brief spell in the summer of 830, but who once more had to make way for Odo as soon as Louis had recovered his power in the Loire valley.[80]

The way was clear for Louis to devote himself to building up a secure power base in Neustria and then to ensuring the region's

[75] Nithard, *Histoire des Fils de Louis le Pieux*, 1.3, ed. P. Lauer, Les Classiques de l'Histoire de France au Moyen Age 7 (Paris, 1926), p. 8; Thegan, *Vita Hludowici*, 36, p. 597; 'Astronomer', *Vita Hludowici*, 44, p. 633; *AB*, a. 830, pp. 1–3; Paschasius Radbert, *Vita Walae*, II.7–10, MGH SS II.551–7.
[76] *Recueil des Historiens des Gaules et de la France*, ed. M. Bouquet, 24 vols. (Paris, 1738–1904), VI.563–5, no. 156.
[77] *Recueil*, ed. Bouquet, VI.566–7, nos. 158–9.
[78] 'Astronomer', *Vita Hludowici*, 45, p. 633.
[79] *AB*, a. 831, p. 4; 'Astronomer', *Vita Hludowici*, 46, p. 634.
[80] 'Astronomer', *Vita Hludowici*, 44, p. 633.

defences against Viking attack. As part of this, he made a novel move and entrusted some form of general responsibility over the Bretons to one of their own number, Nominoe, almost certainly at the Ingelheim assembly.[81] Other provisions followed. By 832, his staunch supporter Rorigo was count of Le Mans, and at Rorigo's suggestion, Louis appointed his own confessor Aldric to the bishopric of the same city in November 832. Aldric worked energetically to restore episcopal rights within his diocese, and thereby to further royal power in the area.[82] At about the same time, Louis made provisions for the defences of the Loire estuary. To this effect, he subdivided the huge county of Poitou on the south bank of the lower Loire, making Rainald, a relative of some of the leading loyal Neustrian and Aquitainian magnates, count of Herbauge.[83] It was also with an eye to strategic considerations of river defences in the Breton marcher region that in 832 Louis refused to approve the foundation of Redon, located as the monastery was at the confluence of the rivers Oust and Vilaine, and on the western boundary of the county of Nantes.[84]

Neither the reconciliations and rearrangements of 831 nor the new scheme for the partition of the empire proposed in the same year did anything to address the original grievances. In 832, Matfrid, who had not recovered the county of Orléans, persuaded Louis' second son, Louis, to invade Alemannia, a province which had been allocated to Charles the Bald.[85] Revolt broke out again in 833, this time led by Lothar and his brothers Louis and Pippin. After the showdown of the Field of Lies at the end of June 833 and the imprisonment of Louis the Pious in the monastery of Saint-Médard at Soissons, Lothar tried to rule the empire in his own name. According to Nithard, his effort failed because Lambert, Hugh, and Matfrid quarrelled amongst themselves as to which of them should be Lothar's right-hand man, and no one bothered to attend to the business of government.[86] After Louis had been

---

[81] Regino of Prüm, *Chronicon*, a. 837, p. 74: 'Murmanus rex Brittonum moritur et Numenoio apud Inglenheim ab imperatore ducatus ipsius gentis traditur.' The arguments of Hubert Guillotel on behalf of 831 resolve the extensive debate over the date of Nominoe's appointment. Chédeville and Guillotel, *Bretagne*, pp. 227–9.

[82] P. Le Maître, 'L'oeuvre d'Aldric du Mans et sa signification', *Francia*, 8 (1980), 43–64.

[83] F. Lot and L. Halphen, *La Règne de Charles le Chauve (840–877). Première partie (840–851)*, Bibliothèque de l'Ecole des Hautes Etudes 175 (Paris, 1909), p. 76 n. 7; Brunterc'h, 'L'extension du ressort politique et religieux du Nantais', pp. 71–8.

[84] *GSR*, 1.8, p. 133, where the strategic arguments are explicit.

[85] *AB*, a. 832, pp. 5–7.

[86] Nithard, *Histoire*, 1.4, p. 16; also Brunterc'h, 'Le duché du Maine', p. 57.

restored to power and reconciled with his sons in March 834, Lambert and Matfrid still held out against the emperor. They concentrated their forces in the Breton march, where they defeated the army sent against them by Wido, count of Le Mans.[87] Wido was killed, together with Odo, count of Orléans, his brother William, count of Blois, an unknown Count Fulbert, and Theoto, abbot of Saint-Martin of Tours.[88] The defeated rebels turned to their patron Lothar for protection. He sheltered them in Italy, where certainly Matfrid was given lands which Lothar had seized during the revolt; many of them died in Italy of plague in 836/7, their Neustrian *honores* not yet reclaimed.[89] By the summer of 834, the revolt against Louis the Pious had degenerated into feuding amongst the Neustrian aristocracy: Matfrid pitted against Odo, Lambert against Wido.

The unrest in the Breton march spilled over into Brittany. We hear of Franks making their way into Brittany in January 834, presumably Lambert's men looking for refuge or for support.[90] More interestingly, we can trace the confusion of loyalties generated by the revolt right down to the level of one Breton village. Two charters of 10 December 833 both recording the same grant of land at Augan in Poutrocoet to Redon suggest that, even at this very local level, uncertainties were felt as to whether Louis or Lothar was the rightful emperor, and sides were taken in the conflict. Of this pair of charters, one was probably drawn up for the donor, the other for the beneficiary.[91] Besides small but significant differences in the wording of the details of the grant itself, the donor's copy makes the grant for the sake of the souls of the donor and his son, and is dated by the regnal year of Lothar; Redon's copy has the grant made for the sake of the souls of the donor and of the emperor, and is dated by Louis the Pious' regnal year.[92] We could not ask for clearer signs that the rivalries

---

[87] The sequence of counts of Le Mans at this time is unclear. It is widely assumed that Wido of Le Mans is the same man who is named in charters up until January 830 as count of Vannes. This identification rests on the two men holding the same name. If indeed they were one and the same, then Wido's opponent in this battle, Lambert, was his brother. The date of his transfer to Le Mans, and the timing of and reasons for Rorigo's removal from the countship are open to debate. Oexle, 'Ebroin', p. 187, cf. Dhondt, *Naissance*, pp. 321–2.

[88] Nithard, *Histoire*, I.5, p. 20; *AB*, a. 834, p. 13; Adrevald, *Miracula Sancti Benedicti*, 20–1, pp. 487–9; 'Astronomer', *Vita Hludowici*, 52, p. 638.

[89] 'Astronomer', *Vita Hludowici*, 56, p. 642; *AB*, a. 837, p. 22; MGH D.Kar. III.239–40, no. 100.   [90] CR 11.   [91] Davies, 'Forgery', p. 268 n. 15.

[92] CR 6 (Redon's version), 23 (donor's version).

that wracked the Carolingian dynasty itself were felt far away
from the high politics of palace life.

Redon's recognition of Louis the Pious was a sign of the
monastic community's determination to seek out Carolingian
patronage, despite Louis having twice refused to favour the
monastery in 832. The monks' support for Louis went hand in
hand with Nominoe's. On 18 June 834, some three months after
Louis had recovered his throne, Nominoe made a small grant to
Redon 'in consideration of our lord emperor Louis' strife and
affliction', in which he requested the monks to pray for the
emperor.[93] In July 834 Nominoe was able to persuade Louis to
change his mind and recognise Redon, and of Nominoe's loyalty
and support for the emperor during the crisis of 833–4 there can
be no doubt. Despite the signs of wavering loyalties at Augan,
Louis' decision of 831 to break with tradition and appoint a
Breton to represent imperial authority amongst the Bretons paid
off, and, with the exception of unrest in 836/7, which ended
when the Bretons gave hostages and returned lands they had
seized, Nominoe kept the Bretons tranquil for the rest of Louis'
reign.[94] Only after the emperor's death did the gamekeeper take
to poaching.

It remains to investigate more closely Nominoe's personal
position from 831 until the end of Louis' reign. Of the man
himself, we know virtually nothing, although it seems probable
that he was a Breton lord whose power lay in the Vannetais.[95] His
choice by Louis makes it quite possible that he was one of those
Bretons who had been given as a hostage to either Charlemagne
or Louis the Pious earlier in the century. His appointment was
evidently not considered important by Frankish commentators of
the day: no contemporary chronicler mentions him at all before
840.[96] Indeed, almost all that we know of him comes from Redon
and its archive. As recorded *c.* 870, Redon tradition maintained
that Nominoe was mandated by Louis to rule 'almost all' of
Brittany, but added that afterwards, he seized the province on his

[93] CR 2.
[94] *AB*, a. 837, p. 22; 'Astronomer', *Vita Hludowici*, 56, p. 642, cf. *GSR*, I.11, p. 141.
[95] See below, p. 130. Two charters refer to him as count of Vannes but the text of both,
including the dating clauses, are too corrupt to permit any reliance to be placed upon
them (CR 250, 252). Suggestions for their date have ranged between 819 (La Borderie)
and 834 (Guillotel). If Nominoe was indeed count of Vannes, it may have been before
or after 831; when and how he replaced Count Wido must remain unknown.
[96] Only Regino, writing 906–15, mentions Nominoe's appointment; above, n. 81.

own initiative.[97] The dating clauses of Breton private charters from February 833 onwards are consistent with this. They refer to Nominoe by a variety of descriptive expressions but no single, specific title of rank.[98] These charters make clear Nominoe's pre-eminent status throughout Brittany both before and after Louis the Pious' death. On the other hand, Louis the Pious' two extant diplomas for Redon both refer to Nominoe as the emperor's *fidelis*.[99] Neither of Louis' diplomas attributes any official rank to Nominoe: from a Carolingian perspective, Nominoe was someone who maintained fidelity to the reigning emperor.

In the only charter of Nominoe's to survive in its entirety, dated 18 June 834, the superscription hails him as imperial representative, *missus imperatoris*,[100] and he is similarly described in the dating clauses of a further five charters from before 840.[101] We may therefore presume that at Ingelheim Louis designated Nominoe as his *missus*. But although his authority came from the emperor, Nominoe held no office, no *honor* in the Carolingian sense, on which his power or status was based. In this respect he was quite unlike those men chosen to act as *missi* elsewhere in the empire, who were always drawn from the ranks of the counts, bishops, abbots, local fiscal officials, and other officeholders of the imperial secular or ecclesiastical administration.[102] The nature of Nominoe's power will be investigated in chapter 5; what is important here is that, on the basis of the surviving documentation, we have no evidence that he ever acted specifically on Louis' behalf. Rather, he was a man of power among the Bretons who was a loyal supporter of the reigning emperor, to whom he had presumably taken an oath of loyalty at Ingelheim. Louis had taken advantage of the drift towards Breton 'state formation' to

---

[97] GSR, I.1, p. 109.

[98] For example, *Nominoe magistro in Britanniam* (CR 7, the earliest of all these references); *Nominoe possidente Brittanniam* (CR 171); *gubernante Nominoe totam Brittanniam* (CR 178); *Nominoe principe in Brittannia* (CR 180); *regnante Nominoe in Brittannia* (CR 199); *Nominoe duce in Britannia* (CR A5). These phrases continue in use until Nominoe's death in 851.

[99] CR A6, A9, of 27 November 834 and 30 August 836 respectively.

[100] CR 2.

[101] CR 148, 177, 179, 200, Morice, *Preuves*, I.271–2. Of these, all except CR 148 and 200 were drafted at Redon.

[102] Cf. J. Hannig, 'Zentrale Kontrolle und regionale Machtbalance. Beobachtungen zum System der karolingischen Königsboten am Beispiel des Mittelrheingebietes', *Archiv für Kulturgeschichte*, 66 (1984), 1–46; J. Hannig, 'Pauperiores vassi de infra palatio? Zur Entstehung der karolingischen Königsbotenorganisation', *Mitteilungen des Instituts für österreichische Geschichtsforschung*, 91 (1983), 309–74.

encourage and recognise Nominoe as his representative in Brittany: for his part, Nominoe was a figurehead of imperial authority for so long as he was both able and willing.

This did not preclude Louis continuing to intervene directly in the affairs of the county of Vannes whenever he so chose. His diplomas of 834 and 836 for Redon conveyed seigneurial rights in certain areas to the abbot, probably in effect confirming grants already made by Nominoe. There is also some evidence that he gave the monastery the privilege of electing its own abbot, and that he may have granted judicial protection and immunity at the same time.[103] In addition, he tried to appoint a Frankish count to Vannes in 836/7, but Breton protest thwarted him.[104]

Louis the Pious' continuing concern with the Vannetais was part of an effort to strengthen his authority in western Neustria as a whole, and to establish his youngest son Charles as his successor there.[105] In 838, the duchy of Le Mans was revived for Charles, and at that date Rorigo was still active and influential in Maine on Louis' behalf.[106] After Lambert's flight to Italy, the county of Nantes was given over to Richowin.[107] Like so many other magnates introduced into Neustria by the Carolingian kings, Richowin was in all probability from a Rhineland background. Adalhard, abbot of Saint-Martin, may also have been given the county of Tours.[108] Charles' lordship of this region, including the Breton march, was confirmed in 839 in the last partition of the empire which Louis was to make before his death.[109] Charles the Bald might hope to continue the *modus vivendi* with Nominoe and the Bretons which Louis had established in the last decade of his reign.

Louis the Pious' dealings with the Bretons were shaped by two main considerations. In the early years of his reign, the reluctance of this Christian people to accept his overlordship offended his profound sense of his empire as the Christian community of the

---

[103] I have argued this in 'Culte impérial et politique frontalière', pp. 133–7.

[104] See above, p. 82. Frankish and Breton sources give conflicting dates; *AB* mentions a Breton revolt in 837 (p. 22), but Redon's house history locates the incident immediately before Louis issued his second diploma for Redon, dated 30 August 836. *GSR*, I.11, p. 141.

[105] A point stressed by J. L. Nelson, 'The last years of Louis the Pious', in *Charlemagne's Heir*, pp. 147–59, at p. 153.

[106] *AB*, a. 838, pp. 24–5; MGH Conc. II.837.

[107] CR A8 (datable to 28 January 834–27 January 835); 195.

[108] Dhondt, *Naissance*, p. 84.   [109] *AB*, a. 839, p. 32.

universal Roman church under his own paternal care. In addition, he gradually became more preoccupied with pressing issues of Carolingian politics: the problems of providing for all his sons, of distributing his patronage appropriately throughout the aristocracy, and of enforcing his rule in areas beyond immediate imperial oversight, in particular the troublesome regions of Neustria. In the last decade of his reign, it was imperative to find a form of lordship over the Bretons that was acceptable to them and to hold on to Brittany despite the unreliability of the counts appointed to the marcher area. Hence, with signs that the Bretons were more and more prepared to band together under a single leader in times of stress, he recognised the Breton Nominoe as his personal agent among the Bretons. Nominoe's loyalty towards Louis suggested that the emperor had made a sensible choice. Louis had recognised that Brittany was a key to the security of that part of his realm. which lay between Paris and Poitiers, and had done what he could to extend his lordship over the Bretons, wherever they were willing to accept it. In effect, he did no more than intensify the traditional forms of Frankish hegemony over subject peoples. No firm administrative network bound the Bretons into the Carolingian empire; apart from the presence of Breton hostages in the imperial court, it was a personal relationship with an individual Breton leader, cemented by an oath of loyalty, that was the essence of Carolingian rule over the Bretons. There is a sharp contrast with those other outlying regions where Merovingian lordship had lapsed and where the Carolingians overcame much opposition to impose their peace, import their aristocratic followers, and create a network of churches bound together under royal patronage. The Bretons remained marginal and often at odds with the Carolingians, only attracting attention when they caused trouble. Their loyalty and obedience were precarious, but precious.

Chapter 4

CAROLINGIAN HEGEMONY AND BRETON REVOLTS, 840–874

The ideal of Latin Christendom united under a single, Carolingian, emperor remained a potent political force long after Louis the Pious' death in 840. But to it was added a second, equally significant political reality: the existence of several legitimate Carolingian kings, Louis' sons and grandsons. Churchmen urged them to rule in a spirit of fraternal love and co-operation, but all of them were intent upon securing and advancing their status, wealth, and retinue, especially at the expense of their fellow rulers. In this competitive climate Charles the Bald manoeuvred and fought to establish his rule over the West Frankish portion of the empire which his father had designated for him. His long reign, from 840 until 877, was marked throughout by fierce rivalry for land and lordship between himself and his brothers, nephews and sons. At stake were the loyalties of Frankish aristocrats, the rich Carolingian fiscal lands of the Rhineland, and the two imperial capitals of Aachen and Rome.[1]

Carolingian imperial ambitions made themselves felt all the way from the centre to the periphery. Dealings with frontier regions provided an opportunity for lavish, ritual displays of hegemony over Danes, Slavs, Beneventans, and Bretons. There was always the possibility of extracting tribute and military assistance from these peoples. Moreover, restive subject peoples could be exploited to distract the attention and destabilise the power of a brother king, for in the second half of the ninth century, one man's opponent was invariably another's ally. So it was with the Bretons. Louis the Pious' lordship over Nominoe

---

[1] On imperial ideas and the ethics of fraternal affection, see U. Penndorf, *Das Problem der 'Reichseinheitsidee' nach der Teilung von Verdun (843)*, Münchener Beiträge zur Mediävistik und Renaissance-Forschung 20 (Munich, 1974); R. Schneider, *Brüdergemeine und Schwurfreundschaft. Die Auflösungsprozess des Karlingerreiches im Spiegel der caritas-Terminologie der karlingischen Teilkönige des 9. Jahrhunderts*, Historische Studien 388 (Lübeck, 1964); W. Mohr, 'Die Krise des kirchlichen Einheitsprogram im Jahre 858', *Archivum Latinitatis Medii Aevi*, 25 (1955), 189–213.

had ended with the emperor's death: Charles the Bald had to compete for Breton loyalty with his Carolingian kin and with his rebellious Frankish magnates. Neither Nominoe nor his successors, however, were easily reconciled to Charles the Bald's overlordship, and their truculent and increasingly aggressive behaviour reopened the problem of how to deal with these 'false Christians' who denied their rightful lord.[2]

Charles the Bald was faced with frequent Breton revolts and raids from 843 onwards. Twice, in 845 and 851, the Bretons badly defeated the Frankish army: on the latter occasion, the king barely escaped with his life and his prestige took a great blow. Charles then resorted to granting blocks of Frankish lands to the Bretons. In 851, Erispoe, the son and successor of Nominoe, was given the marcher counties of Nantes and Rennes, along with land on the southern bank of the mouth of the Loire, the pays de Retz, now detached from Poitou, and in 856, Charles concluded a marriage alliance with him. In 863, Erispoe's slayer and successor, his cousin Salomon, was given land in western Anjou, and four years later, in 867, the entire counties of Avranches and Coutances. Thereafter, Breton revolts ceased. It might seem as though the only way to mitigate the Breton threat was for Charles to dismember his own kingdom, and indeed, this sequence of events has been taken as exemplifying the process whereby the West Frankish kingdom crumbled into independent 'territorial principalities', first at the remoter edges, and then later, in the tenth century, in the Neustrian heartlands.[3] Along with the concessions of Frankish counties came grants of regalia, in 851 to Erispoe and in 868 to Salomon. For the patriotic Breton historiographical tradition, these grants were believed, from at least the fourteenth century onwards, to constitute Frankish recognition that Brittany was a fully independent kingdom, ruled by its own king and free from obligations towards the French crown.[4]

---

[2] This derisive expression is Hincmar of Reims'. He refers to the havoc created by 'pseudochristiani Brittones' in a letter to Hadrian II (PL CXXVI.641) and similarly, to the revolts of 'falsi Christiani, scilicet Britones' in his *De Fide Carolo Regi Servanda* (PL CXXV.966).

[3] Dhondt, *Naissance*, pp. 82–108; K. Brunner, 'Die fränkische Fürstentitel im neunten und zehnten Jahrhundert', in *Intitulatio II*, ed. H. Wolfram, Mitteilungen des Instituts für österreichische Geschichtsforschung Ergänzungsband 24 (Vienna, 1973), pp. 179–340, esp. pp. 262–71.

[4] J. Kerhervé, 'Aux origines d'un sentiment national. Les chroniqueurs bretons de la fin du Moyen Age', *Bulletin de la Société Archéologique du Finistère*, 108 (1980), 165–206;

Certainly, by 877 the political configuration of the Armorican peninsula was profoundly different from the early ninth-century patterns. At the time of Charlemagne's campaigns, the Breton-speaking part of the Armorican peninsula was a conglomerate of petty *regna*; the eastern, Frankish marcher region was under firm Carolingian control, and remained so at the time of Louis the Pious' death. But by 877, Brittany was a single, large, political entity under the rule of a hereditary dynasty, embracing both Frankish and Breton communities. In short, a powerful and quite new bloc had been constituted in the reign of Charles the Bald. Rather than seeking explanations for its emergence in terms of well-worn models of political decay or anti-Carolingian national-ism, this chapter explores a very different dimension of this sequence of events. Just as Carolingian magnate politics in the reign of Charles the Bald only make sense on an empire-wide scale, so too Charles' dealings with the Bretons are most profitably seen in an imperial context. This perspective is of value in two ways. In the first place, the fraternal rivalries and jockeying for power between Charles the Bald and his half-brothers Louis the German and Lothar provide the key to explaining the timing and purpose of Nominoe's behaviour between 840 and 851. Salomon's involvement in West Frankish magnate unrest between 858 and 863 is a further aspect of the competition for lordship over the restive Neustrian aristocracy. In the second place, Charles was experimenting with imperial symbolism many years before his coronation as emperor in 875: I shall show that his schemes for a marriage alliance with Erispoe and his grants of lands and regalia to Erispoe and Salomon are part of a deliberate policy of imperial self-aggrandisement. Not only do they reveal the West Frankish king's careful manipulation of imperial imagery in order to bolster his own prestige, these schemes also demonstrate how Charles created far stronger bonds of obligation and lordship over the Bretons than had hitherto existed. Chapter 5 will then examine how, within this firmly Carolingian context, Breton provincial lordship developed, and will explore the significance for the Bretons of the grants of lands and regalia.

J.-P. Leguay and H. Martin, *Fastes et Malheurs de la Bretagne Ducale, 1213–1532* (Rennes, 1982), pp. 166–8; P. Jeulin, 'L'hommage de la Bretagne en droit et dans les faits', *Annales de Bretagne*, 41 (1934), 380–473.

NOMINOE AND THE REGIME OF BROTHERLY LOVE

Whereas Louis the Pious' dealings with the Bretons are generally only accessible through sources which convey the attitudes of the imperial court, any 'official', court-based record of Charles the Bald's activities ceased after 843.[5] Instead, various chroniclers, annalists, and letter-writers both within and beyond the West Frankish kingdom can be exploited for their differing perspectives on his reign, and for their snippets of information on Breton affairs. Against the guarded statements of Prudentius of Troyes and the garrulous entries of Hincmar of Reims in their respective sections of the so-called Annals of Saint-Bertin can be set the East Frankish perspective of the Annals of Fulda, and the concerns evinced in the correspondence of that busy scholar-politician, Lupus of Ferrières.[6] In general, the record is very much richer than for the preceding half century, especially where regional Neustrian chronicles, such as the Chronicle of Fontenelle (Saint-Wandrille) or the annals for 843 from Angers, are available.

The relative abundance of information, however, does not bring with it any greater understanding of the Bretons. Quite the contrary: the real import of Charles the Bald's Breton problems and his tactics for coping with them receive no attention at all. Only in the wider context of Carolingian political strategies as a whole does the nature of Charles' difficulties with the Bretons become apparent. This is particularly true for two separate periods of his reign. The first is the years until 851, when Nominoe died. Analysis of the frequent revolts of these years will show that they were integral to the competition for lordship between Charles the Bald and his fellow Carolingians in the aftermath of Louis the Pious' death. Charles' inability to force Nominoe to recognise his hegemony was but one aspect of a much wider set of problems created by the emperor Lothar's manoeuvrings to weaken or unseat his half-brother. The second period to be examined is 857–63. On this occasion, the Breton revolts were part of another issue, the efforts of the West Frankish

[5] J. L. Nelson, 'The Annals of St. Bertin', in *Charles the Bald*, pp. 23–40.
[6] See the surveys of H. Löwe, 'Geschichtsschreibung der ausgehenden Karolingerzeit', *DA*, 23 (1967), 1–30, and of W. Wattenbach and W. Levison, *Deutschlands Geschichtsquellen im Mittelalter. Vorzeit und Karolinger. V Die Karolinger vom Vertrag von Verdun bis zum Herrschaftsantritt der Herrscher aus dem sächsischen Hause. Das westfränkische Reich*, re-ed. H. Löwe (Weimar, 1973).

aristocracy to redress the balance of power between themselves and a king whose tactics they were finding too oppressive.

Both these episodes reflect the fundamental dynamic of the politics of Charles the Bald's reign.[7] Louis the Pious had ruled a unitary empire as sole effective emperor, in partnership with an aristocracy whose interests straddled its length and breadth, and in association with an articulate ecclesiastical hierarchy with strong but by no means unanimous views on royal morality and the nature of political obligation. Charles the Bald, by contrast, ruled only the West Frankish portion of this empire, but still in conjunction with an aristocracy whose interests were empire-wide, and with churchmen whose moral concerns and administrative competence also extended beyond the geographical boundaries of Charles' lordship. The treaty of Verdun of August 843 marked the transition, and symbolised an enduring change in the political framework of Latin Christendom from one imperial state to several kingdoms within a notional empire.[8] At Verdun, for the first time since Louis the Pious had died on 20 June 840, Louis the German and Charles the Bald were able to make their elder brother Lothar acknowledge that each had a right to a kingdom of their own. And for the first time since Charlemagne had taken over his brother Carloman's kingdom in 771, the heart of the empire, Francia itself, was divided between brother rulers. This region, the lands from the Seine to the Rhine, was where the Carolingian family had first risen to prominence, where most of their lands and fiscal resources lay, and where many of the Frankish aristocratic families had their origins. Once this area had been divided up, it was never again to be united under one ruler, with the exception of the short imperial rule of Charles the Fat from 885 to 887. The struggle for lands and lordship between the heirs of Louis the Pious was at its fiercest here: and it created eddies which rippled throughout Carolingian society.

Political conflict, anyway endemic to early medieval societies, was intensified by the transition that was formalised at Verdun, for the treaty marked not the end of the struggle but only the end of its first round. It secured for Charles the Bald the kingdom his father had intended for him and which Lothar had agreed under oath in 839 to respect[9], but which, as soon as the old emperor was

---

[7] For a succinct analysis of Charles the Bald's reign, see J. L. Nelson, 'The reign of Charles the Bald: a survey', in *Charles the Bald*, pp. 1–22.
[8] Classen, 'Verträge von Verdun und von Coulaines'.   [9] *AB*, a. 839, p. 32.

dead, Lothar had set about subverting. The partition, however, did nothing to turn Charles' entitlement to rule into effective power, and was an open invitation to Lothar to continue scheming to undermine his youngest brother's position. Both before and after Verdun, the Bretons were a vital ally for Lothar.

From Charles' point of view, the kingdom Louis the Pious had designated for him was not one that would have been easy to rule even without Lothar's meddling. It consisted of three parts – Aquitaine, Neustria, and the lands between the Seine and the Meuse – and was a kingdom which had little coherence but many problems. Only since 838 had he been designated the heir to Neustria, and only since 839 to Aquitaine as well. Louis the Pious' decision to give this southern region to Charles followed upon the death of Charles' half-brother Pippin in December 838, but Pippin's son, Pippin II, was thereby left disappointed and determined to wrest Aquitaine back from his uncle. Ever since Charlemagne had installed his three-year-old son Louis, the future emperor, as subking in Aquitaine in 781, this region had enjoyed a strong sense of regional identity as a subkingdom within the Carolingian empire, and when Louis the Pious died, Charles was having difficulty making some of the Aquitainians accept his lordship. As for Pippin II, he was a natural ally for Lothar, and indeed, fought with him against his uncles Charles and Louis the German at the fraternal battle at Fontenoy on 25 June 841. Neustria, on the other hand, was quite different, except inasmuch as here too Charles had no well-established following. There was no coherent regional identity here; local feuds amongst the aristocracy drove into Charles' camp those at odds with Lothar's men.

Already in the 830s, Lothar had been able to draw upon a considerable Neustrian following.[10] It was natural that, in his efforts to overturn Louis the Pious' deathbed settlement of his empire, and to claim for himself the empire promised by the *Ordinatio Imperii* of 817, he should look to Neustria as the place where he might hope to overturn his half-brother's rule. As he moved north from Italy against Charles and Louis the German in the summer of 840, he tried to win over the Neustrian aristocracy by promising that he would confirm and even increase their *honores*: they reacted 'in fear and in greed'.[11] At the same time as

---

[10] See above, pp. 80–1.   [11] Nithard, *Histoire*, II.1, p. 38.

the news reached Charles that some of the most important men in the West Frankish kingdom had defected to Lothar, Lothar crossed into Neustria. Charles also learned of unrest in Aquitaine and in Brittany.[12] There was an uprising in Le Mans, too.[13] In western Neustria Lothar might hope to unseat Charles.

We can see something of the confusion of loyalties of 840–1, as each man had to calculate where his allegiance was best bestowed, which lord was most likely to respect his *honores*, what weight to give to earlier undertakings.[14] Richowin, count of Nantes, joined Lothar's camp; he may well have had Rhineland interests to protect.[15] Aldric, bishop of Le Mans, recorded his loyalty to the young Charles, whereas his opponent, the abbot of Saint-Calais, joined the uprising. Aldric also reveals the identity of those who went on the rampage through Maine, ravaging whatever they could: men related to the *superiores tyranni* Wido and Hervey.[16] Some of Wido's kinsmen already had a tradition of supporting Lothar, whereas the family of Hervey was amongst Louis' then Charles' most reliable followers in Neustria and Aquitaine. In the aftermath of Fontenoy, leading members of these two families, Lambert and Rainald, count of Herbauge, were also feuding for control of the city of Nantes.[17] Uncertainty over royal lordship brought endemic tensions amongst the local aristocracy to the fore, and made it easy to settle old scores by violence.

In 841, Charles and Lothar were in direct competition for the loyalties of the Neustrian aristocracy. In March of that year, Charles made his way to Le Mans, and won back the support of those who had deserted to Lothar. But after the battle of Fontenoy, Lothar again chased after Charles into western Neustria, hoping to intimidate or destroy his army.[18] Both Charles and Lothar were aware that Breton support was crucial to their respective bids for Neustrian support. In the spring of 841, Charles sent from Le Mans to Nominoe, whose allegiance had

---

[12] Nithard, *Histoire*, II.4, p. 46.

[13] *Gesta Aldrici Episcopi Cenomannensis*, 52, MGH SS xv.i, 325.

[14] Compare Nelson, 'Public *Histories* and private history'; Brunner, *Oppositionelle Gruppen*, pp. 120–9. [15] Nithard, *Histoire*, II.10, p. 74.

[16] *Gesta Aldrici*, 57, p. 327.

[17] Below, p. 94. Adrevald of Fleury commented that 'marchisis Britannici limitis inter se gravi perduellione dissidentibus'. *Miracula Sancti Benedicti*, 33, p. 493. Dhondt, *Naissance*, pp. 85–8. On Count Reynald's relationship to the family in which the name Hervey recurs see works cited in n. 92 p. 54 above.

[18] Nithard, *Histoire*, II.5, III.4, pp. 52, 99–100.

been to the now-deceased emperor Louis, 'desiring to know if he wished to submit himself to Charles' power'. Nominoe agreed, and took an oath of fidelity to Charles.[19] It is quite clear from Nithard's account of these negotiations that Charles was in no position to compel Nominoe's loyalty, which the Breton leader was free to give or withhold as he chose. All the more reason, then, for Lothar to see in Nominoe a valuable potential ally, on whom his hopes of winning Neustria turned. But his advances to Nominoe at the end of 841 were rejected, 'insolently', according to Nithard.[20]

There can be no doubt of Nominoe's initial loyalty to Charles. On 25 January 842, he made a donation to Redon 'in alms for the sake of the king and myself', possibly on the anniversary of his oath to Charles.[21] And the following month, when at Strasbourg Charles and Louis the German exchanged oaths of mutual support in the face of Lothar's persistent aggression, Charles had Breton troops in his army, who joined in the military displays in front of the royal retinues along with Saxons, Gascons, and Austrasians.[22]

Despite Nominoe's support for Charles, the confusion of Carolingian politics was nevertheless deeply felt within Brittany. Nominoe's charter for Redon was by no means the only charter from 841–2 to be dated by reference to the battle of Fontenoy and the strife between the sons of Louis the Pious. A private sale from Sixt, north of Redon in the county of Vannes, for example, was concluded on 19 June 'in the 842nd year of our lord Jesus Christ, the sons of Emperor Louis ruling, there being conflict between them'.[23] Here again, the quarrels within the Carolingian dynasty were registered by a community that lay beyond the area of any direct Frankish lordship.[24]

In the spring of 843, as the negotiations between the three brothers that were to be formalised in August at Verdun were nearing completion, Lothar and his supporters must have given thought as to how to continue to harass Charles the Bald. The deliberate creation of disturbances amongst peoples under only tenuous lordship was a tactic commonly employed by one early medieval ruler to destabilise the regime of another. Charles the

---

[19] Nithard, *Histoire*, II.5, p. 52.   [20] Nithard, *Histoire*, III.4, p. 100.
[21] CR A13; Guillotel, 'Cartulaires de Redon', p. 45.
[22] Nithard, *Histoire*, III.6, p. 110.
[23] CR A16; other references to the turmoil at around the time of Fontenoy are in CR 214, A15, A17.   [24] Similarly, above, p. 81.

Bald probably used this strategy in 853;[25] Lothar was certainly already adept at fomenting trouble along the frontier. During the spring of 841, he had sown unrest amongst the lowest ranks of Saxon society as a means of attacking Louis the German; of the significance of this move to spread the conflict beyond the confines of the Frankish aristocracy Nithard was in no doubt. Lothar had also established the Viking leader Harald on the Frisian island of Walcheren specifically in order that he might harass the Christian subjects of Louis in the area; Louis was in fear of a combined uprising of Danes, Slavs, and Saxon slaves prompted by his half-brother.[26] In 843, Vikings and Bretons offered a similar opportunity for Charles' opponents to get at the West Frankish king behind his back. In June 843, Lambert, almost certainly the son of that Lambert who had held the countship of Nantes in Louis the Pious' reign and who had shown himself a staunch supporter of Lothar, defected from Charles the Bald and made a double bid to drive out of Nantes Charles the Bald's appointee to the office, Rainald. His first attack, in which Rainald was killed, was carried out in co-operation with the Bretons. When this battle had failed to secure Nantes for him, he connived a month later in the spectacular, bloody Viking assault on the city during the celebration of the feast of John the Baptist, on 25 June 843.[27]

For reasons which are quite unknown, Lothar, either directly, or indirectly through Lambert, had been able to persuade Nominoe to defect and help create a distraction and disturbance on the frontiers of Neustria. After the summer of 843, Nominoe never again resumed his former support for Charles the Bald. Instead, he became a persistent and dangerous threat to the security of Neustria, the more so because he appears to have been

---

[25] Charles the Bald was believed to have incited the Bulgars and Slavs to attack Louis the German in 853. *AB*, a. 853, p. 68.

[26] Nithard, *Histoire*, IV.2, pp. 120–2; also *AB*, a. 841, pp. 38–9; *Annales Xantenses*, a. 841, ed. B. von Simson, MGH SSRG (Hanover, 1909), p. 12. On Lothar's tactics, see also Nelson, 'Last years of Louis the Pious', p. 151 n. 23.

[27] *AB*, a. 843, p. 44; *La Chronique de Nantes*, ed. R. Merlet, Collection de Textes pour servir à l'Etude et à l'Enseignement de l'Histoire 19 (Paris, 1896), chap. 6, pp. 14–17. The Chronicle of Nantes is a late compilation, late eleventh-century at the earliest, more probably twelfth/thirteenth century, and was compiled as a piece of invective and polemic against the Bretons. Although it is generally extremely unreliable, chapter 6 is a verbatim transcription of an annal entry which is also preserved in an early eleventh-century manuscript, Angers, BM 817, fos. 135r–6r, and which was probably initially composed late in Charles the Bald's reign.

a partisan of Lothar, in conjunction with Lambert and Pippin II of Aquitaine. For Lambert, intent on reasserting his father's claim to the county of Nantes, and for Pippin, whose claim to the Aquitainian kingdom had the support of many of the magnates south of the Loire, Nominoe was a useful ally. Certainly, in 844, as Lambert continued his feud against those to whom Charles had given Nantes and Rainald's other *honores*, Breton troops were a useful asset.[28]

Dealing with Nominoe was Charles' first priority as soon as the conclusion of the treaty of Verdun had given him security from open attack by Lothar, and in November 843 he marched against the Bretons. Whether he ever proceeded further west than Rennes is not known; this show of force on the Breton border had no traceable effect.[29] Then, as soon as possible thereafter, he struck against Pippin II. But whilst besieging Pippin's supporters in Toulouse in June 844, his enemies attacked simultaneously, and almost certainly in co-ordination. Lambert, with Breton troops to assist him, attacked Charles' loyal supporters in Neustria, Pippin fell on the Frankish army that was on its way south to Charles' assistance and inflicted a devastating defeat on it near Angoulême, whilst Nominoe ravaged Maine.[30]

Charles' position was left severely weakened. In October 844, he and Louis the German had a meeting with Lothar at Thionville, to try to persuade him to stop his plotting against Charles. Nearby at Yütz, a synod of Frankish bishops met at the same time under the presidency of the senior member of the Carolingian family, Charlemagne's bastard son Drogo, bishop of Metz. The bishops urged the three brother kings not to feign their good faith with each other or to engage in 'secret scheming to cause harm', and then set out the ethics of brotherly love and co-operation which were becoming the leitmotiv of later ninth-century political rhetoric.[31] The exhortation must have been directed especially at Lothar, and the upshot of the meetings was the dispatch of messengers to Nominoe, Lambert, and Pippin demanding that they renew their fidelity to Charles, and

---

[28] *AB*, a. 844, p. 46; *Chronicon Aquitanicum*, a. 844, MGH SS II.253.
[29] *Chronicon Aquitanicum*, a. 843, p. 253; *Recueil des Actes de Charles II le Chauve*, ed. G. Tessier, 3 vols. (Paris, 1943–55), I.71–3, no. 28; Guillotel, 'L'action de Charles le Chauve', pp. 10–14.
[30] *AB*, a. 844, pp. 46–8; *Annales Xantenses*, a. 844, p. 13; *AF*, a. 844, pp. 34–5.
[31] Schneider, *Brüdergemeine und Schwurfreundschaft*, esp. p. 144.

threatening military action against them if they persisted in their opposition.[32]

Pippin and Lambert both made their peace in the course of 845.[33] But events took a new turn when Bretons who opposed Nominoe summoned Charles into Brittany in order that they might defect to him in safety. The result was a serious defeat for Charles' small army as it crossed the Vilaine just north of Redon, at Ballon on 22 November 845.[34]

The débâcle revealed the extreme fragility of royal power in western Neustria. It was the result of a virtually complete breakdown of any firm lordship in the Breton border area, for the power of both Nominoe and Charles was insecure. Lupus of Ferrière reports the unrest among the Bretons,[35] whilst charter evidence reveals the complexities of Frankish lordship in the region. Dating clauses are generally indicative of political affiliation: those from within the Breton communities of the Vannetais suggest that here loyalties were uncertain and perhaps divided in the aftermath of Nominoe's defection from Charles in 843. A small private sale of land in Carentoir concluded in May 844 was recorded in a charter dated 'during the reigns of Charles and Lothar and Louis' whilst another charter for the purchase of adjacent land by the same buyer refers to the reign of Charles only. From Avessac, a Breton community immediately across the river from the abbey of Redon, comes a document of 6 May 843/8 recording the donation to Redon of a field dated 'in that time when our lord Lothar is reigning'.[36] Nor was Charles' lordship more secure in the counties of Rennes and Nantes. Almost all those Frankish landowners who made grants to Redon of lands in the Rennais and Nantais between 842 and 849 were supporters of Lothar.[37] To make matters worse, as Charles attacked the Bretons, his own men defected from him.[38]

---

[32] *AB*, a. 844, pp. 48–9; MGH Conc. III.27–35, no. 6; clause 1 includes the caution against indulging in 'occulta nocendi machinatio'.

[33] *AB*, a. 845, p. 50; Lambert was back in Charles' court as a count by December 845: *Actes de Charles le Chauve*, ed. Tessier, I.227, no. 81.

[34] *AB*, a. 845, p. 51; *AF*, a. 845, p. 35; *Chronicon Fontanellense*, a. 846 (*recte* 845), p. 79; *Actes de Charles le Chauve*, ed. Tessier, I.219–23, nos. 78–9.

[35] Lupus, *Correspondance*, I.184, no. 44: 'Britanni, sibi praeter solitum dissidentes, regem nostrum Britanniam versus evocaverunt, ut pars, quae contra Nomenoium sentiebat, ad eum tuto deficeret.'   [36] CR 112, 111, 117.

[37] CR 41, 42, 214, A18, A19. The only grant by a Frank of land in the county of Nantes that mentions Charles the Bald in the dating clause is CR 59.

[38] *AB*, a. 845, p. 51.

Charles' reaction to this collapse of his authority in westernmost Neustria was one of caution. Amidst rumours that both he and his arch-chancellor had been killed, he fled from Ballon back to Le Mans where he regrouped his forces and prepared for, but did not make, another attack.[39] The following summer he again set out towards Brittany with his army, but once more did not fight. Instead he made a formal peace with Nominoe, whose terms are uncertain. It did, however, involve mutual oaths, and therefore some reciprocal obligations.[40] Since this is the first occasion when Prudentius of Troyes applies to the Breton leader the formal title of the rank of *dux*, the peacemaking may have involved Charles' recognition of Nominoe's right to rule the Bretons in return for acknowledgement of Charles' overlordship.[41] It is also likely that at Nominoe's request, Lambert was moved to a county further away from the Breton border, probably to Sens.[42]

Circumstantial evidence suggests that Lothar soon importuned Nominoe to defect again and resume raiding Neustria. At Christmas, 846, the Bretons were raiding the countryside around Bayeux;[43] at Meersen (near Maastricht) in February 847 Charles and Louis the German again met Lothar in an atmosphere of mistrust, to try to persuade him to adhere to the regime of fraternal co-operation and brotherly love. In 846, Louis the German had tried to persuade Lothar to make peace with Charles the Bald, but Lothar's persistence in destabilising the West Frankish kingdom is evident from the statement issued by Louis the German at Meersen, in which he announced that the brothers would be sending messengers urging Pippin II to keep the peace, to the Vikings and to Nominoe, and that Lothar would send messengers to those of his men who had been resisting Charles' lordship, with instructions to desist.[44] As in 844, injunctions to Nominoe and Pippin were issued at the point when tensions between Charles the Bald and Lothar were approaching crisis point. There is every sign that Nominoe was in Lothar's pay.

---

[39] *AB*, a. 845, p. 51; Lupus, *Correspondance*, I.186–96, nos. 45–6.

[40] *AB*, a. 846, p. 52.   [41] Goetz, '*Dux*' und '*Ducatus*', pp. 162–3.

[42] The move of Lambert at Nominoe's request is mentioned in a synodal letter to Nominoe of 850. Lupus of Ferrières, *Correspondance*, II.60, no. 81. The chronology of Lambert's career at this juncture cannot be established with precision. See Brunterc'h, 'Le duché de Maine', pp. 71–2 and n. 254.

[43] *Historia Translationis Corporum Sanctorum Ragnoberti et Zenonis*, AASS Mai. III.621a. The date of the Breton raid mentioned here is established by Lot and Halphen, *Charles le Chauve*, p. 174 n. 1.

[44] *AF*, a. 846, p. 36; MGH Capit. II.69–70, no. 204.

Early in 849, Charles the Bald and Lothar made peace with each other.[45] But Charles the Bald still faced difficulties in Aquitaine, especially in the Spanish march, and as he marched into Aquitaine in the spring and again in the autumn of 849, Nominoe resumed his raids on Neustria.[46] A chronicler writing between 875 and 885 at Saint-Wandrille (to the west of Rouen on the Seine) who was particularly well informed about Breton affairs in the late 840s, associated the restoration of Count Lambert to command of the Breton marcher area with Nominoe's raid on Anjou in 849.[47] But if Charles was relying on Nominoe's former ally to hold Nantes in the face of Breton attacks, he was mistaken, for in 850 Lambert and his brother Warnar defected to Nominoe. At this juncture we can observe the revival of old aristocratic feuds between 'Widonid' and 'Rorigonid' kin groups. Gauzbert, a relative of Rorigo and probably the count of Le Mans, soon afterwards captured Warnar; Nominoe and Lambert retaliated by ravaging Maine 'with unspeakable fury'.[48]

Once again, effective royal authority collapsed and patterns of allegiance in the Breton march returned to a state of extreme confusion. In August 850 Charles the Bald had marched as far as Rennes, garrisoned the city and then withdrawn: Nominoe and Lambert promptly attacked both Rennes and Nantes and captured their garrisons, including Amalric, the man just appointed to hold Nantes.[49] As the rebels plundered the Nantais and Anjou, the king's supporters in the region scattered.[50] Yet in the midst of the uproar, the abbot of Redon sought out the West Frankish king's patronage and protection, and himself offered shelter at Redon to one of Lambert's opponents, Gauzlin, abbot of Rorigo's family monastery of Saint-Maur at Glanfeuil.[51] It is only at Redon that we have evidence that Charles' lordship was still recognised.

The king probably spent the winter of 850–1 making provisions for the defence of Neustria, for he was in Chartres in January 851 and in Tours in February. His presence did not deter Nominoe.

[45] *AB*, a. 849, p. 56; *Chronicon Fontanellense*, a. 849, p. 81.
[46] *AB*, a. 849, pp. 57–8.   [47] *Chronicon Fontanellense*, a. 849, p. 83.
[48] *Chronicon Fontanellense*, a. 850, p. 85.
[49] *Chronicon Fontanellense*, a. 850, p. 85. The detailed chronology of the campaign is worked out by Guillotel, 'L'action de Charles le Chauve', pp. 20–2.
[50] *GSR*, III.5, pp. 201–3.
[51] *GSR*, III.5, pp. 201–3. For Charles' diploma of protection and immunity for Redon, see *Actes de Charles le Chauve*, ed. Tessier, I.348–51, no. 132. This was issued on 3 August 850 at Bonneveau, in eastern Anjou, as Charles was *en route* for Rennes.

The Breton continued raiding, but died on 7 March 851, probably outside Vendôme, to the north-east of Tours.[52] Breton attacks on Neustria continued under the leadership of Lambert, whose feud with the family of Rorigo had not quite run its course. It only ended the following year, 852, when 'little young Gauzbert' succeeded in killing Lambert, and Warnar was tried and sentenced to death by Charles the Bald.[53]

Before marching against the Bretons in August 851, Charles the Bald yet again began to tackle this turmoil by meeting his brothers at Meersen. Some time during the summer all three met together and made an agreement that none would engage in 'schemings and plottings and wicked machinations and harmful activities' to the others' detriment, and that henceforward they would maintain brotherly love 'in pure heart and good conscience and unfeigned faith, without treachery or deception'.[54] The urgent tone of this undertaking suggests that, despite his reconciliation to Charles in 849, Lothar had nevertheless connived at, and perhaps fomented, the unrest on the frontiers of the West Frankish kingdom. He had undoubtedly been the root cause of much of the earlier unrest in western Neustria which so vexed Charles. His meddling was made all the easier by the long-standing rivalries amongst the Neustrian aristocracy, by Charles' conflict with his nephew Pippin and by Nominoe's readiness to play his own game and challenge Charles' overlordship.

These eights years of Breton unrest, from 843 to 851, culminated in another, devastating, defeat for Charles, inflicted by Nominoe's son Erispoe on 22 August 851 at Jengland, a spot within a few miles of the site of his father's victory over Charles in 845.[55] The details of the peace agreement concluded shortly thereafter will be discussed in detail below: they mark a new and quite different phase in Frankish expressions of overlordship over

---

[52] *AB*, a. 851, p. 60; *Chronicon Fontanellense*, a. 851, p. 85; *Annales Engolismenses*, a. 851, MGH SS XVI.486. The place of Nominoe's death is only noted in late medieval sources. Lot and Halphen, *Charles le Chauve*, p. 223 n. 3.

[53] *Chronicon Fontanellense*, a. 851, pp. 85–9. Note that this chronicle distinguishes 'Gauzbertus', 'Gauzbertus iuvenis' and 'Gauzbertus iuvenculus', without, however, specifying their relationship to each other.

[54] MGH Capit. II.72, no. 205, clauses 1–2.

[55] *Chronicon Aquitanicum*, a. 851, p. 253; *Chronicon Fontanellense*, a. 851, p. 87; Audradus Modicus, *Liber Revelationum*, ed. L. Traube, 'O Roma Nobilis. Philologische Untersuchungen aus dem Mittelalter', *Abhandlungen der philosophisch-philologischen Classe der königlichen bayerischen Akademie der Wissenschaften*, 19 (1892), 297–394, at p. 384–5; F. Lot, 'Vivien et Larchamp', *Romania*, 35 (1906), 258–77.

the Bretons. As for the years of Nominoe's revolts against Charles the Bald, they show clearly the extent to which the politics of Neustria and the Breton march were not simply regional squabbles, but were part of a much wider, more complex pattern in which both local rivalries and conflicts amongst the Carolingians themselves interlocked. We can only see these events through the extremely hostile eyes of Frankish chroniclers, and it is therefore impossible to deduce quite what Nominoe's incentives and motives may have been. It is also impossible to judge how far the Bretons were united behind him, or the extent to which his successful plundering expeditions brought in the booty with which to build up his own lordship over the Bretons. Whatever the Breton side of the story may have been, it was Carolingian quarrelling and the failure of the regime of brotherly love that provided the opportunity for Nominoe's sustained and successful opposition to Charles the Bald's claim to hegemony over the Bretons.

THE REVOLT OF 858

Charles the Bald again faced persistent Neustrian unrest between 858 and 863. At the heart of the trouble lay the balance of interests between king and aristocracy, particularly within the old *ducatus Cenomannicus*; as a holder of Neustrian benefices, the Breton leader Salomon was deeply implicated. These revolts sought to adjust that consensus between king and subjects which formed the basis of Frankish government, but derived their seriousness from the availability of other Carolingians always eager to challenge Charles' lordship over his West Frankish subjects. Amongst the pool of Carolingian kings and princes, it was now Louis the German who posed the most persistent threat to Charles the Bald, the emperor Lothar having died in 855. Into the mêlée caused by Louis' readiness to support disaffected West Frankish magnates, Salomon was drawn so fully that not until the Bretons were pacified could Charles regain control over Neustria. To understand how this came about necessitates a brief sketch of Charles' efforts to promote his power in both Neustria and Aquitaine between 851 and 857.

In the aftermath of the battle between Charles the Bald and the Bretons at Jengland, the king undertook a major redistribution of Neustrian *honores*. As part of the peace he made with Erispoe, the Breton leader was given the counties of Rennes and Nantes and the pays de Retz to hold in benefice.[56] Royal authority was in tatters here by this date and Charles had little to lose by such a grant; reasons why it secured Erispoe's fidelity for the rest of his life will be suggested later. The deaths of many of Charles' loyal Neustrian supporters in the battle, especially Vivian, count of Tours, together with the demise the following year of the two worst Frankish trouble-makers, the brothers Lambert and Warnar, provided the king with the opportunity for consolidating his hold on the lower Loire basin and preventing Lothar re-establishing any influence there. In particular, he introduced into Neustria one of his closest supporters, Robert the Strong, giving him the lay abbacy of Marmoutier, and in March 852, the command of a large duchy stretching from Tours and Angers on the Loire to the Seine, equivalent to the royal apanage centred on Le Mans.[57] In addition to rewarding Robert, Charles' aim was undoubtedly to provide effective defence in the face of Viking and Breton raids, and it was through family connections with a large group of Neustrian vassals that Robert was able to rise so very rapidly to predominance in Neustrian politics.[58] The favour shown to Robert was accompanied by an assault on the family of Rorigo, for in March 852, Charles the Bald had Gauzbert of Le Mans executed, apparently without a proper trial.[59] In 852, he also established contact with Salomon, foster-son of Nominoe and cousin of Erispoe, who became his *fidelis* and to whom he entrusted one third of Brittany, presumably those Neustrian lands with which Erispoe had been beneficed the previous year.[60]

After the deaths of Lambert, Warnar, and Nominoe, Neustria was for the moment not a priority for Charles. Instead, he was faced with the insoluble clash of interests with his nephew Pippin II over Aquitaine. This was another instance where conflict within the Carolingian dynasty fed on, and itself sustained, conflicts among the regional aristocracy.[61] Charles the Bald's dilemmas are

---

[56] *AB*, a. 851, pp. 63–4. The eastern boundary of the land granted to Erispoe was probably the river Mayenne. Brunterc'h, 'Géographie historique et hagiographie', p. 44.

[57] Dhondt, *Naissance*, pp. 93–4; Werner, 'Arbeitsweise', pp. 113–15.

[58] Werner, 'Untersuchungen', 19 (1959), pp. 149–69.

[59] *Chronicon Aquitanicum*, a. 852, p. 253; *AF*, a. 854, p. 44; Regino, *Chronicon*, a. 860, p. 78.

[60] *AB*, a. 852, p. 64. CR A35 refers to Erispoe and Salomon as the *dominatores* of the county of Rennes in 853.

[61] J. Martindale, 'Charles the Bald and the government of the kingdom of Aquitaine', in *Charles the Bald*, pp. 115–38.

especially clear in the Aquitainian revolt of 853–4, and in the role in it of the influential and numerous descendants of Rorigo of Le Mans, for of the many aristocratic families with interests throughout the West Frankish kingdom and even beyond, they had the most influence in both Aquitaine and Neustria.[62] In 852, Pippin II had been forcibly tonsured and confined to the cloister. Angered, 'almost all' the Aquitainians defected from Charles the Bald to Louis the German in 853, inviting him to be their king, or to send his son in his stead. As reported in the Annals of Fulda, a source very close to Louis' court circle, their plea to Louis asserted firmly that the whole of Christendom (that is, the Carolingian empire) was their sphere of legitimate political action. If Louis did not free them from Charles' 'tyranny', the only alternative was to seek from foreign and pagan peoples the help that 'orthodox and legitimate' lords would not give them. In 854, Louis sent his son, Louis the Younger, to the Aquitainians, but on his arrival he found that in fact only the relatives of the executed Gauzbert welcomed him, and this because they were greatly offended by Charles the Bald's arbitrary killing of their kinsman.[63] Thus in 853–4, Charles' high-handedness in dealing with one Neustrian magnate had helped trigger a revolt in Aquitaine, which itself gave Louis the German an opening to try to expand his influence at his brother's expense and to provide for his son. And significantly, the magnates distinguished sharply between the political unity of the entire Carolingian world and the pagans and foreigners who lay beyond its frontiers. Charles the Bald dealt with his subjects on the premise that all the Carolingian kingdoms formed a single political whole.

The Aquitainian revolt of 854 had raised the issue of the quality of Charles' rulership, in the form of accusations of oppressive rule. By the summer of 856, this mistrust of the king was not confined to the Aquitainians, but had spread further north.[64] An immediate cause for this can be found in the marriage alliance which Charles concluded with Erispoe in February 856. In addition to betrothing

[62] Oexle, 'Ebroin'.

[63] *AB*, a. 853–4, pp. 67–9; *AF*, a. 853–4, pp. 43–4. The Annals of Fulda reports the Aquitainian request to Louis the German thus: 'ut aut ipse super eos regnum susciperet aut filium suum mitteret, qui eos a Karli regis tyrannide liberaret, ne forte ab extraneis et inimicis fidei cum periculo christianitatis quaerere cogerentur auxilia, quae ab orthodoxis et legitimis dominis invenire nequirent'.

[64] MGH Capit. II.279–85, nos. 262–5.

the king's eldest son, Louis the Stammerer, to Erispoe's daughter, the negotiations established a Neustrian subkingdom equivalent to the duchy of Le Mans for the ten-year-old prince: according to an account of the negotiations written about a decade later by a Neustrian cleric, Louis received the *regnum Neustriae* not from Charles, but from Erispoe, with the consent of the Frankish magnates.[65] Two men in particular stood to lose from this projected marriage alliance between Frank and foreigner. One was Salomon. He was threatened on two counts: the loss of the Neustrian *honores* which he had ruled in Charles' name under Erispoe since 852, and also as the most influential man in his cousin's retinue.[66] The other likely loser was Robert the Strong, who had been given a duchy spanning much of Neustria back in 852, and whose influence would be severely curtailed by the establishment of a princely court at Le Mans. How many others may have felt their interests threatened by such a warm rapprochement with the Bretons or by the introduction of Louis the Stammerer into the region is unknown.

Prudentius of Troyes hints at undercurrents of unrest amongst the Neustrian magnates throughout 857, but the event which triggered off the revolt which reverberated throughout all of Charles' kingdom in 858 was the assassination in November 857 of Erispoe. His slayers were his kinsmen Salomon and an otherwise unknown Breton, Almarchus.[67] As the political crisis came to a head, the news of Erispoe's assassination and the disruption of Charles' plans for Neustria was of great importance to the king's supporters.[68] In the spring of 858, Neustrians and Bretons together drove the young Louis out of Le Mans, who fled to join his father north of the Seine.[69] The leader of the Neustrian rebels was Robert the Strong.[70] The defectors again sent to Louis the German for help, complaining, as in 853, of Charles' oppressively harsh rule. Faced with the choice of supporting one man, his brother, or of assisting the many rebels, Louis finally decided to go to the help of the West Frankish rebels. When he

---

[65] *AB*, a. 856, p. 72; *Actes de Charles le Chauve*, ed. Tessier, 1.481–5, nos. 181–2.
[66] Of the eight diplomas of Erispoe whose witness lists survive, Salomon attests more frequently than anyone else except his own son-in-law Pascweten, and in four out of the five relevant charters, he attests second only to Erispoe himself. CR A31, A32, A40, A44, *Chronique de Nantes*, 14, p. 48.   [67] *AB*, a. 857, 874, pp. 75, 196.
[68] MGH Epp. VIII.i, 51, no. 105.   [69] *AB*, a. 858, p. 77.
[70] Werner, 'Untersuchungen', 19 (1959), p. 151.

reached Orléans in September, Aquitainians, Neustrians, and Bretons came to pledge themselves to him.[71] Like any disaffected Frankish magnate, Salomon had expressed his discontent with Charles by recognising a different Carolingian lord. Once again, the issue for the Bretons was not the acceptance or rejection of Frankish hegemony; as with the Frankish rebels, it was rather a matter of *which* Carolingian it was most advantageous to support.

Peace negotiations in 859–61 to restore fraternal love between Charles and Louis turned on the question of access to patronage and office for the rebels. As always, good lordship in the Middle Ages meant promoting royal interests whilst at the same time balancing out the claims of the competing aristocracy so that as many as possible were rewarded and as few as possible felt unfairly disparaged. The accusations of 'tyranny' which the defectors levelled against Charles are a sign that the king's footing had faltered in this delicate balancing act. Only by restoring to the rebels the lands and *honores* which they had forfeited by defecting could Charles regain their fidelity.[72] But there simply were not enough countships and lay abbacies in Neustria available to satisfy all those who had a claim on them. When Charles received Robert the Strong back into his court in 861, the two men on whose advice he had done so, Guntfrid and Gauzfrid, promptly defected.[73] In 860, Louis the Stammerer received only the lay abbacy of Saint-Martin of Tours, small compensation for the kingdom he had been promised in 856: in 862 he followed the advice of Guntfrid and Gauzfrid and defected to join them, and further insulted his father by marrying without his permission the daughter of one of his own Neustrian supporters, the recently deceased Count Harduin.[74] Gauzfrid was a relative of the Count Gauzbert whose execution in 852 had caused such a stir, in other words a member of an old-established Neustrian family and a descendant of the Rorigo who had held Le Mans early in the century. Guntfrid was a member of the circle of Harduin, who himself had links with 'Rorigonid' interests.[75] Their quarrel was with Robert the Strong, over *honores* traditionally held by their own relatives; when they defected from Charles, they sought out Salomon.

[71] *AB*, a. 858, pp. 78–9; *AF*, a. 858, pp. 49–51; Penndorf, '*Reichseinheitsidee*', pp. 39–40.
[72] *AB*, a. 861, p. 85; MGH Capit. II.152–8, 298–9, nos. 242, 270, cf. *AF*, a. 859, p. 53.
[73] *AB*, a. 861, p. 86.   [74] *AB*, a. 860, 862, pp. 84, 88, 91.
[75] Oexle, 'Ebroin', p. 194.

Although Salomon had sworn fidelity to Charles in 852, he was not yet recognised by him as the legitimate ruler of the Bretons, or as the holder of the Frankish benefices which Erispoe had held. In 859, the Frankish bishops who met at Savonnières near Toul to try and resolve the revolt reminded Salomon of this fidelity and of the fact that the Bretons had always been subject to the Franks, and requested him to resume the traditional tribute payments.[76] For the time being the call went unheeded; instead, Salomon provided a focus for the opposition precipitated by the patronage showered on Robert the Strong. In the spring of 862, Salomon hired the services of a Viking fleet with which to attack Robert, who for his part bought the help of another band of Vikings; he also provided Louis the Stammerer with a large band of troops with which to go after Robert.[77] With help from Louis the German no longer forthcoming – he had made his peace with Charles in 860 – the disaffected Frankish magnates had done what they had threatened to do in 853 and 858: they had turned outside the 'family circle' of Carolingian politics to seek help from foreigners and from pagans.

Salomon, however, was not a complete outsider to the world of Frankish politics. He was a Christian, and he had hereditary claims to rule over the Bretons and to those benefices which Erispoe had held from Charles the Bald. By recognising this, Charles was able to calm Neustria. In 863 he embarked upon a campaign against the Bretons but thought better of it, and at Entramnes, on the left bank of the Mayenne, he made his peace with Salomon and with the remaining Frankish rebels by distributing *honores* to them. Here Charles affirmed with Salomon the peace he had made with Erispoe, adding to his benefices the lay abbacy of Saint-Aubin at Angers and that part of western Anjou which lay between the rivers Mayenne and Sarthe. For his part, Salomon recognised Frankish overlordship by commending himself and swearing fidelity to Charles and by paying tribute.[78] Through traditional rituals of hegemony peace was restored: and the Bretons now controlled western Neustria as far as the gates of Angers itself.

[76] Synod of Savonnières, clause 9, and letter to the Breton bishops, MGH Conc. III.460–1, 480–1. For other provisions of this council regarding the Bretons, see below, p. 155. [77] *AB*, a. 862, pp. 89–90.

[78] *AB*, a. 863, p. 96; Regino, *Chronicon*, a. 866, p. 91. As often, Regino's chronology is wrong here. For further possible provisions of the deal between Charles the Bald and Salomon, see below, p. 112.

Salomon was central to the revolt of 858–63. It was he who had precipitated it by killing Erispoe and helping the Neustrians chase out Louis the Stammerer. Long after the worst of the unrest was over, he remained the focus round which opposition to Charles the Bald gathered, just as a decade or so earlier, it had been Nominoe who provided the opportunity and often the troops for Frankish rebels. But his participation was by no means a rejection of Frankish overlordship, and when peace was achieved in 863, it was accompanied by a return to the normal rituals of hegemony. Certainly, Salomon took advantage of Charles the Bald's difficulties to extend his own sphere of influence further into Neustria, but he did so by competing for benefices and patronage along with the rest of the Neustrian aristocracy, and by switching allegiance to Louis the German at an opportune moment.

SALOMON'S LAST REVOLT

On one further occasion, Salomon was again in a position to move yet further into the circle of the Neustrian magnates, and to adjust the demands of Frankish overlordship yet more in his own favour. Viking raids in the valleys of the Loire and the Seine were frequent and devastating in the middle years of the decade 860–70: in distributing countships and abbacies, Charles had to make as best provision for the defence of his realm as possible, and was mindful that Le Mans was the traditional base from which the defence of western Neustria was organised. Nevertheless, military priorities could not be allowed to override the demands magnates made for patronage for themselves and their own followers. In consequence, patterns of lordship remained very fluid throughout Neustria long after the peace of 863, for officeholders were being switched around very rapidly in the Loire valley, northern Burgundy, and southern Neustria, particularly in 865–6.[79] Military ineptitude led several magnates to lose their offices.[80] Most effective against the Vikings was Robert the Strong, who after his death was hailed at Fulda as a second Maccabaeus. He had been killed at Brissarthe in 866, whilst attacking a band of Vikings

---

[79] *AB*, a. 865–6, pp. 116–34; Werner, 'Untersuchungen', 19 (1959), pp. 155–6, esp. n. 41.
[80] This is explicitly the case for Adalhard, Hugh, and Berengar. *AB*, a. 865, p. 124.

and Bretons who were ravaging the countryside around Le Mans for the second year running.[81] Eventually, Salomon and Charles' cousin on his mother's side, Hugh the Abbot, emerged as the two men both militarily able and acceptable to the local aristocracy. It was they who dominated Neustria during the last decade of Charles the Bald's reign.

In 865 the West Frankish king faced considerable difficulties in Burgundy; it is impossible to establish why the Bretons resumed hostilities at this time, having paid the traditional tribute the previous year.[82] Whatever the reason may have been, in the wake of the casualties at Brissarthe, Frankish animosity towards the Bretons reached a level not recorded since the worst days of Nominoe's plundering raids. Under threat of renewed ravaging of ecclesiastical lands by the Bretons, the Frankish bishops had Pope Nicholas I write to Salomon to recall him to his obligations towards Charles and to urge him to resume paying tribute.[83] Then, in 867, Charles called out his army against the Bretons, but in negotiations conducted between the king and Salomon's son-in-law, Pascweten, at Compiègne in August, a lasting peace was restored. In return for the counties of Avranches and Coutances and a confirmation of all the other Neustrian *honores* already given to Salomon, the fidelity of Salomon and his son towards Charles and his son was assured and a promise of aid against the Vikings made.[84] For the rest of his life, Salomon remained loyal to Charles the Bald, fulfilling his undertaking to provide military aid on two occasions: in 868, when he was also rewarded with a gift of regalia, and again in 873.[85]

By the time of Salomon's assassination in 874, the old *ducatus Cenomannicus* had effectively been dismembered to the Bretons' advantage, for Salomon ruled four entire Frankish counties and parts of two others: Rennes, Nantes, Avranches, Coutances, the pays de Retz and western Anjou. His influence and power in Neustria had grown throughout his lifetime, to the point where, in 867, Charles the Bald acknowledged that he could not hope to secure Neustria without the Bretons as his allies. For Charles, the

---

[81] *AB*, a. 865, 866, pp. 124, 130–1; *AF*, a. 867, p. 66; Regino of Prüm, *Chronicon*, a. 867, pp. 92–3. [82] *AB*, a. 864, p. 113.

[83] Synod of Soissons to Nicholas I, *Chronique de Nantes*, 16, pp. 51–7.

[84] *AB*, a. 867, pp. 136–7, which mentions only the grant of Coutances. Avranches must, however, have been included, and this is confirmed by the *Historia Translationis Sancti Launomari Abbatis Corbionensis in Oppidum Blesas*, AASS OSB iv.ii, 246.

[85] *AB*, a. 868, 873, pp. 151, 192–5; Regino of Prüm, *Chronicon*, a. 873, pp. 105–7.

Breton problem was just one aspect of much larger concerns to make his lordship effective in Neustria and to defend the region against the Vikings, and the deal he finally concluded with Salomon contributed to the tranquillity he enjoyed in Neustria in the last decade of his reign. It is important that at all times, the relationship between Charles and Salomon was played out in terms of the traditional conventions of overlordship: the giving or withholding of tribute, rituals of commendation and the rendering of oaths of fidelity and military aid. There remains to discuss one further, dramatic way in which Frankish overlordship over the Bretons was asserted and maintained by Charles the Bald, one which has hitherto gone quite unnoticed.

IMPERIAL HEGEMONY AND POLITICAL KINSHIP

Carolingian kings often expressed their authority in a metaphor drawn from the strongest social bond they knew: the power of a father over his family and household. To extend and secure political authority, artificial ties of kinship were sometimes constructed. In particular, the strong bonds of spiritual kinship created by baptism were exploited to cement alliances and further political ends. Thus, for example, Louis the Pious had his adult son Lothar sponsor Charles the Bald at his baptism in 823, in the – futile – hope that he would secure Charles' inheritance for him. A generation earlier, the Carolingians' association with the papacy was expressed when Hadrian I sponsored Charlemagne's son Pippin at his baptism, receiving him from the font to become his godfather in 781. Not only did this baptism create a bond between godfather and godson, it also established the close and morally binding relationship of 'compaternity' between spiritual father and natural father.[86]

Spiritual kinship was of the greatest importance at all social levels in the early Middle Ages, binding the Carolingians' subjects to each other in a web of overtly Christian symbolic ties. It was also an ideal means of extending control over the dependent

---

[86] A. Angenendt, 'Taufe und Politik im frühen Mittelalter', *Frühmittelalterliche Studien*, 7 (1973), 143–68; J. H. Lynch, *Godparents and Kinship in Early Medieval Europe* (Princeton, 1986); J. H. Lynch, '*Spiritale vinculum*: the vocabulary of spiritual kinship in early medieval Europe', in *Religion, Culture and Society in Early Medieval Europe. Studies in Honor of Richard E. Sullivan*, ed. T. F. X. Noble and J. J. Contreni, Studies in Medieval Culture 23 (Kalamazoo, 1987), pp. 181–204.

peoples that lined the empire's borders, and of promoting conversion to Christianity amongst them.[87] Conversion and baptismal sponsorship were part of the rituals by which Carolingian imperial overlordship was asserted. On occasion the Christian ceremonial was extended to include the recognition of a new dependent ruler. The most fully documented example of this was the baptism of the Danish king, Harald, at Louis the Pious' court at Mainz in 826. The emperor himself sponsored Harald at the font, the empress Judith sponsored Harald's wife, and Lothar sponsored Harald's son. Before proceeding to mass, Louis gave Harald as a baptismal present a set of royal robes: a purple, jewelled chlamys, gold sandals and cloak, white gloves, and a crown. He also armed him with his own royal sword and gilded sword-belt. The Danish queen and prince received gifts appropriate to their status. After mass, a lavish banquet for Franks and Danes was provided. The following day, the overlordship implicit in the granting of regalia and weapons was made quite explicit when Harald commended himself to Louis and handed over himself and his kingdom into the emperor's service, receiving in return the Frisian county of Rüstringen as a benefice. Louis had in effect adopted Harald as his son, and given him the equivalent of a subkingdom. The bond created was one of *familiaritas*, a truly familial one.[88]

Byzantine precedents had taught the Carolingians how to exploit Christian liturgy for such avowedly imperial ends as the installation of a new client leader. Similar rituals might also be used to turn military defeat into political advantage. Half a century later, the newly installed emperor Charles the Fat was unable to defeat the powerful Viking army encamped under its leader Gottfrid at Elsloo, near Maastricht in 882. Negotiations opened when the Franks sent hostages to the Vikings. Then, when Gottfrid was baptised, the emperor sponsored him, gave him part of Frisia as a benefice, paid a large sum of money to the Vikings and soon after found a Carolingian princess as a bride for the Viking leader in the person of Gisla, daughter of Lothar II. For his

[87] For what follows see A. Angenendt, *Kaiserherrschaft und Königstaufe: Kaiser, Könige und Päpste als geistliche Patrone in der abendländischen Missionsgeschichte*, Arbeiten zur Frühmittelalterforschung 15 (Berlin, 1984).

[88] Ermoldus Nigellus, *In Honorem Hludowici*, IV.283–648, pp. 66–76; *ARF*, a. 826, pp. 169–70; Thegan, *Vita Hludowici*, 33, p. 597; 'Astronomer', *Vita Hludowici*, 40, p. 629; Angenendt, *Kaiserherrschaft*, pp. 215–23.

part, Gottfrid had been created a *consors regni*, the emperor's consort, and returned the Frankish hostages when the ceremony was completed. He swore never to raid the Franks again, but lost his life when accused of complicity with his wife's brother Hugh in a Carolingian counter-plot against Charles the Fat.[89]

The combined subordination of godson to godfather, and of man to lord in these two examples invoked the most compelling of obligations. It blurred the gulf between the Christian, Carolingian world and the pagan lands beyond. It promoted Christianity beyond imperial frontiers, and established a common political morality where hitherto there had been none. Above all, it gave Christian, ritual expression to imperial notions of hierarchy and overlordship.

As a child of three, Charles the Bald had participated in the glittering splendour of Harald's baptism in 826.[90] After his own accession, only Brittany offered him scope for exercising a quasi-imperial hegemony: in 851 Charles turned these imperial gestures to his own advantage and established Erispoe as a client under his own aegis. That Charles and Erispoe were bound together in the spiritual relationship of compaternity is clear from the diplomas which they issued simultaneously for the cathedral of Nantes on 10 February 856, in which each referred to the other as *compater*, cofather.[91] These diplomas were issued when Charles and Erispoe met at Louviers to betroth Erispoe's daughter to Louis the Stammerer, and it is of course possible that the baptismal alliance was created on this occasion. It is much more probable, however, that in 851 Charles had become godfather to a young son of Erispoe's. Prudentius of Troyes' account of the peace concluded between Charles and Erispoe in 851 is remarkable for omitting any reference to the disastrous defeat which the Bretons had just inflicted on the West Frankish king.[92] But when re-read in the light of the accounts of Louis the Pious' baptismal alliance with

---

[89]   *AF*, a. 882, 883, pp. 98–100, 108–9; Regino of Prüm, *Chronicon*, a. 882, pp. 119–20; Angenendt, *Kaiserherrschaft*, pp. 260–2. It is the Mainz recension of the Annals of Fulda (p. 98) that notes that Charles the Fat 'Gotafridum...consortem regni constituit'.

[90]   Ermoldus Nigellus, *In Honorem Hludowici*, IV.419–20, p. 69.

[91]   *Actes de Charles le Chauve*, ed. Tessier, I.482–3, no. 181; *Chronique de Nantes*, 14, pp. 44–8; A. Giry, 'Sur la date de deux diplômes de l'église de Nantes', *Annales de Bretagne*, 13 (1898), 485–508.

[92]   It is possible that the negotiations of the peace of Angers were the secret ones to which Lupus of Ferrières referred; if so, this may help explain Prudentius' reticence. *Correspondance*, II.66, no. 82.

Harald and of Charles the Fat's with Gottfrid, then all the elements of an imperial ceremony of baptismal sponsorship of a client ruler can be identified: all, that is, except mention of the baptism itself. The only difference will have been that Charles could not sponsor the Christian Erispoe himself, and so must have transferred his attention to an infant, probably Erispoe's son Conan.[93] At Angers in 851, Prudentius tells us that Erispoe was given a set of royal robes, just as Harald was in 826. Further, he was given Frankish counties to hold in benefice, as both Harald and Gottfrid were. And Erispoe commended himself with the traditional gesture of the giving of hands, and became Charles' sworn *fidelis*, as did Harald to Louis.[94] Erispoe was feasted as Harald had been, for Lupus of Ferrières hinted that he had over-eaten at the splendid banquets which were served up for the assembled courtiers.[95] Finally, in 856 the betrothal of a member of the *stirps regia* reinforced and extended the new family tie between godfather and godson, as it did when Charles the Fat gave Gisla in marriage to Gottfrid. Just as in 882 Charles the Fat transformed defeat into victory by forming ties of spiritual kinship with Gottfrid, so too in 851 Charles the Bald turned the tables on Erispoe and bound him with the strongest possible obligations.

Erispoe's respect for these undertakings may be the explanation why the Bretons caused no trouble for the Franks throughout his lifetime. In effect, Erispoe was a *consors regni*. That he took part in Frankish administrative procedures is clear from the various diplomas issued during the betrothal ceremony of 856. Amongst the diplomas Charles issued on this occasion, was a grant to the monks of Saint-Philibert at Déas in the pays de Retz of a refuge in Maine 'at the request of our beloved sworn follower and cofather Erispoe' in which Erispoe's intercession conformed to the norms of Carolingian chancery procedure for obtaining a royal diploma.[96] Also of note are the joint diplomas for Nantes issued simultaneously by Erispoe and Charles the Bald. These are quite without precedent in their legal form, in that both are formal grants in their own right: neither confirms the other. Both documents are couched in identical terms; the Carolingian chancery did everything short of issuing one diploma in both

---

[93] Erispoe's only known son Conan attests three of his father's charters: two undatable ones (CR A31, A40) and also the diploma for Nantes of February 856.

[94] *AB*, a. 851, pp. 63–4.   [95] Lupus, *Correspondance*, II.68, no. 83.

[96] *Actes de Charles le Chauve*, ed. Tessier, I.478–80, no. 180.

Province and empire

names.[97] Such close co-operation between the West Frankish king and the Breton client bespeaks an intimacy, trust, and joint lordship which worked to mutual advantage.

In 856, familial obligations between Charles and Erispoe had been further strengthened by the intended marriage, but Salomon's assassination of his cousin the following year temporarily shattered the ties of political kinship between Franks and Bretons. In the aftermath of the revolt of 858–63, Charles set about restoring his quasi-imperial hegemony over the Bretons, by re-establishing a similar rapport with Salomon. The various ritual expressions of alliance were spread out over a period of several years, and it is again probable that the baptismal relationship was created some years before the recognition of Salomon's lordship in western Neustria. The spiritual bond had been affirmed before 869, when Salomon referred in one of his own charters to 'my cofather, the most pious Charles, King of the Franks'.[98] In 867, Bretons and Franks negotiated at Compiègne only after Charles had given hostages to Salomon, in a way reminiscent of Charles the Fat's negotiations with Gottfrid in 882. At Compiègne, Salomon received Frankish benefices through his representative Pascweten, who also swore oaths of fidelity to the West Frankish king on behalf of Salomon and his son. The following year, Salomon was sent a gold and jewelled crown and a complete set of regalia; he also began to be styled *rex* in Breton charters.[99] But since Salomon was not present in person at Charles' court in 867–8, it is likely that the baptismal alliance was created somewhat earlier, on the only occasion after 857 when Salomon and Charles the Bald are known to have met: at Entramnes in 863. We are told that on this occasion, Salomon was present at the Frankish court with 'all' the leading Bretons, and that Charles affirmed with Salomon 'that pact which he had formerly made with Erispoe'.[100] If Salomon's son Wigo, aged perhaps two years, was on that occasion received from the font by Charles the Bald, then it would explain not only why an oath of fidelity had to be taken on his behalf to Charles in 867, but why he was sent, at the normal

---

[97] Above, n. 91.　　　　　[98] CR 241.
[99] *AB*, a. 867, 868, pp. 137, 151; CR 21, 225, 240, 243, 247, 257, Morice, *Preuves*, I.308. Breton charters from 868 onwards do not use the title *rex* at all consistently when referring to Salomon.
[100] Regino of Prüm, *Chronicon*, a. 866 (*recte* 863), p. 91. By the 860s, Salomon travelled with a large and impressive retinue; see Davies, *Small Worlds*, p. 172.

Frankish age of majority of twelve, to swear an oath of fidelity and commend himself to Charles the Bald in person in 873.[101]

Baptismal sponsorship, of Erispoe's son in 851 and of Salomon's son in 863, grants of fiefs in 851 and 867 and of regalia in 851 and 868, a betrothal alliance in 856: such were the means by which Charles the Bald asserted his lordship over the Bretons, reinforcing the more traditional expressions of Frankish hegemony and strengthening the bonds of dependence and obligation in a way which was of mutual prestige. These rituals, redolent of Byzantine precedent, put us in mind of the late antique imperial image, adapted for Charles the Bald in the Golden Gospels, of the ruler receiving the homage of the personified provinces of his realm.[102] For Charles, his rule was the more imperial for having dependent princes of his own creation in his entourage: the deliberately imperial symbolism which he was increasingly adopting in the 860s was enhanced and his own political advantage furthered.[103] For Erispoe and Salomon, their status within Brittany was strengthened; their power, such as it was, now had the trappings of Carolingian regality. Yet Charles' overlordship over the lands west of the Vilaine was for the most part of superficial practical import: the only direct manifestation of it of which there is evidence is his diploma of immunity and protection for Redon.[104] These lavish displays of hegemony were a counterbalance to the raids and defeats which the Bretons were wont to inflict on the Franks. Through them, Charles turned military inferiority into moral superiority.

These ceremonials enhanced Charles' prestige as much as they did Erispoe's and Salomon's. Above all, they were public affirmations of the personal obligations of lordship. Erispoe and Salomon were both accompanied by large retinues when they met with the Frankish king: we can envisage the Bretons looking on as their own lord humbled himself in front of the Frankish king, or as a tiny Breton prince was taken from the font in

---

[101] *AB*, a. 873, p. 193.

[102] R. Deshman, 'Antiquity and empire in the throne of Charles the Bald' (forthcoming in the Festschrift for K. Weitzmann). I am grateful to Professor Deshman for letting me see this paper in typescript.

[103] On Charles the Bald's careful fostering of his imperial image, see in addition to Deshman, J. L. Nelson, 'Translating images of authority: the Christian Roman emperors in the Carolingian world', in *Images of Authority. Essays in Honour of Joyce Reynolds*, ed. M. M. Mackenzie and C. Roueché (Cambridge, 1989), pp. 196–205.

[104] Above, n. 51.

Charles' imperial embrace. In the drama of lordship, in the face-to-face meeting of man and lord, the essence of medieval political obligation was expressed.

It was only to later generations that it looked as if Charles were acknowledging Erispoe and Salomon as independent kings. That this was possible is a reflection both of the Carolingians' skill in manipulating royal symbols, and of the inherent instability of a political system articulated by such intensely personal bonds. For Charles to grant the accoutrements of royalty to the two Bretons no more involved a surrender of power than when Harald came to Louis the Pious' court at Mainz, for when the Danish leader was baptised and adorned with regalia, he was a king-in-waiting, an exile from his own land, hopeful for a throne of his own, powerless except for such support as Louis chose to give him. Similarly, to strengthen Erispoe's and Salomon's position vis-à-vis their own followers posed no threat to Charles' lordship over his own Frankish retinue, just as his gift of royal apparel to the Anglo-Saxon king Æthelwulf, in 855, added to rather than detracted from his own standing.[105] By contrast, Charles carefully controlled the regality of his own sons, and might leave their status utterly ambiguous. In particular, Louis the Stammerer was returned to a command in Neustria in 865, but 'the title of king was neither given back to him nor withheld from him'.[106] In capable Carolingian hands, royal symbolism was potent but ambivalent stuff.

In the case of Salomon, the ambivalence arose from a clear disjuncture between the powerful social and ethical bonds which constrained him in his dealings with Charles the Bald, and his virtual *de facto* independence from Charles. In practice, Salomon had behaved much as Radulf of Thuringia had done after his victory over the Merovingian Sigebert in 639: according to Fredegar, 'Radulf was in transports of pride. He rated himself king of Thuringia...and did not in so many words deny Sigebert's overlordship but in practice he did all he could to resist his power.'[107] Just as Charles' hegemony over the Bretons was expressed through traditional gestures inherited from the Merovingians, so Salomon's attitude to Charles had seventh-century precedents.

[105] *AB*, a. 855, p. 70.
[106] *AB*, a. 865, p. 123, 'nec reddito nec interdicto sibi nomine regio'.
[107] *Chronicle of Fredegar*, IV.87, p. 74.

Charles gave Salomon a personal gift of regalia: he did not create for him the rank and office of king. The most accurate description of Salomon's regality is that of a Redon writer of the early eleventh century: 'Salomon was called king, not because it was true in fact, but because he wore a gold coronet and purple robes by a grant from the Emperor Charles [the Bald], and for this reason was designated by this name.'[108] His use of the title *rex* was a subjective description of his position, not a formal ascription of rank.[109] For Salomon, too, the paraphernalia of kingship were potent but ambivalent.

The Breton leaders' relationship with Charles the Bald was a fragile balance of co-operation and hostility. But they always acknowledged Carolingian hegemony, however nominal it may have been in practice: Nominoe, Erispoe, and Salomon were never lordless. They certainly exploited the tensions within the Carolingian ruling family to their own advantage, on occasion transferring their allegiance to the more distant Lothar or Louis the German. Charles the Bald's difficulty in maintaining his own overlordship over them was part and parcel of the conflicts inherent within Carolingian political life, in which the demands and obligations of lordship were worked out within the Carolingian empire as a whole. Charles' relations with Nominoe and his successors were different from Louis the Pious' Breton problem precisely because after 840 the whole framework of Frankish life had to readjust to accommodate the succession of several legitimate but rival heirs. Charles' great innovation was to draw on his father's symbolism of imperial overlordship and baptismal sponsorship to reinforce his claim to the allegiance of first Erispoe and then Salomon.

[108] *Vita Conwoionis*, 11, in *GSR*, p. 243.
[109] Similarly for Morman; see above, p. 65.

Chapter 5

AN ANATOMY OF POWER

On 17 April 869, some months after receiving Charles the Bald's gift of regalia, Salomon issued a formal charter to Redon. In language self-consciously modelled on that of a Carolingian royal diploma, Salomon, 'by the grace of God prince of all Brittany and a large part of the Gauls' gave the monks lavish gifts and legal privileges, and his beneficence was witnessed by forty-three members of his court. The gifts were jewel-encrusted gold altar furnishings together with liturgical books and relics, and among them was a chasuble worked with gold thread which Salomon declared had been a present to him from 'my cofather Charles, the most pious king of the Franks'. As for the legal privileges, Salomon took Redon into his protection 'in regal custom', remitted all taxes, dues, and services payable to him in favour of the monks, banned all lawsuits against the monastery relating to the activities of the monks and their dependants during the abbacy of the recently deceased Conwoion and freed the monks from all tolls liable on their trading activities.[1] This charter is the fullest statement of how Salomon conceived his position at the height of his power. It alludes to his spiritual kinship with the Carolingian king and expresses his own quasi-royal position. Further, it gives us some hint of the scale of his wealth and of his powers of government. Above all, it is striking for presenting his position in explicitly Carolingian regal terms. Salomon was entitled to wear Carolingian royal vestments: in this charter his power is clothed in Carolingian language.

This charter invites us to consider Salomon's power as the ruler of a province which had been formed by Carolingian ad-

---

[1] CR 241. The charter opens thus: 'In nomine sanctae et individuae Trinitatis, Salomon, gratia Dei, totius Britanniae magneque partis Galliarum princeps, notum sit cunctis Britanniae tam episcopis quam sacerdotibus totoque clero necnon etiam comitibus ceterisque nobilissimis ducibus fortissimisque militibus omnibusque nostre ditioni subditis, quomodo ... '.

ministrative expediency. It offers a point of departure for exploring the organisation of Breton government, for looking at Salomon's lordship over his subjects and for assessing his wealth and resources. It also raises the question of the extent to which both Salomon's and Erispoe's power was strengthened by Charles the Bald's affirmation of Frankish hegemony over Brittany, as manifested by his grants of regalia and of Frankish counties. Hence too there is the issue of the extent to which their position may have differed from Nominoe's. These questions are central to our understanding of the nature of the principality which Nominoe, Erispoe, and Salomon ruled under Carolingian auspices, and of the ways in which Carolingian overlordship was transmuted into Breton government.

Certainly in Charles the Bald's reign, Carolingian hegemony did not affect Brittany through formal institutional processes. Rather, the Breton leaders were able to broadcast their closeness and subordination to their Frankish overlord through a rhetoric of ruling which aped the Carolingians'. Whereas neither of Nominoe's extant charters at all resemble Carolingian diplomas, some of the charters of Erispoe and Salomon and also of Alan I (876–907) reflect their share in Carolingian regality. By borrowing the invocation and formula for legitimation from Charles' diplomas, by adapting his superscription and notification, and by imitating his announcement of a seal, Erispoe, Salomon, and Alan were announcing their status within the Carolingian world and were distancing themselves from their subjects.[2] The most powerful of Charles the Bald's Frankish magnates expressed

---

[2] Some or all of these features are to be found in CR 235, 240, 241, A31; *Chronique de Nantes*, 14, 22 (pp. 44–8, 69–72); *Cartulaire Noir de la Cathédrale d'Angers*, ed. C. Urseau (Paris, 1908), no. 12, pp. 30–2. I have excluded Salomon's charter of immunity for Prüm from consideration either for its language or for the powers of government it mentions because it was drafted by the beneficiary, and closely modelled on the Carolingian diplomas already in Prüm's possession.

It should be noted that the references to princely seals in these charters have occasioned particular controversy, on the grounds that (i) none of these charters survives in the original, (ii) until the late eleventh century, only kings sealed charters, and (iii) the wording of the references to seals in these Breton charters is consistent with eleventh-century not ninth-century practices. However, Charles the Bald expressed his imperial pretensions by sometimes using a pendant gold bull as an alternative to the normal royal seal, an applied wax one. In view of this, it is worth bearing in mind the possibility that the grants of regalia may indeed have included the authorisation to use the lesser, royal form of sealing, Cf. *Actes de Charles le Chauve*, ed. Tessier, III.141–5.

themselves similarly, in ways that were quite compatible with their close political dependence on their king.[3] As Breton power grew in the course of the ninth century, the obvious language for describing it was a Carolingian one.

The rhetoric of ruling, however, is no simple guide to the practicalities of power. Throughout the ninth and early tenth centuries, princely titulature remained extremely variable. Salomon, for example, was styled *dux* or *princeps*, just as Nominoe had been, in addition to the intermittent use of *rex* after 868.[4] Fluidity of titulature suggests fluid structures of authority that were not yet conceived in institutional or official terms. It is not through titulature alone that the growth of princely power can be traced.

Instead, following the lines of enquiry suggested by Salomon's grand charter of 869, this chapter assembles evidence for the nature of Breton lordship and for princely wealth and resources with particular, but not exclusive, reference to Salomon. To do this is no straightforward task. No convenient description of the princely household eases the way. No Breton chronicler recorded the activities or the itinerary of the ruler's court. Instead, the picture has to be compiled using scraps of circumstantial evidence from a variety of sources, principally charters and saints' lives. Foremost among this is material from Redon, but this in itself poses further problems, for it means that almost all the extant evidence pertains only to south-eastern Brittany. It is impossible to make any meaningful assessment of the nature of Breton government in the area beyond Redon's purview: what is known of south-eastern Brittany cannot be put into any useful perspective. The following remarks are offered with this important proviso.

LORDSHIP AND LOCALITY IN NINTH-CENTURY BRITTANY

In any medieval kingdom or lordship, government operated through a consensus between ruler and ruled which had to take account both of tensions between periphery and centre and also of

---

[3] G. Tessier, 'A propos de quelques actes toulousains du IXe siècle', in *Recueil de Travaux Offerts à M. Clovis Brunel*, 2 vols. (Paris, 1955), II.566–80; Airlie, 'Political behaviour', pp. 275–84; Brunner, 'Fränkische Fürstentitel', p. 203.

[4] Exhaustive discussions of Breton princely titulature are provided by W. Kienast, *Der Herzogtitel in Frankreich und Deutschland 9. bis 12. Jahrhundert* (Munich, 1968), pp. 140–61, 434–5, and Brunner, 'Fränkische Fürstentitel', pp. 260–82.

traditions of local self-regulation.[5] This was as true in Brittany as elsewhere. In the first place, there exists no evidence of any well-established tradition of a single Breton rulership before Nominoe passed his position on to his son Erispoe; the leadership of Morman and Wihomarc seems to have been a response to pressing military need, and may have been no more than the temporary leadership of a warband swollen with men from throughout Brittany. Secondly, before the ninth century Brittany was divided amongst several regional rulers. Lastly, at least in south-eastern Brittany, village communities were effectively self-regulating during the ninth century, and doubtless also before, for local landowners and machtierns had little direct contact with their ultimate rulers. Nominoe, Erispoe, and Salomon established their dynastic power unaided by any powerful habit of Breton unity, and in a society with no clear hierarchy of lordship.[6]

Charter dating clauses establish that, whatever Nominoe's status as Louis the Pious' *missus* may have entailed, he claimed authority throughout all of Brittany.[7] Similar claims were made for his successors Erispoe and Salomon, in increasingly assertive language.[8] However, it is hard to discern any consciousness of a Breton political identity underpinning these rulers' position. Awareness of the linguistic identity of the Bretons as a *gens* did not necessarily bring with it any instinct for political cohesion. This emerges particularly clearly from the writings of late ninth-century Breton hagiographers. For them, *Britannia* was a geographical expression: a *regio* not a *patria*. Affinities and loyalties lay instead with the old-established regions which had traditions of their own rulers, Cornouaille (*Cornubia*) in the south-west, and Dumnonée (*Dumnonia*) in the north-west.[9]

---

[5] See especially Reynolds, *Kingdoms and Communities*.
[6] See above, pp. 23–31.   [7] Above, n. 98 p. 83.
[8] For example, CR A34, 'dominante Erispoe, qui dedit, in totam Britanniam et usque ad Medanum fluvium'; CR 79: 'anno .VI. principatus Salomonis in Brittannia'; CR 241: 'Salomon totius Brittannie princeps, qui hanc donationem dedit firmareque rogavit, testis'.
[9] The Bretons are referred to as a *gens* in the prologue to the anonymous first life of Turiau; in his life of Malo (II.13), Bili identifies a man as 'brito natione'. 'Vie antique et inédite de S. Turiau', ed. F. Duine, *Bulletin de la Société Archéologique d'Ille et Vilaine*, 41 (1912), 1–47, at p. 29; Bili, *Vita Machutis, Vie de Saint-Malo, Evêque d'Alet*, ed. G. Le Duc, Dossiers du Centre Régional Archéologique d'Alet B (n.p., 1979), pp. 243–4. On the other hand, Wrdisten writes of the 'Britanniae regio', the 'universa terrae Armoricae regio' but of the 'Cornubiae patria'. (*Vita S. Winwaloei*, II.14, I.18, II.19, pp. 228, 204, 232.) Similarly there is a contrast in Wrmonoc between the 'regio

In the face of local loyalties such as these a single Breton rulership was established. It is therefore not surprising to find clear signs of outright opposition to the rule of Nominoe and all his ninth-century successors. We learn of conflict within Brittany mostly from Frankish chroniclers whose interest was focussed on the repercussions for the stability of the West Frankish kingdom, but they do not allow us to identify any pattern of specifically regional tensions before the late ninth century.

Conflict amongst the Bretons was first noted only after Nominoe had been ruling for nearly fifteen years. Whether his rule had indeed won general recognition until 845 is not known, but in that year Lupus of Ferrières reported that some Bretons (we do not know who) wished to 'defect' from Nominoe to Charles the Bald. It was their request which prompted the Frankish king to lead his army into Brittany, where it was defeated at Ballon. Lupus commented on how unusual it was for the Bretons to be at loggerheads with one another, but he may have had little real knowledge of what went on when the Bretons were not causing trouble for the Franks.[10]

The position of Nominoe and his successors may never have been very secure. In writing his account of Erispoe's murder in 857 in the Annals of Saint-Bertin, Prudentius of Troyes noted that there had been long-standing faction fighting amongst the Bretons.[11] Salomon took a long time to establish his control after the coup against Erispoe, and in the interim there had been considerable unrest and disorder.[12] Dissent amongst the Bretons also brought Salomon's rule to an abrupt end, and Hincmar of Reims described with great relish the details of the conspiracy which resulted in his death in 874.[13]

It is tempting to suggest that Salomon's removal and the protracted power struggle which ensued were the result of regional frustrations which had built up during the seventeen years of his rule. This is certainly true in the case of the Frankish lands which Charles the Bald had made over to Salomon, for Hincmar reports that Franks who had been oppressively treated by Salomon were amongst the rebels.[14] As for Salomon's Breton

---

Armoricae' and the 'Domnonensis patria'. (*Vita Pauli*, 11, 12, 'Vie de Saint Paul de Léon en Bretagne', ed. C. Cuissard, *Revue Celtique*, 5 (1881–2), 413–60, at pp. 437, 438.)   [10] Above, n. 35 p. 96.   [11] *AB*, a. 857, p. 75.
[12] CR 105.   [13] *AB*, a. 874, p. 196.   [14] *AB*, a. 874, p. 196.

assailants, those whose names are known also hint that regional tensions had surfaced. Hincmar identifies Pascweten, Wrhwant, and Wigo son of Riwallon as the Breton leaders of the conspiracy: on the basis of charter evidence, each of these three can be associated with a different interest group. Pascweten is the best known. He was count of Vannes, a wealthy landowner with many estates and salt workings in south-eastern Brittany, a patron of Redon, and a very prominent member of both Erispoe's and Salomon's retinue.[15] As Salomon's son-in-law, he represented Salomon in negotiations with Charles the Bald in 867.[16] Wrhwant, on the other hand, only appears twice in Salomon's court, and was never styled count.[17] He certainly had seigneurial interests in north-eastern Brittany; his one grant to Redon was of jurisdictional rights over part of the *plebs* of Pléchâtel.[18] Pascweten and Wrhwant fought each other for control of Brittany after Salomon's death: their conflict looks like that between the 'ins' and 'outs' at Salomon's court. The third conspirator, Wigo son of Riwallon, was Salomon's nephew. Riwallon himself had been count of Cornouaille for at least part of Salomon's reign.[19] Cornouaille was a region with a particularly strong sense of its own identity in the face of outsiders, and Wigo, never mentioned again after 874, may have seen the coup against Salomon as an opportunity to lessen Salomon's grip here.[20]

Pascweten and Wrhwant had both died by the middle of 876, and the conflict between them was continued by Pascweten's brother Alan and Judicael, son of Erispoe's daughter, until the latter's death, probably in 888 or 889.[21] Alan had inherited his brother's title to the county of Vannes and had extensive interests in the county of Nantes; Judicael had power in part or all of

---

[15] Pascweten is described as count of Vannes in CR 258. His landed interests are recorded in CR 22, 23, 26, 35, 72, 85, 260, 262, A30, A39. He attested the following charters of Erispoe: CR 70, 120, A31, A32, A40, A43, A44, *Chronique de Nantes*, 14, pp. 44–8, and of Salomon: CR 21, 30, 49, 78, 105, 240, 241, 247, 258, Beyer, *Mittelrheinisches Urkundenbuch*, 95, pp. 99–100. [16] Above, p. 112.

[17] CR 21, 257. He also witnessed one charter of Erispoe's, *Chronique de Nantes*, 14, pp. 44–8. [18] CR 243.

[19] 'Tempore quo Salomon Britones rite regebat / Cornubiae rector quoque fuit Rivelen.' Clemens' hymn to Winwaloe, Wrdisten, '*Vita S. Winwaloei*', p. 263; CR 107.

[20] Loyalty to Cornouaille and pride in its glories are expressed by the lament for its fate, oppressed under foreign rulers (the Vikings?, Salomon?) included by Wrdisten in his life of Winwaloe. '*Vita S. Winwaloei*', II.20–1, pp. 232–3.

[21] For discussion of the evidence for the date of Judicael's death, see Chédeville and Guillotel, *Bretagne*, pp. 364–7.

Cornouaille during Salomon's rule.[22] If tensions between eastern and western Brittany did in fact precede Alan's emergence as sole ruler of all of Brittany, then his rule represents the predominance of south-eastern over western Brittany.

The Breton rulers certainly faced opposition from regions unaccustomed to the centralising rule of a single dynasty, and struggles amongst members of the ruling family exacerbated these tensions. No early medieval kingdom or lordship was free from antagonisms such as these. All too often they fed into one another, as Charles the Bald's difficulties in dealing with the Aquitainians and with his nephew Pippin show.[23] We may surmise much the same in Brittany. In particular, it looks as if first Salomon's nephew, Wigo, and later Erispoe's grandson, Judicael, were associated with the resentment felt in western Brittany to rule from the south-east.

We can only guess what methods may have been used to combat these particularist tendencies. But, in any early medieval kingdom or principality, the main forum for consensus and co-operation was always the ruler's court. Thanks to the lengthy witness lists attached to most Breton charters, it is possible to say something of the composition of the retinue which accompanied Nominoe, Erispoe, and Salomon, and to identify the traces of a rudimentary household organisation that may have helped to spread the ruler's power out from beyond his immediate residence into regions unused to his rule.

The Breton rulers moved with their retinue around various rural residences, described by the same Old Breton word used for a machtiern's court, *lis* (sing.; Latin *aula*). At the core of the household was the ruler's family. Nominoe, Erispoe, and Salomon were often accompanied by their close relatives, particularly on grand occasions. Nominoe's wife Arganthael was sitting beside him when he witnessed a donation to Redon made in his *lis* in Renac; when Erispoe met Charles the Bald to betroth his daughter to Louis the Stammerer, his retinue included his wife Marmohec, son Conan, cousin Salomon, together with Salomon's brother Riwallon and son-in-law Pascweten.[24] Although Salo-

---

[22] Regino, *Chronicon*, a. 874, pp. 107–10; CR 201, 235, 238, 239. CR 247 is attested by Judicael, *princeps Poucher*; there is disagreement as to whether the term Poucaer (Poucher) referred in the early Middle Ages to all of Cornouaille or only to that part which later formed the deanery of Poher.   [23] Above, pp. 101–2.
[24] CR 171; *Chronique de Nantes*, 14, pp. 44–8.

mon's wife Wenbrit attested only one of his charters, on numerous other occasions he appeared in the company of his sons Wigo and Riwallon, his brother Riwallon with his son Wigo, and his son-in-law Pascweten.[25] As always in the early Middle Ages, the roots of power and authority lay in the family and household.

The close circle around these Breton rulers also included a few men who acted as their agents or representatives. Worworet went on a mission on Nominoe's behalf to Louis the Pious in 834; he was also a prominent member of Nominoe's retinue, attesting four out of five extant charters which record transactions completed in Nominoe's presence.[26] Other men who put in an occasional appearance at Nominoe's court also acted as representatives when needed. Thus of the men who witnessed Nominoe's own grant to Redon made in Renac on 26 January 842, two, Rihowen and Hencar, were sent by Nominoe to hear accusations which Anauhocar had made to him that Redon had an unlawful claim on land in Avessac; a third man, Driwallon, presided over a different court session again involving Redon.[27]

In contrast to Nominoe's modest court, Salomon's retinue was considerably larger, up to between forty and fifty men at times, including several bishops and abbots. At one such gathering his lavish grant to Redon was made.[28] Also, the number of close associates frequently found in his presence was greater, and we find hints of a rudimentary administrative organisation.[29] In addition to Salomon's relatives, about eight names recur frequently at various times and locations.[30] None of these, however, was among the men described in other charters as Salomon's *missi*, who presided over lawsuits or witnessed transactions on Salomon's behalf.[31] There are, then signs of a distinction between a fairly permanently constituted retinue which travelled around with Salomon, and the use of more local men designated as *missi* to carry out the ruler's business.

The ruler's retinue presumably formed the kernel of his

[25] CR 78, cf. CR 21, 49, 240, 247, 257.
[26] *GSR*, I.10, pp. 137–41; CR 2, 88, 176, A12.   [27] CR A12, cf. CR 61, 124.
[28] Above, p. 116.
[29] Salomon's retinue can be reconstructed from CR 21, 30, 49, 52, 77 (= 100), 78, 85, 105, 109, 240, 241, 247, 257, 258, A48, and Beyer, *Mittelrheinisches Urkundenbuch*, 95, pp. 99–100. See also Davies, *Small Worlds*, pp. 172–3.
[30] Particularly Bran, Bodwan, Urscant, Wrcondelu, Hincant, Sabioc, Sperevi, Omnis, Morweten.
[31] Named *missi* of Salomon are Loiesworet, Litoc (who also appeared as Nominoe's *missus*), Hirdran, and Winic. CR 87, 139, 150, 225, 253.

warband. It certainly did constitute a forum in which lawsuits were heard, benefactions to churches made, and charters issued. Only one stray reference to Salomon's *stabularius*, Winic, a tenant on Redon's land close to Salomon's residence at Plélan, hints at any organised military side to Salomon's household.[32] Of its clerical side, we know a little more. Salomon was frequently accompanied by two clerics, the abbot Finoes and Felix, deacon (later archdeacon) of Vannes and former close companion of Erispoe's.[33] However, the clerical element in Salomon's household had no established secretarial procedures, for it was not capable of coping with the demands of formal correspondence. Nicholas I repeatedly complained to Salomon that his letters lacked not only a seal but also the form of address and respect necessary when communicating with the papacy.[34]

Sparse though this evidence is, it does hint at some effort to develop a princely administrative entourage. A further significant pointer comes in the use in two charters from late in Salomon's reign of the title *comes*, count, for each of a group of four men, all within the inner circle of close associates in frequent attendance upon Salomon. Besides Salomon's son-in-law Pascweten, count of Vannes, and Salomon's brother Riwallon, count of Cornouaille, these were Bran and Morweten, though for which areas they were responsible is not recorded.[35] These references strongly suggest that men very close to Salomon acquired responsibility for government at regional level, within territories defined according to traditional divisions. By the recognition of formal offices in the ruler's court, efforts were being made to bridge the gap between regional identities and princely power.

Corresponding to ancient political divisions, these counties doubtless constituted the basic building blocks out of which the Breton principality was constructed. No surprise need attend the observation that when the firm rule of Alan I gave way to disarray and fragmentation in the early tenth century, counts became even more prominent. Alan died in 907, and his son Rudalt inherited the county of Vannes.[36] Meanwhile, Cornouaille seems to have passed first to Alan's son-in-law Matuedoe, who fled from the Viking invasions to England some time after 913,[37]

---

[32] CR 223.   [33] CR 30, 70, 78, 85, 105, 120, 240, 247, A31, A44, A48.
[34] Nicholas I, epp. 122, 126, 127, MGH Epp. vi.639–40, 646–7, 648–9.
[35] CR 21, 247.   [36] CR 274, 278.
[37] CR 268, 275 + 276, *Chronique de Nantes*, 27, pp. 82–3.

and at some stage to one Wrmaelon, whose charters also express his claim to rule throughout Brittany.[38] Meanwhile, the family of Judicael Berengar (whose name suggests mixed Frankish and Breton ancestry) established itself in the county of Rennes.[39]

It makes sense to view the beginnings of princely administration as a response to the challenge faced by Nominoe, Erispoe, and Salomon in ruling a newly unified territory, one which grew in size as Charles the Bald conceded more and more land to the Bretons. Old regional loyalties, divisions between Franks and Bretons and sheer problems of distance all had to be faced. The rulers began to establish a simple hierarchy of officeholders drawn from among their own family and close followers. But the fact that family feuding and regional loyalties surfaced in 874 argues that they had by no means succeeded in overcoming formidable challenges to their power.

The county of Vannes – the old kingdom of Broweroch – was probably the region in which Nominoe's family originated.[40] There is some evidence that Nominoe may have been count of Vannes at one time;[41] certainly Pascweten, Alan I, and his son Rudalt each held the county in their turn. Although the charter evidence does not reveal anything about their powers as counts of Vannes, the Redon material can be used to ask more general questions about the relationship of the Breton rulers to the village communities in this area.

Of immediate note is the virtual lack of evidence for contact between the rulers and the machtierns who regulated day-to-day village affairs.[42] Only a very few machtierns ever made a recorded appearance at the princely court, even when it met in the immediate vicinity of their own *plebs*. Even less frequently was a machtiern a channel of communication between ruler and villagers. There is only one known occasion: when Salomon used a machtiern's wife as his representative, to inform the inhabitants of Pleucadeuc that he had alienated property within that *plebs*. The event was so unusual that the charter writer felt called to comment on the arrangement.[43] More commonly, Nominoe and Salomon established contact with local affairs through *missi*. (No

---

[38] CR 276, 279; *Cartulaire de Landévennec*, 24, pp. 560–2.
[39] R. Merlet, 'Origine de la famille des Bérenger, comtes de Rennes', in *Mélanges F. Lot* (Paris, 1925), pp. 549–61; Chédeville and Guillotel, *Bretagne*, pp. 393–5.
[40] Below, pp. 129–31.   [41] Above, n. 95, p. 82.
[42] A point emphasised by Davies, *Small Worlds*, p. 206.   [43] CR 257.

missus of Erispoe's is known.) Some of these men were local landowners who occasionally appeared in the princely retinue, and with one exception, each is only ever once recorded as a *missus*.[44] Probably nominated *ad hoc* to carry out specific tasks, *missi* were sent to preside over judicial disputes that had been aired in the ruler's presence, to represent the ruler in property transactions, and were sometimes also recorded as witnesses to transactions to which the ruler was not party.[45] In these ways, they contributed to such links as existed between ruler's court and village locality in south-eastern Brittany.

Further contacts between ruler's court and local communities are also evident in some of the surviving records of lawsuits. Charters suggest a fairly clear grouping of disputes into those problems resolved entirely within the community of the *plebs*, local issues brought to the ruler's attention which he dealt with by sending a *missus* or other representative to preside over a local court in the vicinity of the parties concerned, and cases involving machtierns or powerful landowners which the ruler was inclined to judge himself.[46] Salomon's charter of 869 for Redon makes it clear that he claimed the power to restrict the grievances which might be brought to court, and this may imply that in practice he enjoyed more wide-ranging judicial powers than the surviving cases of disputes reveal.[47] Certainly, his declaration that he was taking Redon into his own legal protection – therefore justiciable only in the ruler's court – was, as his charter made explicit, the use of an essentially royal right. However, as even the most powerful early medieval ruler knew, the right to hear and decide a case was by no means always matched by ability to enforce the ruling, and in this Salomon was no exception, any more than were his predecessors.[48] His government's judicial claims were one thing, its powers of policing another. His court formed an important forum where locally powerful landowners pitted their strength against Salomon's judicial prerogatives.

At the heart of all the issues which have been considered so far lies the most important one of all, obligation and loyalty. We simply do not know whether Nominoe, Erispoe, and Salomon

---

[44] The exception is Litoc, once *missus* for Nominoe and twice for Salomon. CR 106, 139, 150.　　[45] CR 61, 87, 111, 124, 139, 150, 180, 192, 225, 253, 261, 277, A39.

[46] For further details, see Davies, 'Disputes, their conduct and their settlement'; Davies, 'People and places in dispute'.　　[47] Above, p. 116.

[48] CR 21, 105, 242, 247, 261.

expected any active service or loyalty from all those who lived in the area under their rule. We have seen that in the 840s, the villages of the Vilaine valley did not always agree about which lord they recognised; and it is a moot question whether those whom Lupus of Ferrières describes as 'defecting' from Nominoe to Charles the Bald in 845 would have recognised this accusation of treachery in their own actions, or whether they would have denied ever having had any obligation of loyalty to Nominoe at all.[49] Certainly from the Carolingians' point of view, the Breton rulers had little authority to make commitments on behalf of their subjects, for Nithard commented that in 841 Nominoe took his oath to Charles the Bald having first taken the advice of very many of the Bretons, and in 863, Charles extracted an oath of loyalty not just from Salomon, but from all the Breton *primores* who accompanied him to the Frankish court.[50] At the level of Carolingian politics, the ability of the Breton rulers to command the loyalty of the Bretons was very limited.

Occasionally, we learn of men identified as the loyal followers, *fideles*, of their ruler. The word itself does imply some recognition of moral and political obligation on the part of subject to lord, but it is only a very few men who are so designated, and they are men known on independent grounds to have been particularly close associates of their ruler, such as Felix, not only *fidelis* but also *familiarissimus* of Salomon,[51] or Coledoch, *fidelis* of Alan I and also his advisor and supporter.[52] The evidence is too sparse to indicate how many people were touched by this obligation of fidelity, whether it was a general one, or was associated with closeness to the king and service at his court or in his warband. Two charters, however, offer hints that it may have been through the constraints of loyalty that another bridge was made between ruler and village communities. The first records how Deurhoiarn, son of the machtiern Riwalt, killed Catworet (in all probability the son of another machtiern).[53] Catworet had entered into some sort of recognised relationship with Nominoe by 'commending' himself to him, quite probably by an oath, and was Nominoe's *fidelis*.[54] On his death, it was not his kin but Nominoe who exacted

[49] Above, p. 96. [50] Nithard, *Histoire*, II.5, p. 52; *AB*, a. 863, p. 96.
[51] CR 243. [52] *Chronique de Nantes*, 22, pp. 68–72; CR 272 (= A53).
[53] CR 107; for Catworet son of Ratuili see CR 1, *GSR*, I.3, pp. 115–19.
[54] CR 107: 'indicat carta quomodo Catuuoret se comendavit ad Nominoe, et dum esset illi fidelis, occidit eum Deurhoiarn filius Riuualt'.

compensation. This may represent some close bond between this machtiernly family and Nominoe. In the second document, from 913, Alan I's son Rudalt is explicitly described as of superior status – the *senior* – of Bishop Bili of Vannes and his brother Riwalt. Bili and Riwalt themselves had within their service three brothers who had despoiled some of Redon's lands. By petitioning Rudalt, the abbot of Redon was able to have the bishop and his brother bring their own subjects to justice.[55] Here, there is a firm notion of a hierarchy of power and responsibility. Only by the cultivation of such obligations could Nominoe and his successors have turned their claim to rule all of Brittany into some practical reality of power.

Whether these scraps of evidence represent the tip of an iceberg, or the sum total of the instances of loyal followers of the Breton rulers is unknown. The truth probably lies somewhere in between. Although we know that the abbot of Redon expected his tenants to offer him 'fidelity', and that other local landowners might have men under their own power, it does not seem that retinues of faithful subjects were either universal or taken for granted.[56] It would perhaps be surprising if they were. One of the most striking aspects of social organisations in south-eastern Brittany is precisely the *lack* of evidence for close connections between the upper echelons, that of the ruler and his retinue, and the village communities around Redon. The *plebes* were little affected by the extension of Carolingian hegemony over Brittany, or by the growing power of the Breton rulers. In terms of local judicial conventions, of mechanisms for transferring property and registering the transactions, of the status and functions of machtierns, nothing much changed significantly in the course of the ninth century, except as a result of the growth of Redon's landed endowments and seigneurial concerns.[57] No adequate hierarchy of authority or lordship was available to enable those who claimed the greatest power in Brittany to penetrate and influence the everyday life of most Breton communities. The emergence of an embryonic princely administration, the growth of the ruler's retinue into a large and impressive gathering, the appointment of a few counts and of various *missi*, the

[55] CR 274.
[56] On the abbot of Redon's demands for 'fidelity' from its men, see Davies, *Small Worlds*, pp. 185–6. For other references to the 'men' of landowners, see CR 86+169+170, 111.   [57] Davies, *Small Worlds*, pp. 210–13.

encouragement of men with a close relationship and active obedience towards the ruler: all were important steps towards the creation of a strong and united principality. There is every sign that Salomon's or Alan's power to command was significantly greater than had been Nominoe's. Yet the impression remains that by the early tenth century, princely power was still precarious, uneven in its impact, spasmodic in its efficiency and uncertain of the loyalty it could command.

THE RESOURCES FOR RULING

In addition to the evidence which Salomon's charter of 869 for Redon provides of the scope and power of his government, it also offers an indication of the wealth at his disposal and of the fiscal rights which he enjoyed. Wealth was as important a constituent of princely power as networks of communication and the prestige of lordship. Land and movables provided the means for displays of power, for gifts to churches, for rewarding followers and fulfilling the Franks' demands for tribute, or for paying off the Vikings. By and large, the charter evidence pertains to the expenditure rather than the accumulation of wealth, and so no clear picture can be established of the means by which the Breton rulers came by either their lands or their income. Enough is known, however, to be able to show that Nominoe's dynasty was by far the richest in south-eastern Brittany, but that he and his successors were nevertheless always seeking to supplement their resources by whatever means possible. It is improbable that they had access to any types of income within Breton-speaking regions that were not also available to the rest of the aristocratic elite. In terms of the resources for ruling, quantity rather than nature set the rulers apart from their Breton followers.

We know most about the rulers' landed possessions, thanks to their patronage of Redon. Amongst the landowners of south-eastern Brittany, Nominoe and his successors were pre-eminent, if not in terms of their total holdings, then certainly in terms of their generosity towards Redon. Although Nominoe's own donations of land were not particularly extensive, being confined to one plot of land within Bains and a rather longer grant of land in Avessac and Brain,[58] the long list of land grants made by his

[58] CR 2, A13.

successors marks his family out as by far the wealthiest to patronise the monastery, far exceeding all other substantial landed proprietors. Erispoe's benefactions to Redon all lay further east than his father's: land at Piriac in the Guérande peninsula, a salt working at Guérande itself and land at Grand-Fougeray.[59] In addition, he possessed a small monastery somewhere in the vicinity of Vannes, which passed to Redon via the priest to whom Erispoe had initially given it.[60] Salomon was especially generous, granting land in Grand-Fougeray, Plélan, Pleucadeuc, Guer, Pancé, and a very large estate at Bourg-des-Comptes.[61] Pascweten had particularly extensive holdings amongst the saltpans of the Guérande and also land in Grand-Fougeray and Péaule.[62] Judging by the massive penalties for infringing some of his grants, they were of huge estates indeed.[63] Alan's one donation to Redon was of land in Grand-Fougeray.[64]

The lands which Nominoe and his family gave to Redon were thus concentrated in the eastern Vannetais, in the rich salt-producing region of the Guérande peninsula and in the north-western corner of the county of Nantes. We may demonstrate that this must have been the area within which their main landed resources were concentrated. All the estates which the rulers gave to Redon lay within the area where the monastery was acquiring lands from other donors. Either Redon chose not to accept donations of distant properties, or the rulers had no resources outside the south-east with which to endow the monks. Remoteness, however, was no hindrance to Redon on other occasions, for the monks accepted a gift of land nearly 100 km away at Cléguérec, and later fought to retain it.[65] This suggests the conclusion that Nominoe's family did not have lands in other parts of Brittany. Hagiographical traditions reinforce the impression that the landed wealth of Nominoe's family was concentrated in the south-east. Other than Redon, the only churches which remembered traditions of Nominoe's generosity were Léhon and the community of St Guenaël on the Ile de

[59] CR 77 (= 100), A34, A43.
[60] CR A40, A45.
[61] CR 30, 49, 52, 78, 237, 241, 257, A48.
[62] CR 22, 23, 26, 35, 72, 85, 260, 262, A30, A39. For the identification of the *plebs Gablah* of CR 260 with Péaule, see Tonnerre, 'Pays de la basse Vilaine', p. 68.
[63] Monetary sanctions were typically twice the value of the land being conveyed; CR35, 260, 262 all stipulate fines of 1,000 *solidi* for infringing the grant.
[64] CR 239.
[65] CR 247.

Groix.[66] None of the saints' lives from Alet, Saint-Pol, Dol, and Landévennec so much as mentions any of the Breton rulers. The disposition of the lands of Nominoe and his family suggests strongly that the family was indeed local to the south-eastern frontier region.

On occasion, princely resources were supplemented by duly acquired lands. Nominoe received land in Campénéac as compensation for the killing of his follower Catworet, and Salomon was made heir to the lands and seigneurial interests of the powerful woman Roiantdreh in Sévignac, Médréac and Plumaugat.[67] On other occasions, lands came their way by more dubious means. Like most early medieval ruling dynasties, generosity towards their own foundation was counterbalanced by expropriation of the lands of other churches and by a readiness to exploit the endowment of their favoured house. One reason why Nominoe had aroused such hostility in Neustria was that he did not spare churches on his raiding expeditions, and in 850 he was also accused by Frankish bishops of seizing ecclesiastical monies for his own use.[68] In 860, Salomon restored to Ansbold, abbot of Prüm, the Lotharingian monastery's lands in the county of Rennes which had fallen into his own hands.[69] In 866, Frankish bishops complained to Pope Nicholas I that the Bretons had taken all the property of the church of Nantes, and Alan I referred explicitly to his predecessors' despoliation of the cathedral when he made a grant to the bishop of Nantes.[70] He also restored to Redon seigneurial rights in *Ardon* which had formed part of Redon's original endowment but which Alan's predecessors had seized.[71] This readiness to prey on church lands hints at a thirst for access to ever greater resources.

Scraps of evidence that suggest an association between church lands and military service may be a further reflection of the rulers' constant and driving need for lands. Two of the three relevant pieces of information relate to Redon. In the first place, in 868,

---

[66] *Miracula Maglorii*, 7, 'Miracles de Saint Magloire et fondation du monastère de Léhon', ed. A. de La Borderie, *Mémoires de la Société Archéologique et Historique des Côtes-du-Nord*, 2nd ser., 4 (1891), 224–411, at pp. 238–43; *Vita Sancti Guenaili*, 3, AASS Nov. I.678.   [67] CR 107, 109.

[68] Lupus, *Correspondance*, II.54–6, no. 81; see also Regino, *Chronicon*, a. 862, p. 80.

[69] Beyer, *Mittelrheinisches Urkundenbuch*, 95, pp. 99–100; Lupus, *Correspondance*, II.166–8, no. 116.   [70] *Chronique de Nantes*, 16, 22, pp. 54, 68–72.

[71] CR 235, and see Davies, *Small Worlds*, p. 192 n. 22 on the uncertainty over the location of *Ardon*.

Salomon's *stabularius*, Winic, held by precarial tenure land which the monastery owned in Plélan.[72] Secondly, in 851, a man called Risweten who had been deprived of his family inheritance by (presumably) his father's grant of land to Redon demanded that Abbot Conwoion either restore his inheritance to him or install him on another estate and provide him with a horse and armour. Risweten was bought off with 20 *solidi* with which to buy himself a war-horse.[73] The expectation that the monastery would supply land, horse, and armour to enable Risweten to perform his military service suggests that Redon may have repaid princely generosity by maintaining cavalry levies. The third piece of evidence is not datable, is highly circumstantial, and pertains not to Redon but to north-eastern Brittany and the monastery of Saint-Magloire. A miracle story in the late ninth- or early tenth-century *Miracula Maglorii* tells us how the owner of the isle of Guernsey died and, in return for burial in the monastery church, left as a bequest his ornately harnessed horse with a golden girth and all its trappings, golden spurs, and a sword, and how the dead man's son seized them back.[74] Here again aristocratic, mounted warriors associated themselves with a church. The Carolingians based much of their power upon the exploitation of church lands; it would not be surprising if Nominoe and his successors made an effort to capitalise on the huge resources of Redon, and to turn ecclesiastical endowments in eastern Brittany to their own benefit.[75] Other Frankish influences certainly filtered through into this area; it also provided the springboard for Breton raids into Neustria and itself endured repeated Viking attacks.

Like their sixth-century predecessors described by Gregory of Tours, and like their contemporary Frankish opponents, the ninth-century Breton rulers thrived on warfare. A natural supplement to their landed wealth were therefore the spoils of war. When the Bretons joined Lambert in attacking Rainald, count of Nantes in 843, they seized huge numbers of prisoners, many of whom were subsequently sold at great profit.[76] Similarly

---

[72] CR 223.   [73] *GSR*, I.7, pp. 127–31.
[74] 'Miracles de Saint Magloire', 6, p. 237. It is not clear from the context whether this story refers to the period before the monks of Saint-Magloire moved from the island of Sark to Léhon on the mainland.
[75] Compare J. L. Nelson, 'The Church's military service in the ninth century: a contemporary comparative view?', *Studies in Church History*, 20 (1983), 15–30 (reprinted in *Politics and Ritual*, pp. 117–32).
[76] *Chronique de Nantes*, 6, p. 14.

in 850, when Lambert and Nominoe ravaged Maine, aristocratic captives were taken back to Brittany (presumably to be ransomed later) whilst the unarmed peasants were released.[77] Particularly profitable for the Bretons was their tremendous victory over Charles the Bald in 851. Together with his brother Tredoc, Risweten responded to Erispoe's summons to arms in the hope of acquiring spoils, armour, and clothing.[78] Had the brothers not been killed, they would have been in luck. After two days of heavy fighting, Charles fled from the battlefield, leaving his royal pavilion, tents, and regalia together with large quantities of military supplies to be plundered by the Bretons, who returned from the campaign laden with Frankish treasures, weapons, and captives.[79] Every bit as much as the Carolingian empire, ninth-century Brittany was an 'economy of plunder'.[80]

Landed wealth and the gains of war were supplemented by dues, renders, payments, and services. However, among the problems on which the voluminous Redon material is least forthcoming are the nature of seigneurial income and the question of whether taxes were paid, and if so, to whom.[81] Possible forms of income to which Nominoe, Erispoe, and Salomon may have been entitled are best assessed against the background of the exactions taken by the landowning elite as a whole. The following paragraphs will show that there is no firm evidence that any of the rulers was in receipt of any income due to him solely in his capacity as the ultimate leader of the Bretons. The rulers were, however, in receipt of the same kinds of payments as other major landlords, secular or ecclesiastical.

One form of payment for which the evidence is quite clear is the rent payable by tenants to landlords. Either in cash or in kind, or a combination of the two, annual payments were made by those who worked land they did not possess to those who did own that land.[82] Several of Pascweten's large estates generated rental income whose precise sums are recorded; the same must also have been true for most of the rulers' other properties.[83]

---

[77] *Chronicon Fontanellense*, a. 850, p. 85.   [78] *GSR*, I.7, pp. 127–31.
[79] Regino, *Chronicon*, a. 860, p. 79, referring to the battle of Jengland in 851.
[80] Compare Reuter, 'Plunder and tribute'. See also R. R. Davies, *Conquest, Coexistence and Change. Wales 1063–1415* (Oxford, 1987), p. 157, on the transition in twelfth-century Wales from an 'economy of plunder' to an 'economy of profiteering'.
[81] Compare Davies, *Small Worlds*, pp. 205–7.
[82] For example, CR 35, 98, 127, 163, 253, 260, 262. Davies, *Small Worlds*, pp. 49–50.
[83] CR 35, 260, 262.

Province and empire

Some landlords were also in a position to exact charges on property which they did not own. Thus when Redon was given the small monastery of *Castel-Uwel* in Avessac, the donor stipulated that the monks continue to pay the annual *census* due to the church of St Samson at Dol.[84] Similarly, although Redon acquired the lands in Plumaugat which had formerly belonged to the priest Ritweten, there were still dues and services there to be rendered to Roiantdreh, and some time after having been given the land, Abbot Conwoion petitioned her to remit all the obligations with which it was encumbered.[85] The origins of the entitlement to dues of this nature cannot be established; perhaps this represents the remnants of some former taxation or tribute-taking system.

Some powerful lords (both men and women) exercised seigneurial rights over entire *plebes*. The full range of these rights is uncertain, and it is open to debate whether the privileges over one *plebs* were the same as over another. Within Bains, however, these privileges included the right to take tolls on the traffic on the river Oust near Redon, access to the lands of Bronwinoc, and some rights over the church of Bains.[86] Such perquisites are most frequently encountered in the context of princely generosity to Redon. In a series of donations commencing immediately after its foundation, Redon gained control over a substantial number of *plebes*, some of which were clustered in the immediate vicinity of the abbey church, others scattered further afield. These grants all read as if land were being transferred, yet in practice they represent the surrender to the abbey of rights of lordship over the *plebes* in question.[87] Although none of the charters specifies the nature of the rights being conveyed, these grants are nevertheless another useful general indicator of the resources at the disposal of

[84] CR 97.   [85] CR 189, 190.
[86] CR 106, 185. *GSR*, 1.7, p. 127 describes Conwoion and the prior of Redon going 'ad ecclesiam suam quae nuncupatur Bain'. I take the possessive pronoun to imply some form of seigneurial right over the church. That rights over churches were seigneurial perquisites is clearer from the charter donating the *plebs* of *Anast* (now Maure) with its church and dependent chapels to the Angevin monastery of Saint-Maur of Glanfeuil. M. Planiol, 'La donation d'Anowareth', *Annales de Bretagne*, 9 (1893–4), 216–37.
[87] That these were grants of rights of lordship and not of land is clear from the fact that buying and selling of land by private individuals continued within *plebes* after they had passed into the control of the church. It is not clear to me exactly what rights of lordship were being conveyed. For one possible interpretation, see Davies, *Small Worlds*, pp. 192–8.

Nominoe's family. With confirmation first from Louis the Pious and then from Charles the Bald, Nominoe and Erispoe between them gave Redon the *plebs* of Bains, in which the monastery was situated, and the adjacent *plebes* of Renac, Brain, and *Ardon*, all lying immediately north of Redon in the fork between the Vilaine and the Oust.[88] Erispoe also added Locmariaquer at the entrance to the Gulf of Morbihan.[89] Salomon gave half of Pléchâtel on the Nantais side of the Vilaine, and Wrhwant its other half.[90] In addition to restoring *Ardon*, Alan I extended the group of *plebes* that formed the compact block next to Redon by granting the abbey Massérac, on the opposite bank of the Vilaine to Brain, and also handed over Marsac and Bouvron, farther to the south-east.[91] The last grant was of half of the *plebs* of Guipry, which Alan had given to his nephew Ewen and Bili, Bishop of Vannes; Bili and Matuedoe together passed it on to Redon in 913.[92] Quite whatever the rights over these *plebes* which the rulers alienated to Redon may have been, it is the scale of their generosity that deserves comment. There are extant only two other charters in which *plebes* were granted out: one, the grant of a single, large *plebs* to the monastery of Saint-Maur at Glanfeuil near Angers, the other the grant to Salomon by Roiantdreh of her rights over the *plebs* of Sévignac.[93] By contrast, Nominoe, Erispoe, and Alan could each spare several *plebes* for Redon. The ruling dynasty was as pre-eminent in this respect as it was in terms of its landed wealth.

In common with other members of the Breton landed elite, Nominoe, Erispoe, Salomon, Pascweten, and Alan owned lands, had access to rental income, and enjoyed seigneurial rights over *plebes*. It is very much less certain that they had any types of income unique to them in their capacity as rulers. Only one

[88] CR A6, A9, A28, A32, A44, *GSR*, i.10–11, pp. 137–43. Redon seems to have acquired Bains piecemeal, and possibly also Renac, but the charter evidence is conflicting as to whether the abbey was in control of both *plebes* in their entirety by the time of Erispoe's accession in 851. I have argued elsewhere ('Culte impérial et politique frontalière') that Louis the Pious' role was limited to confirming Nominoe's grants: the point remains controversial. Davies, *Small Worlds*, pp. 192–3, esp. n. 23. Charles the Bald's diploma is a reaffirmation of the contents of Louis the Pious' diplomas.

[89] CR 70.

[90] CR 243. The statement in this charter that Pléchâtel lay within the county of Rennes is a later addition reflecting eleventh-century boundary changes. Brunterc'h, 'Puissance temporelle', pp. 60–1; Chédeville and Guillotel, *Bretagne*, p. 358.

[91] CR 235, 238, A51 + A52.   [92] CR 276.

[93] Planiol, 'Donation d'Anowareth'; CR 109.

charter relates explicitly to Nominoe's fiscal rights, and it does not make clear whether the unpaid obligations that were owing to him in Guillac were due to him in his capacity as landlord, lord of a *plebs*, or for some other reason.[94] Although there are hagiographical references to pre-Carolingian Breton rulers exempting church lands from taxation, there is almost no evidence whatsoever that anyone levied taxes specifically for the support of any ruler in the ninth century, and the sole reference to a *census regia* may refer to a levy paid to the Carolingian king and not the Breton leader.[95]

In understanding princely entitlements, the most helpful document yet again is Salomon's generous charter of 869 for Redon. In its characteristically Carolingian language, this refers to Salomon's public purse, *nostrum publicum*. This may be another part of the borrowed Carolingian rhetoric, or possibly a reference to Salomon's resources in Frankish Brittany, to be discussed later. The charter's fiscal clauses exempt the abbey from everything due to Salomon and his men by way of *pastus caballorum et canum*, *angaria*, and *omnia debita*. It is worth examining closely to what these terms refer. *Omnia debita* is too unspecific to get us much further; any of the forms of aristocratic income already described, or something else, could be intended. The other two terms reveal that Salomon could claim certain important labour services. *Angaria* were transport services. Exacted by the state under the Roman empire, evidence for their continuation into the early Middle Ages comes from Carolingian polyptychs and capitularies. Saint-Germain-des-Prés, for example, demanded specific and complex cartage obligations from its tenants, which enabled the monks both to bring foodstuffs into the abbey and to engage in long-distance trade. Similarly on the estates of Prüm, *angaria* formed one of the types of transport services which the workers on the monastic estates fulfilled.[96] In Brittany, it is the implication

---

94 CR 108.
95 The exemption of lands from all *census* is described by Wrmonoc in his *Vita Pauli*, 18, 19, pp. 449, 452. CR 136 stipulates that land sold in Guillac on 9 April 831/36/42 was liable to the *census regis*. Given the possible dates for this charter, it is quite probable that the king in question was either Louis the Pious or Charles the Bald.
96 J.-P. Devroey, 'Un monastère dans l'économie d'échanges: les services de transport à l'abbaye Saint-Germain-des-Prés au IXᵉ siècle', *Annales: Economies, Sociétés, Civilisations,* 39 (1984), 570–98; J.-P. Devroey, 'Les services de transport à l'abbaye de Prüm au IXᵉ siècle', *Revue du Nord*, 61 (1979), 543–69. See also capitularies, nos. 93 clause 5, 180 clause 26, 297 clause 14, MGH Capit., I.196, 375, II.437.

136

of Salomon's charter that the monks had hitherto been performing transport services for Salomon. He, however, was not the only person who exacted them; in 869 the thug Pricient who terrorised Redon was accused of usurping monastic land and also subjecting the lands to *opus et angarium et pastum canum et caballorum*.[97] The third and last reference to transport services is from a charter of 892. This implies that, like Prüm and Saint-Germain, Redon might exact *angaria* in its own right, for it is stated that land given to Redon by one of Alan I's followers was not subject to *angaria* unless performed for the monks.[98] The provision of fodder for horses and sometimes also the feeding of dogs, *pastus caballorum et canum* (and sometimes in Old Breton, *loch-caballis*), which Salomon remitted and which Pricient demanded, occurs more frequently than *angaria*.[99] It is almost always mentioned in exemption clauses, as a charge with which a particular piece of land is not burdened. In view of the importance of war-horses in early medieval Brittany, it makes sense to interpret this particular exaction as a reference to some aspect of the maintenance of those mounted troops for which the Bretons were famous.[100] Provisions for feeding dogs are a reminder of the importance of hunting in the early Middle Ages. Further, in a society in which not only rulers but also aristocrats had their own mounted retinues, it would be surprising if all members of the warrior elite were not in a position to extract some similar right of pasturage from lands in their possession or under their lordship.

There is certainly no unequivocal evidence that anyone other than Salomon had a legal entitlement to *angaria* or *pastus caballorum*. However, what we know of other aspects of early medieval Breton society makes it much more likely that other members of the warrior aristocracy did indeed have rights to transportation and pasturage. The difficulty in identifying rights or resources which distinguished the rulers from their followers is one indication of the lack of formal structures of power in early medieval Brittany, and of the lack of a firm differentiation between powerful subjects and their ruler. This also makes it impossible to gauge the fiscal burden borne by village com-

---

[97] CR 242.   [98] CR 272.

[99] CR 50, 52, 78, 126, 241, 242, 263, A29. Occasional Frankish references to the exemption of land from this obligation confirm that it was not unique to Brittany. Formulary of Marculf, II.1, MGH Form. p. 72; MGH Capit. II.331, no. 274 clause 11.

[100] Above, pp. 19–20.

munities. Whether growing princely power was translated into new or heavier tax obligations, whether these were uniformly distributed, and indeed whether *plebes* were affected by the establishment of a strong ruling dynasty are crucial questions which the evidence leaves unanswered.[101]

Within the Breton-speaking regions, Nominoe's family are not known to have enjoyed any of the fiscal prerogatives of rulership commonly reserved for early medieval rulers or their appointed deputies, such as the right to strike coin, to take the profits of justice, or to collect tolls. For the most part, and perhaps even in its entirety, their resources resembled those of the landowners in their own entourage. Land and the rent it generated together with seigneurial rights over *plebes* and over various lands in other people's ownership formed their main identifiable resources. Plunder and expropriated church lands were an important supplement. The obligation to provide mounted fighting-men may have been a significant charge on the lands of major churches, at least in eastern Brittany. The scanty references to labour services are hard to interpret; were we in a position to know more about them, they might prove to be the key to the system which generated the rulers' wealth and military power. Significantly, there is no sign that the nature of these resources changed during the three-quarters of a century between Nominoe's appointment as Louis' *missus* in 831 and Alan I's death in 907. To identify the ways in which the Breton rulers' resources were transformed during these decades, we must look to the Frankish counties which Charles the Bald entrusted to Erispoe and Salomon.

WEALTH AND LORDSHIP IN FRANKISH BRITTANY

Throughout the ninth century, the power of the Breton rulers within Breton-speaking regions grew, both in terms of the vigour of their lordship and of their wealth and financial resources. Yet from 851 onwards, their power was extended into Neustria by Charles the Bald's grants of the counties of Rennes and Nantes and the pays de Retz to Erispoe in 851, of western Anjou and of the Cotentin and Avranchin to Salomon in 863 and 867 respectively. Made in return for Breton fidelity, these concessions

---

[101] Compare Davies, *Small Worlds*, pp. 201–10.

and Salomon.[112] Within the area entrusted to Salomon in 867, were extensive properties in the county of Avranches, some of which he passed on to a Breton, Gurhamius, and also lands at *Canabiacum* in the county of Coutances, which Alan I gave to the cathedral of Nantes.[113]

The extensive resources within Frankish Brittany which Erispoe, Salomon, and Alan had gained increased their wealth and their powers of patronage. Churches and Breton secular lords were among the beneficiaries of this. It is less clear, however, that the number of men loyal to them increased commensurately. Salomon's Frankish subjects were instrumental in the coup of 874 which ended his life. Throughout his reign, Salomon's entourage remained almost exclusively Breton. At most, one or two Franks appeared in his retinue on more than one occasion; even when his court met in Frankish territory, its composition remained overwhelmingly Breton.[114]

Fiscal and administrative powers within a Carolingian county brought no automatic entitlement to the loyalty of its inhabitants. No more than when a Carolingian king granted an *honor* to one of his Frankish followers can the grants to Erispoe and Salomon have interrupted or severed existing ties of lordship and loyalty. Cadilo, for example, owned land near Nantes, and is known to have been a vassal of Robert the Strong in 859.[115] The bishops of the sees within the area under Breton control remained loyal to Charles rather than to Salomon in the conflicts of the 860s, and Charles explicitly reserved control of the bishopric of Coutances for himself.[116] The Bretons had to win the fidelity of their Frankish subjects: when and by what means Salomon's successors achieved this is a crucial question on which the evidence is unfortunately virtually non-existent.

Such support as Erispoe, Salomon, and Alan did attract within their Frankish lands were strands in a complex web of lordship and fidelity, at whose centre was ultimately the king.

[112] CR A34, 21; Beyer, *Mittelrheinisches Urkundenbuch*, 95, pp. 99–100.
[113] *Translatio Launomari*, p. 246; *Chronique de Nantes*, 22, pp. 68–72. *Canabiacum* is tentatively identified as Cavigny by Chédeville and Guillotel, *Bretagne*, p. 366.
[114] Besides a handful of Frankish names which only appear once each, such as Gosbert (CR 30) or Frutgaud and Matfred (Beyer, *Mittelrheinisches Urkundenbuch*, 95, pp. 99–100), three Frankish names recur in Salomon's charters, Ratfred, Bernahart, and Bertwalt. Names, however, are no reliable indication of men whose origins lay in the Frankish lands, for Ratfred was machtiern of Sixt and brother of Ratuili (CR 221, A17). There was also a *Bertwalt filius Bili* who owned land in Sérent (CR 263).
[115] Above, p. 55.   [116] Below, pp. 158–9.

Furthermore, by handing over these lands to be administered by the Bretons, Charles the Bald was not thereby relinquishing his claim to authority there. Erispoe held Nantes, Rennes, and the pays de Retz as a benefice, in return for his fidelity.[117] Salomon affirmed his fidelity in 863 and 867. Charles' continued lordship over Nantes is quite clear in the joint grant he and Erispoe made to the cathedral in 856.[118] But it is above all from a consideration of numismatic evidence that the subtle political balance between Carolingian lordship and practical Breton control is most evident. Coin evidence stresses the full economic implications of the shifting patterns of hegemony and lordship.

One of the most sensitive indicators of the strength of royal power in the early Middle Ages is the degree to which a tight and effective control was kept over the minting of coin. Metrological analysis of surviving coins may offer insight into fiscal policy and its implementation. It can show how rigorously legislation against counterfeiting was enforced, and the extent of centrally co-ordinated control over regional mints. Like his father and grandfather, Charles the Bald operated a vigorous and stringently controlled monetary regime. His issues of coin fall into two main groups, of which the first type was minted in a limited number of places between 840 and 864. A major reform of the coinage in 864 introduced a distinctive new coin type, which was struck in many more places than the first had been. The new coin was characterised by the legend GRATIA D-I REX surrounding the royal monogram on the obverse with the mint name on the reverse.[119] This latter coin type subsequently became immobilised, and continued to be used by Charles the Fat and Charles the Simple, making it sometimes difficult to ascertain to which Charles a coin pertains. Charles the Bald's first coinage was not issued from the mints at either Rennes or Nantes, whilst his second was. GDR coins from both cities were included in hoards deposited before or immediately after Charles the Bald's death in 877, and of their attribution to him there is no doubt.[120] Therefore, despite Salomon's control over Nantes and Rennes, Charles the Bald retained sufficient authority there to implement a new coinage in his own name in 864 or shortly thereafter.

[117] *Actes de Charles le Chauve*, ed. Tessier, 1.482, no. 181.
[118] *Actes de Charles le Chauve*, ed. Tessier, 1.482, no. 181.
[119] Metcalf, 'Sketch of the currency'.
[120] Van Rey, 'Münzprägung Karls des Kahlen', pp. 168–9.

Many coins from Rennes bearing Carolingian monograms and post-dating Charles the Bald's death are extant.[121] Not until the very end of the tenth century, however, did a Breton ruler, Conan I (d. 992), issue coins bearing his own name.[122] But long before then, royal control over Neustrian mints had lapsed, and instead in several places counts and bishops had begun to strike coin in their own name.[123] At what points the mints at Nantes and Rennes passed into effective Breton control is far from clear, but this must have happened long before the time of Conan I. In common with other Neustrian mints in the late ninth and early tenth centuries, the mint at Rennes struck coins at gradually falling weights after the death of Charles the Bald, and at Rennes, as at Angers, Le Mans, and Tours, this may be one token of waning royal authority.[124] Further analysis of the output of the mint at Rennes may help to clarify the true nature of the Bretons' lordship over the Carolingian marcher region and to pinpoint the process whereby this important regalian prerogative was acquired by the Bretons for themselves. Though as yet poorly understood, the translation of Carolingian hegemony into hard cash and the resources for ruling was central to the political transformation which Brittany underwent in the late ninth and tenth centuries.

Access to, and control of, trading centres and monetised economies was an important step in the increase and consolidation of the power of emergent kingdoms on the Slav and Scandinavian peripheries of early medieval Europe. For the Breton rulers, their Frankish lands, especially Nantes and Rennes, gave them access to financial resources of a nature and scale quite different from whatever they enjoyed west of the Vilaine. The transfer to them of the resources of the Carolingian king gave them fiscal prerogatives and sources of wealth unmatched by those of their subjects. In the event, most of what Charles the Bald had granted out on a temporary basis passed permanently into Breton

---

[121] The history of the mint at Rennes is complicated by the existence of large numbers of apparently forged coins found in two hoards in Burgundy, at Chalon-sur-Saône and Bourgneuf-Val-d'Or. It has recently been suggested by Metcalf and Northover (as n. 124) that they were forged in Burgundy.

[122] A. Bigot, *Essai sur les Monnaies du Royaume et Duché de Bretagne* (Paris, 1857), pp. 35–6.

[123] F. Dumas-Dubourg, *Le Trésor de Fécamp et le Monnayage en France Occidentale pendant le second moitié du Xe siècle* (Paris, 1971).

[124] Lafaurie, 'Deux trésors monétaires carolingiens'; D. M. Metcalf and J. P. Northover, 'Carolingian and Viking coins from the Cuerdale hoard: an interpretation and comparison of their metal contents', *The Numismatic Chronicle*, 148 (1988), 97–116.

hands.[125] Despite the lack of a strong following among his Frankish subjects, Salomon evidently built up his power sufficiently that Breton control over the Frankish benefices was not seriously jeopardised by the turmoil in Brittany after 874.

By the end of Charles the Bald's reign, Brittany was a large and influential Neustrian principality, firmly under Carolingian hegemony, but in practice free from day-to-day administrative control by the West Frankish king. What was the nature of this principality? Most fundamentally, it did not correspond to any ancient political or ethnic division whose identity was rooted in a pre-Carolingian past, such as was Bavaria's. Like Flanders, Normandy or Lotharingia, it was essentially a Carolingian creation, and is best assessed as such. Unlike some early medieval principalities whose boundaries tended to fluctuate easily, it was a region with an unusually clear territorial coherence, for on three sides, its frontier was the sea. In contrast with other marcher regions of the Carolingian empire, it was not a protective buffer against ever more barbarous peoples beyond. On its landward side, clear administrative boundaries, analogous to those which marked out one Carolingian county from another throughout the empire, constituted a firm division of political responsibility, though one which was often breached by Breton raiders. Nevertheless, Brittany was not an area of jurisdiction neatly demarcated from the West Frankish kingdom. Whether our standpoint is the Vilaine, the frontier until 851, or the Mayenne, the boundary-line from 851 until extended to the Sarthe in 863, the frontier was criss-crossed by a web of economic interests, property ties, judicial privileges, and obligations of lordship. For example, from shortly after its foundation, Redon was accumulating lands in the counties of Rennes and Nantes, and had substantial endowments there before 851. From 850 onwards, all its lands formed a discrete jurisdictional entity as a result of Charles the Bald's grant of immunity and protection. Also, the abbey of Prüm maintained its distant possessions in the county of Rennes: they too formed an immunity and were detached from normal local administrative constraints. Bonds of obligation and loyalty were similarly interwoven. Salomon and Charles both had interests in Rennes, Nantes, and the Cotentin peninsula. Their

---

[125] See below, pp. 195–6.

claims for allegiance conflicted or complemented each other as the quicksands of West Frankish political manoeuvring shifted. Furthermore, Salomon's power over Breton-speaking communities must have far outweighed Charles the Bald's very attenuated hegemony, for although Charles' overlordship touched and constrained Salomon himself, it did not extend to intervention in local Breton village affairs, unlike Louis the Pious' efforts at control through his counts.

Militarily, Salomon's Brittany was strong; politically it was strong enough to survive the turbulence which followed his death. Nevertheless, it was not a particularly cohesive polity. It had no ethnic identity based upon perceived common origin or culture, and language divided Salomon's subjects in a way whose effects cannot be gauged. Princely power ran up against regional loyalties and local self-sufficiency. The composition of Salomon's retinue, and in particular the absence of a Frankish component to it, suggests that no notion that all his subjects together formed a political 'nation' had yet emerged.

The coherence of this principality was essentially personal and dynastic. Nominoe, Erispoe, Salomon, and Alan I were as strong as their power to exact loyalty and extract revenue. Some areas of Brittany, notably the south-eastern region around Redon where the rulers' resources appear to have been concentrated, must have been much more intensively governed than others, such as the far north-west. Even within the south-east, the area which is open to investigation, princely power was not uniformly effective. Despite Brittany's notional territorial limits, the personal lordship and private wealth of its ruling family provided the province with its identity and ruling authority. Political coherence crystallised around this family's leadership.

This is doubly true. It was not simply that the acceptance of the lordship of Nominoe and his descendants by their Breton subjects fostered political development. Rather, the fact that this process was *simultaneously* accompanied by the recognition and acceptance of Nominoe, Erispoe, and Salomon by their Carolingian overlords provides the key to the development of this principality. Nominoe, Erispoe, and Salomon were at all times under the lordship of the Carolingian dynasty, rebellions against Charles the Bald notwithstanding. The regalia and benefices granted by the West Frankish king provided the resources and the status which differentiated Erispoe and Salomon from their subjects much more sharply than Nominoe had ever been. The more regal their position, the more they partook of the symbolism, rituals, and power politics of the Carolingian world. The emergence of the Breton principality cannot be divorced from its Carolingian context.

Chapter 6

CHURCHES AND LEARNING IN CAROLINGIAN BRITTANY

In sending Hatto, archbishop of Mainz, his collection of canons, Regino of Prüm remarked: 'Just as the various nations of peoples are distinguished from each other by race, customs, language and laws, so the holy universal church throughout the world although joined together in unity of faith nevertheless differs from place to place in ecclesiastical customs. Some customs in ecclesiastical practices are found in the kingdoms of the Gauls and of Germany, others are found in the eastern kingdoms and in overseas places.'[1] In ecclesiastical and cultural life as in political society, the bedrock of the Carolingian empire was regional identity and local custom. Historians have tended to be mesmerised by the brilliance of Carolingian court culture and by its rhetoric of unity, but wherever scholars have searched with an eye for nuanced difference, they have found evidence that substantiates Regino's comments. The early medieval church was a medley of characteristically regional habits, in bible texts, canon law, and liturgy as in manuscript illumination and script or saints' cults.[2] However, just as at the apogee of Carolingian power the royal court exercised a strong centripetal pull against the grain of local political life, so too the religious and cultural life of Carolingian provinces was profoundly affected by central influences, demands, and expectations.

These influences were of two very different types. In the first place, building on the efforts of Pippin III and Carloman,

---

[1] Regino, *Epistula ad Hathonem archiepiscopum missa*, see *Chronicon*, ed. Kurze, p. xx.

[2] Fundamental here is Kottje, 'Einheit und Vielfalt'. On the bible, see B. Fischer, 'Bibeltext und Bibelreform unter Karl dem Grossen', in *Karl der Grosse*, II.156–216. On script and manuscript culture, see B. Bischoff, *Latin Palaeography: Antiquity and the Middle Ages*, trans. D. Ganz and D. Ó Cróinín (Cambridge, 1990), pp. 114–18, and R. McKitterick, 'Carolingian book production: some problems', *The Library*, 6th ser., 12 (1990), 1–33. On saints' cults, see T. Head, *Hagiography and the Cult of Saints: The Diocese of Orléans, 800–1200* (Cambridge, 1990), pp. 1–57.

Charlemagne enunciated a programme of reform of all aspects of ecclesiastical life which set common standards for all his realms. In these reforms, deference to Rome for liturgical, canonical, and spiritual authority went hand in hand with the emergence of an articulate, hierarchically structured Frankish episcopate which was a willing partner in the royal efforts to improve the quality of religious life throughout Carolingian society. From the jurisdiction of archbishops to the sexual mores of the laity, nothing was left unaffected.[3] Charlemagne had read 'how the holy Josiah by visiting, correcting and admonishing, strove to recall the kingdom given to him by God to the worship of the true God' and set out to follow this example.[4] His vision was of a realm unified as much spiritually as politically.

The impact of central directives doubtless depended upon the reforming zeal of individual bishops and upon the degree of intractability of the problems each faced locally.[5] Whatever efforts were taken to modify ecclesiastical and religious practices, the initiatives inevitably interacted with long-established local customs and conventions. Although Carolingian bishops subscribed to a common ideal, in practice they presided over a network of regionally distinctive churches, in each of which pre-existing laws, religious practices, and literary traditions blended in different ways with centrally generated influences. Nowhere did ecclesiastical culture fully conform to the normative standards proclaimed by royal legislation.

Although Charlemagne's programme arguably culminated in the comprehensive reform legislation of the early years of Louis the Pious' reign, Louis' reign also inaugurated the breakdown of the unanimity of purpose which had bound Charlemagne's bishops together. Under the strain of the political tensions of his reign, and in particular of the disputes over the shape which the

---

[3] On the episcopal hierarchy, see E. Lesne, *La Hiérarchie Episcopale. Provinces, Metropolitains, Primats en Gaule et Germanie depuis la Réforme de Saint Boniface jusqu'à la Mort d'Hincmar*, Mémoires et Travaux des Facultés Catholiques de Lille 1 (Lille, 1905). Carolingian reform legislation is effectively and succinctly surveyed by Wallace-Hadrill, *Frankish Church*, pp. 258–78. As to its implementation, see R. McKitterick, *The Frankish Churches and the Carolingian Reforms, 789–895* (London, 1977).　　　[4] *Admonitio Generalis* of 789, MGH Capit. 1.54, no. 22.

[5] McKitterick, *Frankish Church*, pp. 45–79. Two contrasting case studies are Le Maître, 'L'oeuvre d'Aldric du Mans', and A. Dierkens, 'La christianisation des campagnes de l'empire de Louis le Pieux: l'exemple du diocèse de Liège sous l'épiscopat de Walcaud (c.809–c.831)', in *Charlemagne's Heir*, pp. 309–29.

succession to the emperor should take, the *navis ecclesiae* struck the shoals of political conflict.[6] The Franks had never subscribed to a single theory of empire: the revolts of the later years of Louis' reign and the division of the empire after his death encouraged divergent views on the correct relation of secular to ecclesiastical power. Political conflict left the church increasingly prey to the needs and ambitions of secular magnates and of kings. By the middle of the ninth century, reform ideals could only be forwarded against the backdrop of a tangle of competing interests as kings, popes, archbishops, and bishops all struggled to define and protect their own niche in the hierarchy.[7] It is little surprise that the conflicts of the middle and later years of the ninth century provided opportunities for the fostering of regional identities (whether of subkingdom, province, locality, or diocese), and for efforts to redefine the relationship of ecclesiastical centre and locality.

Meanwhile, the second, very different centralising force wrought other changes in the Carolingian church. A series of outstandingly able and legally minded popes made a great effort to assert juridical influence over secular and ecclesiastical officeholders alike. Building upon the work of Leo IV (847–55), popes Nicholas I (858–67), Hadrian II (867–72), and John VIII (872–82) vigorously pressed the rights of the see of St Peter to arbitrate in matters of canon law.[8] These men took particular interest in settling issues at dispute within the Carolingian episcopate itself, in protecting the rights of the church from lay encroachment, and in trying to regulate the conduct of kings wherever it threatened the peace and good order of the Christian community.[9]

---

[6] The metaphor is that of the preamble to the canons of the council of Coulaines of 843. MGH Conc. III.14, no. 3.

[7] There is no satisfactory account of the ninth-century church which gives adequate analysis of the many differing interest-groups and perspectives within it. A general impression can, however, be gleaned from the suggestive remarks of I. S. Robinson, 'Church and papacy', in *Cambridge History of Medieval Political Thought*, ed. Burns, pp. 252–305, and from E. Amann, *L'Epoque Carolingienne*, Histoire de l'Eglise depuis les Origines jusqu'à Nos Jours, gen. eds. A. Fliche and V. Martin, 6 (Paris, 1947); Y. M.-J. Congar, *L'Ecclésiologie du Haut Moyen Age* (Paris, 1968), pp. 131–246; J. Devisse, *Hincmar, Archevêque de Reims 845–882*, 3 vols. (Geneva, 1975–6); Kaiser, *Bischofsherrschaft*.

[8] Amann, *Epoque Carolingienne*, pp. 367–439; W. Ullmann, *The Growth of Papal Government in the Middle Ages* (3rd edn, London, 1970), pp. 190–228.

[9] See especially J. Fried, 'Laienadel und Papst in der Frühzeit der französischen und deutschen Geschichte', in *Aspekte der Nationenbildung im Mittelalter. Ergebnisse der*

In effect, by the reign of Charles the Bald, the Frankish church was a quicksand of disputed jurisdictions as regional interests tugged against the pull of Rome and as outspoken bishops ran up against the desire of kings and secular magnates to control the church and its resources. *Causes célèbres* such as the divorce of Lothar II or the dispute between Hincmar of Reims and his nephew and namesake of Laon shared with more humdrum cases a common background in disagreements about the correct relation of secular to ecclesiastical lordship, and in fluid jurisdictional patterns within the ecclesiastical hierarchy itself. It is no coincidence that this was the environment in which the hugely influential series of pseudo-Isidorian False Decretals was produced to forward episcopal rights in the face of royal and metropolitan pressure.[10] By contrast, wherever issues of power, autonomy, or jurisdiction were not at stake, kings and bishops worked hard together to revitalise the reform programme and to sustain cultural and intellectual life. Despite being wracked with conflicts, the Carolingian church still took its identity from a common moral and intellectual purpose that transcended regional manifestations and preoccupations.

Perhaps no other province of the Carolingian empire reveals the clash of centralising influence with local culture and regional ecclesiastical identity as clearly as Brittany. From a Frankish and papal perspective, the church in Brittany presented obvious problems. Breton ecclesiastical practices did not match up to the high standards of Carolingian reformers, and Breton bishops were reluctant to accede to subordination within a juridically defined hierarchy. From a Breton perspective, Carolingian efforts to use the church as an instrument of political control were resented and rejected. The result was bitter conflict in the reign of Charles the Bald over the correct place of Brittany within the ordering of the Catholic church. This struggle between the Bretons on the one hand and the Frankish church and the papacy on the other was a microcosm of the juridical uncertainties and conflicts which characterised the Carolingian church as a whole.

On the eve of the Carolingian conquest, Breton ecclesiastical

Marburger Rundgespräche 1972–75, ed. H. Beumann and W. Schröder (Sigmaringen, 1978), pp. 367–406.
[10] Ullmann, *Growth of Papal Government*, pp. 178–89; H. Fuhrmann, *Einfluss und Verbreitung der pseudoisidorischen Fälschungen*, 3 vols., MGH Schriften 24 (Stuttgart, 1972–4).

culture was notably unlike that of adjacent Neustria. A plethora of extremely local saints' cults and a literate culture indebted to Britain and Ireland were among its more distinctive features. As the ninth century wore on, however, contacts between Breton and Frankish churches gradually increased, and the extension of Breton rule over western Neustria must have facilitated interchanges still further. In this environment, the impact of Carolingian reform legislation and of the cultural changes promoted by the Carolingian renaissance began to be felt. Although Frankish norms of ecclesiastical organisation seem to have had minimal impact on Breton churches at very local level, the higher echelons of the church were open to Carolingian cultural influence and to papal guidance in a wide range of pastoral matters and points of canon law. In effect, many of the ambivalences and tensions of relationships between Bretons and Franks in the secular sphere were also played out within the church: disputes about symbols of authority and the corresponding powers of lordship were combined with considerable Frankish influence among the Breton elite whilst leaving life at village level effectively untouched by the changes.

BRETON CHURCHES UNDER FRANKISH LORDSHIP

All the bishoprics of the Armorican peninsula fell within the ecclesiastical province whose metropolitan see was Tours. Although Breton settlement in the western and central regions of the peninsula had disrupted the diocesan structure of the late Roman province, the sixth-century bishops of Tours had nevertheless made some efforts to assert their jurisdiction over the newcomers. In practice, however, their authority seems to have gone unheeded, and churches in Brittany developed in virtual isolation from their Romano-Frankish neighbours.[11]

Cut off as they were from the mainstream of Merovingian ecclesiastical life, Breton churches may well have evolved their own conventions. Yet owing to the almost complete lack of contemporary evidence, it is impossible to make any realistic comment on Breton religious organisation on the eve of the Carolingian conquest of the peninsula. Two points in particular

[11] See above, pp. 11–12, 15–16.

remain open to debate. The first questions whether bishoprics and lesser ecclesiastical subdivisions corresponded to secular divisions of power, and whether they had firm territorial boundaries. The second asks whether there was any substantive difference between communities of monks and communities of secular clergy.[12]

Both these issues indirectly concern the extent to which the church was able to stand apart from secular power structures. Everywhere it was characteristic of the earlier Middle Ages that, except at periods of vigorous reforming zeal, church offices and property were readily assimilated more or less completely into secular society as desirable sources of prestige and power. Equally frequently, monastic communities initially marked out by ascetic rigour slid gradually into a lifestyle hardly distinguishable from that of the married, propertied secular clergy. Western Neustria in the early eighth century was not exempt from this trend,[13] and there is certainly no reason to think that the areas of Breton settlement were any different. Much of the thrust of the Carolingian reform movement, especially in its early phases, was precisely to try to tease apart sacred and secular and to distinguish clergy from laity.

Whilst the first stirrings of the reformers' drive to disentangle bishoprics from secular subordination and to reorganise the episcopal hierarchy reached the Loire valley in the reign of Pippin III, not until the reign of Louis the Pious did the bishop of Le Mans recover his influence and reform his diocesan clergy.[14] Carolingian reform probably did not reach the dioceses of Rennes and Nantes until an equally late date. As for the Breton dioceses further to the west, Frankish reaction to whatever sort of ecclesiastical organisation existed is unknown. Imperial fostering of reform is, however, implied by the mission to Brittany *in Dei servitio et nostro* of Ingilfred, abbot of the monastery of St John the

---

[12] Traditional wisdom on these points (summed by up Chédeville and Guillotel, *Bretagne*, pp. 113–51) is predicated upon a sharp distinction between secular and monastic clergy in Brittany throughout the early Middle Ages. This tacit assumption is increasingly being questioned to notable effect elsewhere: see J. Semmler, 'Mönche und Kanoniker im Frankreiche Pippins III. und Karls der Grossen', in *Untersuchungen zu Kloster und Stift*, Veröffentlichungen des Max-Planck-Instituts für Geschichte 68 (Göttingen, 1980), pp. 78–111; also many of the essays in *Pastoral Care before the Parish*, ed. J. Blair and R. Sharpe (Leicester, forthcoming). In Brittany, sources only permit clear differentiation between communities of secular clergy and of monks from the middle of the ninth century.   [13] Above, pp. 46–7.

[14] Ewig, 'Saint Chrodegang', p. 44; Le Maître, 'L'oeuvre d'Aldric du Mans'.

Baptist in Angers, and perhaps also by the presence at the imperial court of two Breton bishops in 834.[15] At the very least, reform certainly did mean being brought back under the jurisdiction of Tours.[16] Most plausibly, this occurred early in Louis the Pious' reign, at about the same time as the introduction into Brittany of Louis' monastic reforms.[17]

The essence of a metropolitan's authority lay in the right to consecrate the suffragans within his archdiocese. In addition to being a sanctification to office, consecration was also an enactment of hierarchy, and the submission of bishop to metropolitan was formalised in the profession of faith and obedience which the new bishop made to his superior at his consecration.[18] The Bretons were to deny this hierarchy of profession and consecration in Charles the Bald's reign. From a Carolingian and a papal point of view, however, the right ordering of political life and of the church were inseparably associated. Bishops and counts linked court to locality through their joint work as *missi*. Also, an appropriate ecclesiastical hierarchy was one which matched the obligations of secular lordship. In 798, Leo III granted the Bavarians their own archbishopric on the grounds that the province was now fully brought to order under Charlemagne's lordship.[19] At the height of the conflict between Salomon and the Frankish church in Charles the Bald's reign, Nicholas I made a

[15] *Formulae Imperiales e Curia Ludovici Pii*, 6, MGH Form. p. 291. The date of Ingilfred's journey to Brittany is not known. The visit of Felix of Quimper and Ermor of Alet to Louis' court at Thionville is recorded in *GSR*, I.10, p. 137.

[16] That the authority of Tours over the Breton bishops was effective for a time is clearly implied by the complaint made by the Frankish bishops in 866 that for about twenty years the Breton bishops had not taken part in synods of the diocese of Tours nor gone to Tours for consecration. *Chronique de Nantes*, 16, pp. 52–3.

[17] Above, pp. 71–2.

[18] In contrast to Anglo-Saxon England, no text of a Frankish episcopal profession survives and it has been suggested that the profession was generally given orally: *Canterbury Professions*, ed. M. Richter, Canterbury and York Society 67 (Torquay, 1973), p. xi. Hincmar does, however, refer to the written draft of a profession: *De Praedestinatione dissertatio posterior*, 21, PL cxxv.182. Within the province of Tours, mention is made of profession to the archbishop in the formal notification of the consecration of Electramn of Rennes in 866 issued by his consecrating bishops. H. Quentin, 'Lettre de Nicholas I pour le concile de Soissons et formules ecclésiastiques de la province de Tours dans un manuscrit de Nicholas Le Fèvre', *Le Moyen Age*, 17 (1904), 97–114.

[19] Leo III, ep. 3, MGH Epp. v.58–9: 'Quoniam provincia ipsa mirifice a filio nostro domno Carolo excellentissimo rege Francorum et Langobardorum atque patricio Romanorum penitus ex omni parte, sicut decuit, *ordinata est*, idcirco convenit nos ipso nempe ecclesiastico moderamine *in sacro ordine* fideliter atque spiritualiter secundum canonicam censuram ipsam *ordinare* Baiowariorum provinciam.' Italics mine.

similar point to the Bretons, that acknowledgement of the rightful ecclesiastical hierarchy would bring with it peace, concord, and *omnis legitimus ordo*, whilst failure to obey would result in scandal, discord, and shame.[20] That part of the Carolingian effort to discipline Breton churches which has left most trace is the drive for 'order', in other words, for submission to the authority and spiritual lordship of the Frankish hierarchy and the papacy.

'ORDER' IN THE EPISCOPAL HIERARCHY

Breton episcopal politics in the middle of the ninth century constitute a dramatic saga of the rejection of both metropolitan and papal authority. Neither side won in this clash of interest between regional political aspirations and a hierarchy determined to see due canonical process respected. The issues and passions first raised by Nominoe and Salomon nevertheless had a long life, for the question as to whether Breton bishops were subject to Tours was not finally resolved until 1199.[21]

The trouble started when Nominoe deposed all five Breton bishops at a 'synod' at *Coitlouh* in 849. Precisely how this was achieved is far from certain, for there are irreconcilable contradictions among the surviving accounts, none of which is precisely datable and most of which are highly tendentious. In particular, the sequence of events leading up to the expulsions is unclear, as is the nature of the charges preferred against the bishops.[22] Allegations of simony certainly reached Leo IV, who wrote both to the Breton bishops and to Nominoe informing them that cases could only be brought in front of a panel of twelve bishops, with the testimony of seventy-two sworn

---

[20] Nicholas I, ep. 107, MGH Epp. vi.622.
[21] B.-A. Pocquet du Haut-Jussé, *Les Papes et les Ducs de Bretagne*, 2 vols., Bibliothèque de l'Ecole Française d'Athènes et de Rome 133 (Paris, 1928).
[22] In addition to the papal correspondence on which my analysis is based, there are also narrative accounts of dubious reliability in the *Gesta Sanctorum Rotonensium*, in the Chronicle of Nantes, and in an eleventh-century *Indiculus de episcoporum Britonum depositione*. W. Hartmann has recently assembled a convenient dossier of all the relevant texts in MGH Conc. iii.185–93. His editorial comments, together with the remarks of Chédeville and Guillotel, *Bretagne*, pp. 266–72, supersede all older accounts. There is no need to rehearse here all the possible ways to reconstruct what happened; see the bibliography in Chédeville and Guillotel, *Bretagne*, p. 295. However, neither of these latest analyses is uncontroversial or definitive, and it should be noted that Hartmann errs in concluding that only four bishops were deposed.

witnesses.[23] Fifteen to twenty years later, Nicholas I reiterated the comments of an earlier letter of Benedict III (now lost), to the effect that he believed that under pressure from Nominoe and other laymen, the Breton bishops had been forced to admit to crimes which they had not definitely committed, and that in papal eyes, judgement against them on such evidence was no true judgement.[24] The angry letter which a West Frankish synod (meeting at Angers or Tours) sent to Nominoe in the summer of 850, alleged that Nominoe had refused to accept delivery of a papal letter and had rejected it sight unseen, and took note that he had replaced those whom he had uncanonically deposed with his own hirelings.[25] These *mercennarii* were not recognised by either the pope or the Frankish church, which excommunicated them.[26] Nominoe responded to this letter by sacking the cities of Rennes and Nantes and then expelling the Frankish bishop of Nantes whom he again replaced with his own nominee.[27]

Ten years later, when Salomon was in revolt against Charles the Bald, the Frankish bishops in synod at Savonnières in 859 wrote to four Breton bishops whom they did recognise as legitimate, urging them not to have anything to do with the excommunicated men and requesting them to urge Salomon to renew his fidelity to the West Frankish king.[28] Comparison of the names of the addressees of this letter with bishops mentioned in the dating clauses of Breton charters enables the deposed bishops and their replacements to be identified. In several cases, the fates of the displaced men are also known. Susannus, bishop of Vannes since 838, went into exile among the Franks and was still alive in 866.[29] His replacement at Vannes was Courantgen.[30] Salocon of

[23] Leo IV, ep. 16, MGH Epp. v.593–6 (and reprinted MGH Conc. iii.187–9). This letter survives without its dating clause and cannot be assigned to a precise point in the dispute.

[24] Nicholas I, ep. 107, MGH Epp. vi.619–22. This letter is also undated, but must have been written in either 863 or 866. [25] MGH Conc. iii.202–7.

[26] Nicholas I, ep. 107, MGH Epp. vi.622. The excommunication is mentioned by the Frankish bishops meeting at Savonnières in 859 in a letter to those Bretons with whom they were in communion. MGH Conc. iii.480–1.

[27] Above, p. 98; Leo IV, ep. 20, MGH Epp. v.598.

[28] Council of Savonnières, letter to the Breton bishops: MGH Conc. iii.480–1. F. Lot pointed out that the addressees must have been recognised as legitimate by the Frankish church (though he misidentified their sees). 'Le schisme breton du IXᵉ siècle', in his *Mélanges d'Histoire Bretonne* (Paris, 1907), pp. 58–96, at pp. 89–90.

[29] Letter of the Council of Soissons to Nicholas I, *Chronique de Nantes*, 16, pp. 54–5. Accusations that the Breton bishops were guilty of simony were made at Redon, where Susannus was held to be the worst perpetrator. *GSR*, ii.10, p. 175.

[30] He is noted frequently in Redon charters from 14 May 850 to 7 August 868.

Dol also went into exile among the Franks and was also living in 866.[31] He entered the monastery of Flavigny and on occasion acted as *coepiscopus* to Jonas of Autun.[32] Quite what had happened after his deposition is unclear: the name of his immediate replacement is not recorded, but his successor but one, Festinian, was recognised as legitimate by the Frankish church whilst Salocon was still alive.[33] At Quimper, Felix was replaced by Anaweten, and at Saint-Pol, Garnobrius made way for Clutwoion.[34] Both these two deposed bishops remained in Brittany, and it is most likely that it was they who were the Breton bishops whom Salomon is known to have summarily reinstated in 865–6.[35] At Alet, Mahen seems to have replaced Rethwalatr, but nothing further is known of either man.[36] At Nantes, Actard's place was usurped by Gislard, who appears to have occupied the see for about a year before being exiled to the monastery of Saint-Martin at Tours on the orders of Charles the Bald.[37] Restored to Nantes, Actard was one of the most staunch upholders of ecclesiastical authority in the face of its continuing erosion by the Bretons.

That Nominoe was able to summon all five Breton bishops together and then dismiss them is testimony to his control over the church throughout the Breton lands. Extravagant only in scale, his action is readily comprehensible as a direct attempt to further that control. Bishoprics were often pawns in secular politics. In the seventh century, Frankish magnates were occasionally prepared to kill in order to seize control of episcopal sees, and even in the relatively cleansed atmosphere of the ninth-

---

[31] *Chronique de Nantes*, 16, p. 54.
[32] Egil of Sens, *Eulogium Historicum*, AASS OSB iv.ii, 237–41; Hugh of Flavigny, *Chronicon*, a. 865 misdates Salocon's death (MGH SS viii.355). Salocon was regarded as an outstandingly holy man at Flavigny.
[33] Cf. F. Lot, 'Festien, "archévêque" de Dol', in his *Mélanges*, pp. 14–32.
[34] Felix: council of Savonnières, MGH Conc. iii.480 (where his see is misidentified); *GSR* ii.10, p. 179. Anaweten: CR 30, A31. Garnobrius: also council of Savonnières, on which see Chédeville and Guillotel, *Bretagne*, p. 268. Clutwoion: CR A31; Bili, *Vie de Saint-Malo*, ii.18, p. 254.
[35] As reported to Nicholas I by the council of Soissons. *Chronique de Nantes*, 16, p. 55.
[36] See H. Guillotel, 'Les évêques d'Alet du IXe au milieu du XIIe siècle', *Annales de la Société d'Histoire et d'Archéologie de l'Arrondissement de Saint-Malo* (1979), 251–66, at pp. 255–7.
[37] Hincmar, ep. 31 *Ad quemdam episcopum*, PL cxxvi.210–30, at col. 218. The suggestion of Duchesne (*Fastes Episcopaux*, ii.369) that Actard was restored when Charles the Bald made peace with Erispoe in 851 is likely to be correct. For a different reconstruction of Gislard's career, see Kaiser, *Bischofsherrschaft*, pp. 121, 130.

century Carolingian church, bishops might still find themselves summarily displaced.[38] The events of the synod of *Coitlouh* are a sign that by the middle of the ninth century the Breton episcopate was sufficiently rich and influential to be worth dominating. Furthermore, the remonstrations of the West Frankish bishops with Nominoe in 850 evidently fell on deaf ears, and coming as the episcopal crisis did at the height of his career of political recalcitrance towards Charles the Bald, Nominoe's behaviour was an additional statement of his determination to distance himself from the immediate overlordship of the West Frankish king.

That Nominoe's uncanonical dismissal of five bishops in 849 created such a furore is no surprise. The dispute concerned obedience to authority, and to canon law procedures laid down for the entire church. In the eyes of the West Frankish bishops, Nominoe's most heinous action was his refusal to receive a letter from the pope.[39] But since Nominoe was not even prepared to hear what the pope had to say, there was nothing the church could do except threaten him with anathema.[40]

When Nicholas I was enthroned in 858, Breton bishops had effectively been removed from the jurisdiction of Tours for nearly a decade, and the sees of Rennes and Nantes had also fallen under Breton hegemony.[41] Nominoe's bishops had been excommunicated; they did not go to Tours for consecration, instead consecrating each other in a highly irregular manner, and they did not attend provincial synods or general councils of the Frankish church.[42] They certainly cannot have offered professions of obedience. There were four bishops whom the Frankish church did recognise – two of the deposed men, the bishop of Dol and the bishop of Rennes – but although summoned to the synod of Savonnières in 859, they did not attend.[43] Nicholas continued his predecessors' efforts to get a canonical hearing of the case against the deposed bishops, and in a letter sent to Salomon in either 863 or 866, he elaborated upon the appropriate procedures. Leo IV

---

[38] Examples of the fates of Merovingian bishops are provided by G. Scheibelreiter, *Der Bischof in der Merowingischer Zeit*, Veröffentlichungen des Instituts für österreichische Geschichtsforschung 27 (Vienna, 1983), pp. 258–66. For Carolingian examples of bishops who were deposed and replaced for reasons of secular politics see council of Savonnières, clauses 4–5 (MGH Conc. III.459) and Nicholas I, ep. 108, MGH Epp. VI.623.   [39] MGH Conc. III.205–6.   [40] MGH Conc. III.206.
[41] There is no evidence as to how the dispute was conducted during Erispoe's rule.
[42] See the complaints made to Nicholas I by the council of Soissons in 866. *Chronique de Nantes*, 16, pp. 52–3. Their mode of consecration is commented on by John VIII, ep. 92, MGH Epp. VII.87–8.   [43] MGH Conc. III.480–1.

had specified that the case must be heard by twelve bishops, but Nicholas added the rider that the metropolitan archbishop must also be on the panel and amongst those who gave judgement. In addition, he suggested that if the Bretons were not prepared to have their case heard by the archbishop of Tours, two of the deposed bishops and two of their replacements should go to Rome, along with an envoy of Salomon's, in order that the case might be heard directly by the papacy.[44]

The problem of how the archbishop of Tours might bring the Bretons to heel was made more complicated when even his theoretical right to jurisdiction was challenged. At some point, most probably in the early 860s, the Bretons began to deny that Tours had ever been their metropolitan and tried to make the case instead that their archiepiscopal see was Dol.[45] Nicholas I's initial reaction to Salomon's request to send the archiepiscopal pallium to Festinian of Dol was to set out the correct procedure for such a request, to demand evidence that earlier bishops of Dol had received the pallium and to require a written profession of faith and of obedience to the papacy from Festinian, as normally sent by an archbishop.[46] When satisfactory evidence was not forthcoming, the request was refused and appears to have been dropped thereafter.[47]

Salomon's archiepiscopal schemes never had the support of all the bishoprics over which he ruled. Not surprisingly, the Frankish sees of Rennes and Nantes remained firm adherents of Tours, and at least one Breton see, Alet, would appear to have continued to recognise Tours in preference to Dol.[48] Lacking the full support

---

[44] Nicholas I, ep. 107, MGH Epp. vi.619–22.

[45] The main evidence for the effort to make Dol into an archbishopric is four of Nicholas' letters, nos. 107, 122, 126 and 127 (MGH Epp. vi.619–22, 639–40, 646–9). It is clear from the two of these which are dated (no. 122: 26 May 865, and no. 127: 17 May 866) that the issue had already been raised by early in 865, but since letter 107 must date from either 863 or 866, it is possible that the status of Dol had been brought into question somewhat earlier. Eleventh-century assertions that it was Nominoe who made Dol into an archbishopric are implausible for the reasons set out in J. M. H. Smith, 'The "archbishopric" of Dol and the ecclesiastical politics of ninth-century Brittany', *Studies in Church History*, 18 (1982), 59–70, at pp. 63–6.

[46] Nicholas I, ep. 122, MGH Epp. vi.639–40. For the format of an archbishop's profession, declaring obedience directly to St Peter and the papacy, see MGH Epp. viii.i, 1–2, no. 1.

[47] Nicholas I, ep. 127, MGH Epp. vi.648–9. For the unsatisfactory documentation which Salomon did send to Rome, see Smith, '"Archbishopric" of Dol', p. 66.

[48] Rennes: a new bishop was consecrated in 866, and notice of his ordination by Herard of Tours, Actard of Nantes, and Robert of Le Mans is extent. Quentin, 'Lettre de Nicholas I ... et formules ecclésiastiques', pp. 109–10. Nantes: after Actard's translation

of his bishops, why then did Salomon request the pallium for Festinian? Certainly not, as has been claimed, so that he could consecrate Salomon king.[49] It is far more likely to have been a move to resolve the affair of the deposed bishops. Nicholas had stipulated that an archbishop must preside over the trial of the deposed bishops, and, indeed, one of his reasons for declining to promote Festinian had been that there were only seven bishoprics in Brittany, not the twelve needed to constitute a judicial panel.[50] In trying to get Festinian appointed archbishop, Salomon perhaps hoped to break the deadlock by having the ejected bishops tried by a Breton metropolitan. Only by replicating within Brittany the hierarchical structure of the Carolingian church did Salomon stand a chance of resolving the situation to everyone's advantage. But he failed, and until Gregory VII sent the pallium to Dol in 1076, the archiepiscopal status of Dol was only realised in hagiographical propaganda.[51]

As Nicholas saw it, the issue was clear. It was one of the obedience needed to uphold the right ordering of society, which would only be achieved if canonical procedures were followed. After Charlemagne's death, the only circumstances in which ninth- and tenth-century popes were prepared to establish new archdioceses were for missionary churches in areas where conversion was proceeding apace; Hamburg in 832, Magdeburg in 968, Gnesen in 1000, Gran in 1001. Brittany did not qualify for a new archbishopric, the Bretons lacked valid proof that Dol had ever been an archbishopric, and the church hierarchy was not to be altered at whim. The keys to Nicholas' reaction were *disciplina*

to the archbishopric of Tours (below, n. 53) he consecrated Ermengar, formerly deacon of Nantes, to the see. Duchesne, *Fastes Episcopaux*, II.367. Also, his successors Fulcher and Isaiah were signatories to Tours charters. E. Mabille, 'Les invasions normandes dans la Loire et les pérégrinations du corps de Saint Martin. Pièces justificatives', *Bibliothèque de l'Ecole des Chartes*, 30 (1869), 423–60, nos. 9, 12, at pp. 442–5, 451–4. Alet: in reworking the life of Malo between 866 and 872, Bili added a scene in which Malo went to Tours for his episcopal consecration. *Vie de Saint-Malo*, I.40, p. 121.

49 Cf. W. Kienast, *Studien über die französischen Volksstämme des Frühmittelalters*, Pariser Historische Studien 7 (Stuttgart, 1968), pp. 121–3 and further references there. The only ninth-century 'evidence' for the anointing of a Breton ruler is a reference to Alan I receiving the last rites during an illness from which he subsequently recovered: see Chédeville and Guillotel, *Bretagne*, p. 360.

50 Ep. 127, MGH Epp. VI.648.

51 Chédeville and Tonnerre, *Bretagne Féodale*, pp. 259–60. A group of (probably) late ninth-century *vitae* from Dol portray the founding saint of Dol and his successors as archbishops. See Lapidge and Sharpe, *Bibliography*, nos. 932, 951, 952.

and *lex*. He quoted to Salomon his biblical namesake, saying, 'Hear, my son, the instruction of thy father, and forsake not the law of thy mother.'[52] This was, of course, that the Breton bishops were all subject to the archbishop of Tours.

It is hard to trace what happened after Nicholas died in 867. By then, Salomon had made a lasting peace with Charles the Bald, and as the deposed bishops died, the dispute over their status will have lost its fervour. There is no mention of the issue in the correspondence of Hadrian II, who presumably left it in the hands of Actard, formerly bishop of Nantes and from 871 archbishop of Tours. Actard had intimate first-hand experience of the Bretons, having been temporarily ejected from his see in 850 and having played a leading role in the council of Soissons in 866.[53] To help in the fight against the Breton usurpers, Hadrian II equipped Actard with a copy of the *Capitula Angilramni*. The *Capitula Angilramni* were that part of the collection of False Decretals which aimed precisely at strengthening metropolitan and papal rights to hear accusations against bishops and at preventing secular rulers bringing charges against bishops or trying them.[54] Actard's efforts were continued by his successor at Tours, Adalard, who drew John VIII's attention to the persisting Breton episcopal intransigence at the synod of Troyes in 878. John's letter threatening the Bretons with anathema is the last that is heard of the matter for another century.[55]

The political conflict between Nominoe, Erispoe, and Salomon on the one hand and Charles the Bald on the other was articulated through traditional tokens of lordship, especially the giving or withholding of oaths, and by the grants of the symbols of royal rulership. Similarly, the Bretons' dispute with the archbishops of

---

[52] Nicholas I, ep. 107, quoting Proverbs 1:8, MGH Epp. VI.621.

[53] Actard's own career is another, minor, example of the conflicts within the hierarchy of the Carolingian church. His translation to Tours was requested by Charles the Bald. Hincmar attempted to block it by arguing that it was uncanonical but Hadrian II approved it, citing the testimony of the False Decretals in his favour. Hadrian II, epp. 7–10, 34–6, MGH Epp. VI.704–12, 738–46; Charles the Bald to Nicholas I, *Sacrorum Conciliorum Nova et Amplissima Collectio*, ed. J.-D. Mansi, 31 vols. (Florence, 1759–98), XV.800; Charles the Bald to Hadrian II, PL CXXIV.876–81; Hincmar to Hadrian and to an unknown bishop, PL CXXVI.641–8, 210–30.

[54] Hadrian II, ep. 11, MGH Epp. VI.712, and see Fuhrmann, *Einfluss und Verbreitung*, II.278.

[55] John VIII, ep. 92, MGH Epp. VII.87–8. The issue thereafter was dormant but not dead: an isolated letter of John XIII (956–72) survives which shows that the matter was still in the air in the late tenth century. PL CXXVI.959–60 (where it is misattributed to John VIII).

Tours and the papacy was a dispute about the symbols of spiritual lordship and authority. Episcopal professions of obedience were the ecclesiastical equivalent of oaths of fidelity; the archiepiscopal pallium was a token of rank and authority conferred to mark its recipient's place in the church hierarchy and in recognition of his acknowledgement of Rome's superiority. Behind the conflict about symbols, however, lay fundamental questions of power and authority. How to prevent laymen from trying and deposing bishops and priests, whether the papacy could find ways of constraining obdurate rulers, and what the nature of metropolitan authority was: all these questions were stirred up by the events which started at *Coitlouh*.

Similar juridical problems were under intense discussion by Carolingian churchmen for much of the ninth century. They were most clearly articulated in the voluminous writings of Hincmar of Reims, his adversaries and correspondents. Hincmar's own archdiocese was split between West Francia and Lotharingia, two kingdoms whose rulers were frequently ill-disposed to one another, and his high sense of his own metropolitan authority was under frequent challenge from his suffragans. It was probably early in Hincmar's episcopate and within his archdiocese that the pseudo-Isidorian decretals were forged; that the same texts were also appropriate to the conflict with the Bretons is an indication that comparable problems were facing the church in western Neustria as in the heart of the Carolingian empire.

The threat to the archbishopric of Tours was of evident concern to the Carolingian church as a whole. On several occasions, the affairs of the province of Tours found a place on the agenda of several synods of bishops of more than one kingdom: at Savonnières in 859, Soissons in 866, and finally Troyes in 878.[56] As the sentiment of the unity of the Carolingian empire long outlasted its division into separate kingdoms, so too the moral unity and sense of common purpose of the Carolingian church which had been built out of the Franko-papal alliance also lasted, transcending the growing political divisions.

---

[56] For the other business discussed at these synods see W. Hartmann, *Die Synoden der Karolingerzeit im Frankenreich und in Italien* (Paderborn, 1989).

THE INFLUENCE OF THE CAROLINGIAN RENAISSANCE

In launching and succouring reform of the church, the Carolingian rulers gave a far-reaching stimulus to learning and culture. Royal impetus interacted with local differences and changing circumstances, with the effect that 'the ultimate product and contribution of the Carolingian renaissance was precisely this tension between the demands of an official culture and its diverse manifestations'.[57] For example, the Anglo-Saxon origins of Fulda and the Irish connections of Sankt Gallen or Reichenau were evident in the persistence of insular influences in these churches; in parts of Bavaria and Alemmania, Christian Latin teachings were made available in written form in Old High German; churches in the middle Loire valley were more concerned to copy classical texts than to produce de luxe bibles.[58] As for Brittany, it is possible to detect, albeit only in outline, something of how that tension was manifested thanks to the survival of a substantial number of early medieval manuscripts and saints' lives.

Only very occasionally is it possible to identify the routes of communication which brought knowledge of Carolingian cultural standards into the region. What we can do, however, is to map in general terms the growing contacts between Breton churches and the wider world, contacts which provided the ambience in which cultural exchange took place. Although Nominoe and Salomon had effectively cut Breton bishoprics off from the synodical processes and canonical hierarchy of the province of Tours, the result was in no way to isolate Breton clerics from Frankish influences. On the contrary, from about 850 onwards increasing contacts can be traced between Breton churches and churches elsewhere in the Carolingian world.

Three places in particular stand out as areas of significantly close interchange: the lower Seine valley, the churches and monasteries of the middle Loire valley, and Rome. The church of Dol had links with the lower Seine valley. Samson had also founded a monastery at *Pental*, now Saint-Samson-sur-Risle near the

[57] J. J. Contreni, 'The Carolingian renaissance', in *Renaissances before the Renaissance: Cultural Revivals of Late Antiquity and the Middle Ages*, ed. W. Treadgold (Stanford, 1984), pp. 59–74, at p. 68.
[58] P. Riché, *Les Ecoles et l'Enseignement dans l'Occident Chrétien de la fin du Ve siècle au milieu du XIe siècle* (Paris, 1979), pp. 87–110; McKitterick, 'Carolingian book production'; J. F. Kenny, *The Sources for the Early History of Ireland: Ecclesiastical. An Introduction and Guide* (New York, 1929), pp. 486–621.

confluence of the Risle and Seine, and although this is last mentioned in 833, the cathedral of Dol continued to own land in the neighbourhood until 1613, and several parishes here formed enclaves of the diocese of Dol until the French Revolution.[59] These jurisdictional and property ties help explain why in the middle of the ninth century, a bishop of Dol became abbot of the monastery of La-Croix-Saint-Leufroi (dép. Eure).[60] This may also have been the route by which Breton manuscripts later reached Norman monasteries in the vicinity of the lower Seine basin.[61] As for the Loire valley, contacts with the monasteries and churches of Angers, Tours, and Orléans were maintained throughout the ninth and tenth centuries. Right on the border between Neustria and Brittany from 851, Angers was something of an ecclesiastical entrepot, even before two of the city's monasteries acquired Breton lay abbots.[62] Monks of Redon came here to steal relics for their church.[63] The nearby monastery of Glanfeuil had Breton monks in the community, welcomed Breton pilgrims, and accepted land in Brittany from one of them, and, having provided guidance in the observance of the Benedictine Rule to the founding monks of Redon, remained in close communication with the Breton community.[64] Upstream at Tours, the Bretons are known to have kept in touch with the clergy of the church of Saint-Martin rather than with the cathedral. Few instances of personal contact are known, but the dissemination into Brittany of the bible text associated with Alcuin is most likely to have been the result of communication between Bretons and the churches of their metropolitan see.[65] Further up the Loire, the monastery of Fleury in the diocese of

---

[59] L. Musset, 'Saint-Samson-sur-Risle', in *Annuaire des Cinq Départements de la Normandie, Congrès de Pont-Audemer* (Caen, 1961), pp. 11–18; H. Guillotel, 'Les origines du ressort de l'évêché de Dol', *MSHAB*, 54 (1977), 31–68.

[60] For John of Dol see above, n. 28 p. 15.

[61] From Fécamp comes the canon and penitential collection BN Lat. 3182; from Jumièges a Breton manuscript of Isidore's *Etymologiae*, BL Harley 3941. Both of these are glossed in Old Breton.

[62] Salomon was given the lay abbacy of Saint-Aubin in 863: *AB*, a. 863, p. 96. Alan I had the lay abbacy of Saint-Serge within his gift: *Cartulaire Noir*, 12, pp. 30–2.

[63] *GSR*, II.9, pp. 171–5.

[64] Planiol, 'Donation d'Anowareth', pp. 233–7; *GSR*, I.2, III.5, pp. 113–15, 201–3.

[65] One of the founding monks of Redon was well known to the monks at Saint-Martin: *GSR*, I.9, pp. 135–7. For pilgrims sent from Saint-Martin to the shrine of Maglorius, see *Miracula Sancti Maglorii*, 6, *Catalogus Codicum Hagiographicorum Latinorum in Bibliotheca Nationali Parisiensi*, 4 vols. (Brussels, 1889–93), III.312–14. For the influence of the Tourangelle bible text, see below, pp. 169–70.

Orléans was a well-known meeting place of insular and Carolingian influences. Travel here from Brittany can only be documented in the tenth century, but the closeness of these contacts together with the hint of Breton influence on the scripts used at Fleury suggests that this was nothing new.[66] Contacts such as these hint at the routes by which works by Carolingian authors may have entered Brittany.

Rome occupied a rather different place in the web of links between Brittany and the wider world. The veneration in which the Bretons held St Peter is suggested by Salomon's unfulfilled vow to go to pray at his tomb, a vow which was commuted into sumptuous gifts, and by Alan I's pledge to give a tithe of all his property to Rome if he were to defeat the Vikings.[67] Interestingly, the traffic between Brittany and Rome was two-way, for not only did Breton monks seek permission to go on pilgrimage to the shrine of St Peter, but the presence of relics of the martyred pope Marcellinus at Redon attracted to Brittany those whom the pope sent on public penance round the major shrines of Latin Christendom and the Holy Land.[68] Such travellers brought news into Brittany – of a renegade Breton monk who had returned to the monastic life in Pavia – and spread the reputation of an obscure Breton saint to an Apennine city.[69] When correspondence between popes and Breton bishops quickened in the second half of the ninth century, there can have been no lack of carriers for the letters.

Against this background the evidence for Carolingian cultural influence in Brittany may best be assessed. The evidence itself falls into two categories, manuscript and textual. As for the first, there exist upwards of 150 manuscripts for which a Breton origin in the

[66] One specific example is Bern, Burgerbibliothek 277, a copy of Ambrose's *De Officiis Ministrorum* which Mabbo, bishop of Saint-Pol-de-Léon, gave to Fleury when he retired there in about 958. Other contacts are conveniently summarised by L. Gougaud, 'Les relations de l'abbaye de Fleury-sur-Loire avec la Bretagne et les îles britanniques, X^e–XIe siècle', *MSHAB*, 4 (1923), 3–30. Bischoff, *Latin Palaeography*, p. 90, suggests possible Breton influence on Fleury script. See also M. Mostert, *The Library of Fleury: A Provisional List of Manuscripts* (Hilversum, 1989).
[67] CR 89; Regino, *Chronicon*, a. 890, p. 135.
[68] CR A2; *GSR*, III.1, 8, pp. 189–93, 207–13; John VIII, ep. 44, MGH Epp. VII.299–300. For a Frankish pilgrim who made his way independently to Brittany see *Itinerarium Bernardi*, pp. 97–8, 99.
[69] *GSR*, II.5, p. 163; for the circumstances in which the cult of Winwaloe was introduced to Arezzo, see R. Fawtier, 'Une rédaction inédite de la vie de saint Guénolé', *Mélanges d'Archéologie et d'Histoire de l'Ecole Française de Rome*, 32 (1912), 27–44.

period up to the eleventh century has been posited.[70] However, only in a very few cases is it possible to date them within more specific confines than very general chronological bands. With the exception of the handful of manuscripts firmly attributed to the monastery of Landévennec, no place of origin can be suggested for any manuscript, and so it is not known whether the vast majority are witnesses to the learning of the secular church or to monastic centres. Only a few have ever been the subject of any detailed textual or palaeographical study, and of the organisation and functioning of the scriptoria which produced them, we remain ignorant. All are books salvaged by Breton monks and clerics as they fled from the Vikings which have therefore survived in libraries outside Brittany. The second category of evidence is the modest collection of works composed by Breton authors in the ninth and tenth centuries. Apart from one short set of annals from Redon and possibly one metrical treatise on the priestly office, there is only a corpus of hagiography.[71] The authors of some of these saints' lives are known, as are the approximate dates at which they were writing, but most of the *vitae* are anonymous and some of those for which a ninth–century origin has been claimed may be of a rather later date.[72] Study of these works is made more problematic by lack of satisfactory editions of most of the texts in question. Until an exhaustive, technical study of the culture of early medieval Brittany is done, the following tentative remarks are offered as a brief and interim sketch.

[70] The longest published list is that of J.-L. Deuffic, 'La production manuscrite des scriptoria bretons (VIIe–XIe siècles)', in *Landévennec et le Monachisme Breton*, ed. Simon, pp. 289–321. Some of these entries are doubtful; in other respects the list is certainly incomplete.

[71] The annals, which are from Redon, are both brief and fragmentary: B. Bischoff, 'Annales Rotonenses (um 919)', in B. Bischoff, *Analecta Novissima. Texte des vierten bis sechzehnten Jahrhunderts*, Quellen und Untersuchungen zur lateinischen Philologie des Mittelalters 7 (Stuttgart, 1984), pp. 103–5. Liosmonoc, author of the metrical *Libellus Sacerdotalis*, is accepted to have been a Breton, but it is not known where he wrote: one recent suggestion is Fleury. See the editorial comments in MGH Poet. IV.278–95 and J. Fontaine, 'De la pluralité à l'unité dans le "latin carolingien"', *Settimane*, 27 (1979), 765–805, at p. 801 n. 49.

[72] For editions of Breton Latin saints' lives, see Lapidge and Sharpe, *Bibliography*. Brief surveys of the corpus are provided by Wattenbach, Levison, and Löwe, *Deutschlands Geschichtsquellen*, pp. 600–5; P. Riché, 'Les hagiographes bretons et la renaissance carolingienne', in *Bulletin Philologique et Historique du Comité des Travaux Historiques et Scientifiques, année 1966* (Paris, 1968), pp. 651–9; F. Kerlouégan, 'Les vies des saints bretons les plus anciennes dans leurs rapports avec les îles britanniques', in *Insular Latin Studies*, ed. M. Herren, Papers in Mediaeval Studies 1 (Toronto, 1981), pp. 195–213.

In no way is it possible to talk about early medieval Brittany as a province with its own easily identifiable cultural identity. The boundaries of the region changed dramatically in the second half of the ninth century to combine two zones of distinct languages and cultural traditions. The cultural life of all of Neustria west of Tours is an uncharted field: modest libraries and writing centres there must have been, but manuscripts from them have not been identified, with the possible exception of a tiny handful from Angers.[73] Here, the context of written Latin was the evolving 'proto-Romance' vernacular culture, but when Breton lordship was extended over much of this region, several monasteries acquired Breton abbots.[74] The cultural consequences of this must remain speculative, and, since not a single manuscript or saint's life can be confidently attributed to any church within that part of Neustria which had passed under Breton rule, the region cannot be discussed to any profit.[75] The following remarks are specific to the area of Breton speech. Besides clear internal evidence, the presence of Old Breton words and phrases glossing Latin texts provides the most secure means of locating a manuscript's origins. In Brittany, Latin was a remote, learned language with no connection whatsoever to everyday speech. As François Kerlouégan has put it, 'Latin seems to have evolved in Brittany in the same way as French in the colonies.'[76] Glosses suggest ways in which the very different grammar and syntax of Latin were mastered by Breton speakers.[77] Apart from the use of Latin to record land grants, there is little sign of a vigorous written culture, Latin or vernacular, before the ninth century.[78]

[73] J. Vezin, 'Les scriptoria de Neustrie 650–850', in *La Neustrie*, ed. Atsma, II.307–18, surveys Neustrian scriptoria from west to east, starting in Tours, but at p. 311 n. 21 suggests a possible origin in Angers for three manuscripts.

[74] For Breton lay abbots at Angers, see above n. 62. Mont-Saint-Michel also had a Breton abbot, Phinimontius, at some point in the late ninth century: *Itinerarium Bernardi*, p. 98.

[75] Both Donatus' life of Ermenland and the anonymous life of Melanius of Rennes were written within this area, but neither is known to have been written after Breton rule was established. Wattenbach, Levison, and Löwe, *Deutschlands Geschichtsquellen*, pp. 589–92. On the Aquitainian bank of the Loire, Ermentarius wrote his life and miracles of St Philibert before the pays de Retz passed under Breton lordship.

[76] F. Kerlouégan, 'Une mode stylistique dans la prose latine des pays celtiques', *EC*, 13 (1972–3), 275–97, quotation from intervention on p. 297.

[77] L. Fleuriot, *Dictionnaire des Gloses en Vieux Breton* (Paris, 1964); P.-Y. Lambert, 'Les gloses grammaticales brittoniques', *EC*, 24 (1987), 285–308.

[78] For pre-Carolingian archives, see above, p. 22 at n. 56. The only two extant works which have a claim to have been written in pre-Carolingian Brittany are the *Exerpta*

Confining attention to the manuscript culture of the Breton-speaking region, most immediately striking is the continuing influence of the British Isles. The most obvious sign of this, long ago pointed out by W. M. Lindsay, is the palaeographical evidence: the earliest extant Breton manuscripts are written in insular script.[79] The oldest of these, a gospel book from the turn of the eighth/ninth century is written in an insular half-uncial and has many affinities with Irish gospels.[80] The few Breton manuscripts datable to the first half of the ninth century are written in a minuscule script with some Caroline influence but mostly insular characteristics.[81] A further indication that Breton cultural contacts with the British Isles persisted long after the initial period of migration and settlement is the preservation of British and Irish texts in Breton manuscripts, or in ways which show evidence of having been transmitted through Brittany. The *De Excidio Britanniae* of Gildas is the most significant British work, and notable among the Irish texts in this respect are the eighth-century *Collectio Canonum Hibernensis* and the *Hisperica Famina*, usually accepted to be of seventh-century Irish origin.[82] That such

---

de Libris Romanorum et Francorum and the first life of Samson of Dol. On these, see above, p. 20 n. 49, and p. 15 n. 28. On the lack of evidence for a well-developed vernacular culture see C. Brett, 'Breton Latin literature as evidence for literature in the vernacular, AD 800–1300', *Cambridge Medieval Celtic Studies*, 18 (1989), 1–25.

[79] W. M. Lindsay, 'Breton scriptoria: their Latin abbreviation symbols', *Zentralblatt für Bibliothekswesen*, 29 (1912), 264–72.

[80] BN Nouv. Acq. Lat. 1587. For details, see P. McGurk, 'The gospel book in Celtic lands before AD 850: contents and arrangement', in *Irland und die Christenheit: Bibelstudien und Mission*, ed. P. Ní Chatháin and M. Richter (Stuttgart, 1987), pp. 165–89, esp. p. 176.

[81] Orléans, BM 221 (a compendium of canonical material with many Breton glosses), Orléans, BM 302 (Sedulius, *Carmen Paschale* with Breton glosses), Leiden, Universiteits-Bibliotheek Voss. Lat. F.96A (bilingual Breton/Latin medical treatise). On the basis of decoration and text, rather than script, McGurk (as previous note) has argued for a Breton origin for two other early gospels, BL Egerton 609 and Würzburg, Universitätsbibliothek M.p.th.f.67. See also Bischoff, *Latin Palaeography*, p. 90.

[82] The fragment of Gildas, *De Excidio Britanniae* is Reims, BM 414, fos. 78–9; for the identification and significance to the text history of Gildas see W. H. Davies, 'The Church in Wales', in *Christianity in Britain, 300–700*, ed. Barley and Hanson, pp. 131–50, at p. 147 n. 73; D. N. Dumville, 'Sub-Roman Britain: history and legend', *History*, n.s., 62 (1977), 173–92, at pp. 183–4.

For comments on the relevant manuscripts of the *Collectio Canonun Hibernensis*, see H. Wasserschleben, *Die irische Kanonensammlung* (2nd edn, Leipzig, 1885), pp. lxiii–lxxv. On the manuscripts of the *Hisperica Famina* see below, n. 98, also P. Grosjean, 'Confusa caligo: remarques sur les *hisperica famina*', *Celtica*, 3 (1956), 35–85, at pp. 37–40, and *The Hisperica Famina I: The A-text*, ed. M. Herren (Toronto, 1974),

texts were copied and glossed throughout the Carolingian period testifies to the continuing insular influence on Breton Latin culture.[83] Finally, the vernacular glosses which upwards of forty manuscripts bear are witness to complex and close cross-channel links.[84] Scribes of several Breton manuscripts recopied Old Welsh and/or Old Irish glosses from the archetypes they were using; in two cases the Old Breton glosses depend on Old Irish glosses to the same works in a way which suggests that Breton churches continued to have access to speakers of Irish.[85] Hagiography provides a rather different aspect to these cross-channel contacts. In the ninth century, several authors relied on British sources for information.[86] Furthermore, in Brittany as in Wales, saints' lives were an important form of historical writing, and drew their substance at least in part from oral origin tales. But it seems that, as the Breton legends were developed and elaborated in the eleventh and twelfth centuries, this was done under Welsh influence.[87] Thus, despite the lack of direct evidence for

pp. 7–11. For other Irish Latin texts transmitted partly via Brittany, see R. Kottje, 'Überlieferung und Rezeption der irischen Bussbücher auf dem Kontinent', in *Die Iren und Europa im früheren Mittelalter*, ed. H. Löwe, 2 vols. (Stuttgart, 1982), 1.511–24; A. Wilmart, *Analecta Reginensia: Extraits des Manuscrits Latins de la Reine Christine Conservés au Vatican*, Studi e Testi 59 (Vatican City, 1933), pp. 29–112; R. E. McNally, '*Dies dominica*: two Hiberno-Latin texts', *Mediaeval Studies*, 22 (1960), 355–61. See also the general remarks of D. N. Dumville, 'Some British aspects of the earliest Irish Christianity', in *Irland und Europa: die Kirche im Frühmittelalter*, ed. P. Ní Chatháin and M. Richter (Stuttgart, 1984), pp. 16–24, at pp. 21–2.

[83] Manuscripts of Irish canonical and penitential collections with Breton glosses of the late ninth/early tenth century are BL Cotton Otho E.xiii; BN Lat. 12021; Cambridge, Corpus Christi College 279; Orléans, BM 221; Oxford, Bodleian Library Hatton 42. Of the same date is a fragmentary glossed manuscript of the *Hisperica Famina*, Luxemburg, Bibliothèque Royale Grand-Ducale 89.

[84] Published in 1964, Fleuriot's *Dictionnaire* lists thirty-six glossed manuscripts; a few more have been discovered since.

[85] Recopied Old Welsh and Old Irish glosses are discussed by Fleuriot, *Dictionnaire*, pp. 8–9, and by P.-Y. Lambert, 'Les gloses du manuscrit B. N. Latin 10290', *EC*, 19 (1982), 173–213. On the Old Breton glosses with Old Irish antecedents in Angers, BM 477, see P.-Y. Lambert, 'Les commentaires celtiques à Bède le Vénérable', *EC*, 20 (1983), 119–43, and 21 (1984), 185–206. For the glosses to Bern, Burgerbibliothek 167, see P.-Y. Lambert, 'Les gloses celtiques aux commentaires de Virgile', *EC*, 23 (1986), 81–128. For either a Welsh or an Irish exemplar behind the only manuscript of the A-text of the *Hisperica Famina* see M. Lapidge, 'Latin learning in dark age Wales: some prolegomena', in *Proceedings of the Seventh International Congress of Celtic Studies, Oxford 1983*, ed. D. E. Evans, J. G. Griffith, and E. M. Jope (Oxford, 1986), pp. 91–107, at n. 58.

[86] Bili, *Vie de Saint-Malo*, 1.25, pp. 85–7; Wrmonoc, 'Vie de Saint Paul de Léon', 1.10, p. 436. See also Kerlouégan, 'Vies des saints bretons', pp. 200–1.

[87] Brett, 'Breton Latin literature', pp. 15–18.

communication between Brittany and other Celtic-speaking regions, it is nevertheless clear that Breton churches remained influenced by Wales and Ireland, and to some extent culturally indebted to them throughout the early Middle Ages.

From about the middle of the ninth century, this heavily insular culture changed perceptibly. Continental cultural and ecclesi-astical influences swept into the region, and although they by no means totally eroded the traditional orientation towards Wales and Ireland, intellectual life was appreciably different by the early tenth century. Whereas not more than a half-dozen manuscripts can be dated to the first half of the ninth century, Breton manuscript production increased rapidly after the mid-century, reaching a peak at the end of the century before suddenly ceasing in about 920, when churches were abandoned in the face of Viking onslaught. All these later ninth- and early tenth-century manuscripts are characterised by a round and often rather uneven Caroline minuscule script, and many insular abbreviations together with the syntax marks and Latin orthography commonly found in early Welsh manuscripts.[88] Frankish influence, however, is not only traceable in the change in preferred script. The choice of texts copied also betrays it. In the first place, there are a few authors closely connected with the Carolingian renaissance whose work is known to have been copied in Brittany: Alcuin, Smaragdus, and Amalarius.[89] In the second place, the text of Breton gospel books and their accompanying liturgical materials show clear signs that Carolingian influences were displacing older traditions. Of the two Breton gospel books of which detailed studies have so far been published, one that was written at

---

[88] Lindsay, 'Breton scriptoria'. Many more Breton manuscripts have been identified since Lindsay wrote. I am grateful to David Dumville for sharing with me his views on the chronology of Breton manuscript production.

[89] Fragments of Alcuin's Grammar are preserved in Merseburg, Domstiftbibliothek I.204. Amalarius, *Liber Officialis*: BN Nouv. Acq. Lat. 1983. There is a second Breton copy of this work, written at Landévennec in 952, in Cambridge, Corpus Christi College 192. Smaragdus' commentary on Donatus: BN Lat. 13029. All these manuscripts are glossed in Breton; see L. Fleuriot, 'Nouvelles gloses vieilles-bretonnes à Amalarius', *EC*, 11 (1964–7), 415–64; L. Holtz and P.-Y. Lambert, 'La tradition ancienne du *Liber in partibus Donati* de Smaragde de Saint-Mihiel', *Revue d'Histoire des Textes*, 16 (1986), 171–211, at pp. 174–8, 201–7. Also relevant here is a collection of theological and philosophical excerpts assembled in the circle of Alcuin preserved in a late ninth-century Breton manuscript, Munich, Bayerische Staatsbibliothek Clm 18961. See C. E. Ineichen-Eder, 'Theologisches und philosophisches Lehrmaterial aus dem Alkuin-Kreise', *DA*, 34 (1978), 192–201.

Landévennec late in the century has a blend of insular and Alcuinian textual readings, the other (of undetermined origin) opens with a capitulary of readings for feast days of a type that was widely diffused in the Carolingian liturgical reforms of the late eighth century.[90] In total, about twenty-five ninth-/tenth-century gospel books have been claimed to be of certain or probable or possible Breton origin, and throughout this group Carolingian, usually specifically Tourangelle, influences predominate over insular affiliations.[91] In all these respects, the traces of cultural osmosis are unmistakable.

Most of the remaining manuscripts copied in Brittany in the late ninth and early tenth centuries fall into several well-defined though overlapping categories. The first of these are texts of practical value for priests in fulfilling their ministry, texts which they would need in addition to the gospel books. As well as Amalarius' *Liber Officialis* and the clerical handbook in hisperic verse of Liosmonoc, Ambrose's *De officiis ministrorum* may have been known by the third quarter of the tenth century.[92] From both before and after the hiatus in Breton manuscript production occasioned by the Viking invasions are the compilations of canonical, penitential, and biblical material which are of obviously Irish flavour.[93] Probably for use by a preacher was the collection of biblical and patristic extracts in an early tenth-century manuscript now in the Vatican.[94] All this material suggests a

---

[90]   For the Harkness gospel from Landévennec, now New York Public Library 115, see C. R. Morey, E. K. Rand, and C. H. Kraeling, 'The gospel-book of Landévennec (the Harkness gospels) in the New York Public Library', *Art Studies*, 8 (1931), 225–86, esp. pp. 238–57. For the Bradfer-Lawrence gospels in the Fitzwilliam Museum, Cambridge, see J. J. G. Alexander and F. Wormald, *An Early Breton Gospel Book*, The Roxburghe Club (Cambridge, 1977), esp. p. 2.

[91]   McGurk, 'Gospel book in Celtic lands', p. 175, summarising the findings of his forthcoming study of Breton gospel books. Lists of Breton gospel books, none of which completely agree with each other, are given by McGurk, nn. 2, 45; Alexander and Wormald, *Early Breton Gospel Book*, pp. 13–23; B. Fischer, 'Zur Überlieferung des lateinischen Textes der Evangelien', *Cahiers de la Revue Théologique de Louvain*, 19 (1987), 51–104, at pp. 65–7.

[92]   For Amalarius, see above, n. 89. Ambrose: Bern, Burgerbibliothek, 277. This manuscript was given to Fleury by Mabbo of Saint-Pol on his retirement there, and may be of Fleury origin. Mostert, *Library of Fleury*, p. 69. Liosmonoc: BN Lat. 13386, fos. 208–20.

[93]   In addition to the glossed manuscripts cited in n. 83 above is BN Lat. 3182 of the second half of the tenth century.

[94]   Vatican, Biblioteca Apostolica Reg. Lat. 49. For commentary on this manuscript see the references cited by Deuffic, 'Production manuscrite', p. 317.

concern with ecclesiastical organisation and an active, preaching ministry, and it is to be hoped that further study will reveal how these texts were compiled and used.

In a second category and also of practical value, though in a very different way, are several medical manuscripts.[95]

By far the largest category, with several subdivisions, is of texts to be read in schoolroom or library. In a literary vein, poetry is represented by Virgil with Servius' commentary,[96] Sedulius' *Carmen Paschale*,[97] the *Hisperica Famina*,[98] and a Hiberno–Latin devotional alphabetical poem.[99] History is represented by Orosius and a fragment of Gildas.[100] Apart from a complete *De Civitate Dei* of Augustine and one possible manuscript of Ambrose on Luke,[101] patristic theology is conspicuous only by its absence, but there is one copy of a collection of philosophical and theological extracts originally put together in Alcuin's circle.[102] Computistical collections and calendars include Bede's two treatises *De Ratione Temporum* and *De Natura Rerum*.[103] As for general reference, there are two glossed copies of Isidore's *Etymologiae*.[104]

---

[95] BN Nouv. Acq. Lat. 1616; Leiden, Universiteits-Bibliotheek Voss. Lat. F.96A; Sankt Gallen, Stiftsbibliothek 759.   [96] Bern, Burgerbibliothek 167.

[97] Orléans, BM 302.

[98] BN Lat. 11411, fos. 101–2; Luxemburg, Bibliothèque Royale Grand-Ducale 89; Vatican, Biblioteca Apostolica Reg. Lat. 81, fos. 1–12. Between them, these manuscripts preserve all the four known recensions of the *famina*. The only complete recension is that in the Vatican manuscript, whose scribe Liosmonoc may have been writing at Fleury. See *Hisperica Famina I*, ed. Herren, pp. 7–10.

[99] Saint-Omer, BM 666. On the text, see Kenney, *Sources for the Early History of Ireland*, p. 258, no. 86.

[100] Vatican, Biblioteca Apostolica Reg. Lat. 296 is a glossed manuscript of Orosius' *Historia Contra Paganos*. A strong early Breton interest in Orosius is suggested by the survival of four eleventh-/twelfth-century manuscripts bearing glosses copied from early Breton exemplars: Bern, Burgerbibliothek 160; Vatican, Biblioteca Apostolica Lat. 1974 and Reg. Lat. 691, and Venice, Biblioteca Marciana, Zanetti 349. The fragment of Gildas, *De Excidio Britanniae* is Reims, BM 414, fos. 78–9.

[101] Augustine: BN Lat. 2051. Ambrose: Orléans, BM 73, fos. 78–189 (which may rather come from Fleury).   [102] Munich, Bayerische Staatsbibliothek Clm 18961.

[103] Angers, BM 476, 477 both contain Bede's *De Ratione Temporum*, the latter also his *De Natura Rerum*; there are also computistical texts in BN Nouv. Acq. Lat. 1616, originating in Brittany or possibly the Orléanais. Copenhagen, Kongelige Bibliotek Thott 239 is an incomplete calendar table from Landévennec.

[104] BL Harley 3941; the second manuscript is made up of disjointed leaves now Gotha, Landesbibliothek MBR 1.147 + New York, Pierpont Morgan Library G 28 + Herdringen, Archiv der Grafen von Fürstenburg, frag. s.n. + Hanover, Kestner-Museum, Culemann Kat. 1.45 (366) + Paderborn, Bibliothek der Erzbischöflichen philosophisch-theologischen Akademie, frag. 10 + Weimar, Staatsarchiv Hardenburg-Sammlung 12a and 14a. For the glosses to these manuscripts, see L. Fleuriot, 'Gloses inédites en vieux-breton', *EC*, 16 (1979), 197–210.

There are two glossaries[105] and a huge number of grammatical works, all of which are glossed in Breton, sometimes very heavily: three copies of Priscian's Grammar and one of his *Periegesis*,[106] one of Eutyches' *De Conjugatione Verborum*,[107] one of Nonius Marcellus' *De Proprietate Sermonum*[108] in addition to the Grammar of Alcuin and Smaragdus on Donatus.[109]

Almost all of the manuscripts in this third group are of overwhelmingly pedagogical character. Grammar, so prominent in this collection, was a subject in which Irish scholars excelled and was the basis on which the Carolingian educational reforms and biblical studies were built. Bede's *De Ratione Temporum* and *De Natura Rerum* were handbooks for teaching computus. Virgil and Sedulius were both standard early medieval classroom texts. Isidore also had a firm place in any basic early medieval education; Orosius was also readily available in the ninth century. It is precisely these manuscripts which were glossed, often in great detail, in Old Breton. Glossing never extended beyond words or short phrases tied closely to understanding the literal sense of the text: it was designed to help readers who were struggling to acquire a mastery of both the contents of a treatise and of Latin grammar and vocabulary.

Most of those extant Breton manuscripts which show some degree of Carolingian influence on script, content, or both are thus either of direct educational use or designed to help priests carry out their pastoral obligations. So marked is this that it has prompted the suggestion that we have here the traces of 'a deliberate, tightly organised revival of learning' of which the techniques and orthography of glossing formed a part.[110] Although this revival drew on both insular (especially Irish) and Frankish resources, it is hard to see where the model for such an educational programme could have come in the late ninth century, if not from the Carolingian church. It was in the Frankish lands of the late eighth and early ninth centuries that the

---

[105] Leiden, Universiteits-Bibliothek Voss. Lat. F.24 is a Latin glossary which is glossed in Old Breton, Old English, and Old High German; Angers, BM 477, fos. 1–8 is a Greek–Latin glossary.

[106] *Institutiones Grammaticales*: BN Lat. 10289 and 10290; Vatican, Biblioteca Apostolica Lat. 1480; *Periegesis*: BN Lat. 4839, fos. 1–20.

[107] Oxford, Bodleian Library Auct. F.4.32 (St Dunstan's Classbook), fos. 2–9.

[108] BL Harley 2719.

[109] Alcuin: Merseburg, Domstiftsbibliothek I.204; Smaragdus: BN Lat. 13029.

[110] Brett, 'Breton Latin literature', p. 11.

standard medieval curriculum developed, a curriculum based around the liberal arts, especially grammar.[111] What little we know of education in Wales at this time, or for that matter in Anglo-Saxon England, does not suggest the same pre-occupations.[112] Of the texts studied in ninth-century Brittany, only Gildas' *De Excidio* would have been quite out of place in a Frankish context. We are left to conclude that this educational revival was a home-grown Breton achievement, or that the manuscripts offer an indirect reflection of effective Carolingian influence. Perhaps it is not too far-fetched to speculate whether Salomon may have initiated and directed this revival, yet again copying the example of his Carolingian overlord.

The only way to assess how successful this educational revival may have been is to turn to the Breton corpus of saints' lives. This both fleshes out the picture, and suggests some further nuances. The heavy pedagogical emphasis on grammar directs our attention to the Latinity of ninth-century Breton hagiographers. Two writers' styles have been recently analysed, with notable results. The *Gesta Sanctorum Rotonensium* was written by an unknown author at Redon, after the death of the founder Conwoion but before the monks abandoned their monastery in fear of the Vikings.[113] His Latin is simple in both syntax and vocabulary, and often homiletic in quality. Nevertheless, it is also correct, generally conforming to the rules of classical Latin, free of both solecisms and elaborate rhetoric.[114] Although the *Gesta* is an idiosyncratic blend of hagiography and house-history which fits neatly into no established genre, it is in all respects except format typical of the mainstream of Carolingian hagiographical endeavour. At the other extreme, both figuratively and geo-graphically is the *Vita Pauli Aureliani* written in 884 by Wrmonoc, a monk of Landévennec, in response to a commission from the bishop of Saint-Pol. It is thus closely contemporary with the *Gesta Sanctorum Rotonensium* but comes from the other end of Brittany. From Wrdisten, his master at Landévennec, Wrmonoc learned a

---

[111] B. Bischoff, 'Die Bibliothek im Dienste der Schule', *Settimane*, 19 (1972), 385–415; J. J. Contreni, 'Going to school in Carolingian Europe', in *Aspects of Carolingian Learning*, ed. R. E. Sullivan (forthcoming). I am grateful to John Contreni for permission to cite this paper in advance of publication.

[112] Compare Lapidge, 'Latin learning in dark age Wales'; D. A. Bullough, 'The educational tradition in England from Alfred to Aelfric: teaching *utriusque linguae*', *Settimane*, 19 (1972), 453–94. [113] See introduction to *GSR*, pp. 1–11.

[114] Introduction to *GSR*, pp. 63, 70–1.

prose style in the tradition of the elaborate and highly rhetorical Latin of late antiquity as preserved in Britain, above all in the writings of Gildas.[115] As hagiographers and Latin stylists, Wrdisten and Wrmonoc had nothing in common with the norms of Carolingian hagiography; nor did they write for cult centres organised around the veneration of their saints' mortal remains, as Frankish hagiographers generally did.[116] Rather, from their monastic milieu, Wrdisten and Wrmonoc harked back to the grammatical and rhetorical traditions of the fifth and sixth centuries: they suggest a schoolroom where Gildas was a set text, and where Carolingian methods of education had not yet penetrated.

The work of Breton hagiographers also allows us to see that the extant manuscripts do not accurately represent the contents of the libraries to which these writers had access. The reading of the hagiographers is instructive in this respect. Wrdisten prefaced his paired prose and verse lives of Winwaloe (eponymous founder of Landévennec) with a list of his principal *auctores*: Augustine, Cassiodorus, Isidore, Gregory the Great, John Chrysostom, and Abbot Pymen (that is, the *Apophthegmata Patrum*).[117] Detailed textual work has refined and added to this list by revealing Wrdisten's great debt to Gregory the Great's homilies on Ezechiel and Isidore's *Sententiae*, whole paragraphs of both of which are quoted verbatim, and also his use of Augustine's *De Civitate Dei* and *De Magistro*, and Cassiodorus' *Expositio Psalmorum*. Among those authors whom Wrdisten used but did not name are Cassian, Eugenius of Toledo, Sulpicius Severus, Orosius, and Aldhelm. He also knew the Physiologus and the *Disticha Catonis*, and the monastic Rules of both Benedict and Columbanus. A special place in his writing is held by Virgil and Gildas. Both were quoted, but also exercised a deep stylistic influence over Wrdisten's verse and prose styles; from Gildas Wrdisten acquired his sense of the past.[118] A reading of Wrmonoc brings only one addition to this

---

[115] F. Kerlouégan, 'Approche stylistique du latin de la *Vita Pauli Aureliani*', in *Landévennec et le Monachisme Breton*, ed. Simon, pp. 207–17; Kerlouégan, 'Une mode stylistique'. The place of Gildas in Late Latin grammatical and rhetorical educational traditions is established by M. Lapidge, 'Gildas' education and the Latin culture of sub-Roman Britain', in *Gildas: New Approaches*, ed. Lapidge and Dumville, pp. 27–50.

[116] J. M. H. Smith, 'Oral and written: saints, miracles and relics in Brittany, c. 850–1250', *Speculum*, 65 (1990), 309–43.   [117] Wrdisten, '*Vita S. Winwaloei*', p. 174.

[118] The readings underlying the work of Wrdisten and other Breton hagiographers are identified by J. Raison de Cleuziou, 'De quelques sources de la vie de Saint Guénolé', *Bulletin et Mémoires de la Société d'Emulation des Côtes-du-Nord*, 88 (1960), 29–35; J.

list, but a significant one: knowledge of at least one line of Boethius' *De Consolatione Philosophiae*.[119] Of the surviving Breton manuscripts, only two gospel books and an incomplete computus table and calendar are securely attributed to Landévennec before its destruction by the Vikings in 914:[120] Wrdisten and Wrmonoc allow us to see how extensive were the classical and patristic resources available in westernmost Brittany.

When we turn eastwards to hagiographers living near the linguistic and political border zone with Francia, a somewhat different pattern emerges. Writing at Alet between 866 and 872, Bili's greatest debt was to Venantius Fortunatus, whose saints' lives he plagiarised mercilessly. He also borrowed passages from Smaragdus, from the *Vita S. Fursei*, the *Passio SS. Cosmae et Damiani* and the *Vita S. Silvestri*.[121] The subject matter and structure of his work shows a familiarity with the demands of a shrine housing the bodily relics of his subject, St Malo, and with the expectations of an audience attuned to the conventions of Carolingian hagiography.[122] A similar pattern of knowledge of the conventions of the mainstream of continental hagiography is also evident at Redon, where the author of the *Gesta Sanctorum Rotonensium* was much influenced by the Dialogues of Gregory the Great, and also had access to the account in the *Liber Pontificalis* of the life of the martyred Marcellinus, whose relics Redon

Raison de Cleuziou, 'Landévennec et les destinées de la Cornouaille', *Bulletin et Mémoires de la Société d'Emulation des Côtes-du-Nord*, 93 (1965), 7–26; F. Kerlouégan, 'Les citations d'auteurs latins profanes dans les vies des saints bretons carolingiennes', *EC*, 18 (1981), 181–95; F. Kerlouégan, 'Les citations d'auteurs latins chrétiens dans les vies des saints bretons carolingiennes', *EC*, 19 (1982), 215–57; N. Wright, 'Some further Vergilian borrowings in Breton hagiography of the Carolingian period', *EC*, 20 (1983), 161–75; N. Wright, 'Knowledge of Christian Latin poets and historians in early medieval Brittany', *EC*, 23 (1986), 163–85.
[119] F. Kerlouégan, 'Une citation de la *Consolatio Philosphiae* (III, mètre 9) de Boèce dans la *vita Pauli* d'Uurmonoc', *EC*, 24 (1987), 309–14. I am grateful to Neil Wright for his opinion that, of the passage of Boethius cited by Kerlouégan, we may accept that Wrmonoc knew the third line.
[120] Manuscripts of certain Landévennec origin are the Harkness gospels (New York Public Library 115) and the Leofric gospels (Oxford, Bodleian Library Auct. D.2.16), the incomplete calendar and computus in Copenhagen, Konegelige Bibliotek Thott 239, and the Amalarius written in 952, now Cambridge, Corpus Christi College 192.
[121] See L. Duchesne, 'La vie de Saint Malo: étude critique', *Revue Celtique*, 11 (1890), 1–22; A. Poncelet, 'Une source de la vie de S. Malo par Bili', *Analecta Bollandiana*, 24 (1905), 483–6, and the crucial review of Le Duc's edition of Bili, *Analecta Bollandiana*, 101 (1983), 194–6. There is no trace of any classical author in Bili. Kerlouégan, 'Citations d'auteurs latins profanes', p. 192.
[122] Smith, 'Oral and written', pp. 331–4.

acquired. The anonymous author also knew two works of Bede, the *In Lucae Evangelium Expositio* and his *Homelia I in Quadragesima*. As for style and diction, Gregory the Great and Virgil were the two writers whose influence in the *Gesta* is most noticeable.[123]

Hagiography reveals something of the contents of the libraries available to Breton writers. More than that, however, it suggests strongly that Carolingian cultural influences were not felt uniformly throughout Brittany. In terms of their Latinity, their literary resources, and their very notion of the appropriate structure and content of a saint's life, writers in the east differed markedly from those in the west. In churches within easy reach of the Frankish lands such as Alet and Redon, writers had available books comparable in nature if not in number to those of Frankish churches, and produced hagiography which is unremarkable by Carolingian standards. In the west, on the other hand, the libraries and Latinity suggest that cultural contact with Frankish learning of the eighth and ninth centuries was very much less. All that both regions clearly did have in common was an interest in Virgil. The pattern which emerges from this, of a gradual westwards diffusion of Carolingian learning need hardly surprise. What it does do, however, is provide a cultural framework within which further work on dating and locating early Breton manuscripts may proceed.

The Viking invasions left Breton churches unoccupied for one to two decades in the tenth century, and aborted the gradual dissemination of Carolingian influence. When Breton manuscript production resumed after *c.* 950, it did so under the influence of the Anglo–Saxon churches to which Breton monks had fled.[124] For the period up until *c.* 910, however, the combined evidence of manuscripts and hagiography indicates some of the effects of the movement of pilgrims and penitents, books and relics between Brittany and other continental churches. Slowly but surely the region was beginning a cultural and intellectual reorientation towards its landward neighbours. That insular influence remained strong in the practical handbooks compiled for priests suggests either that all the surviving manuscripts of

---

[123] Introduction to *GSR*, pp. 64–9.
[124] To be elucidated by D. N. Dumville's forthcoming paper on the Corpus Amalarius in the memorial volume for L. Fleuriot.

canonical and penitential material come from nearer to western than to eastern Brittany, or that Carolingian influence was more easily absorbed in classrooms and libraries than in pastoral centres. In Brittany, metropolitan and local culture interacted with a complexity that has yet to be fully explored, but which certainly provides a cultural counterpoint to the jurisdictional tensions which under Nominoe and Salomon had set Breton and Frankish bishops at loggerheads.

Although there is no manuscript evidence that Carolingian legislation for the reform of ecclesiastical organisation or the improvement of pastoral care reached Brittany before the Viking invasions, some knowledge of the norms upheld in Carolingian reform legislation did filter through, primarily through correspondence with the papacy. But it is a moot point whether church life was touched in any fundamental way by awareness of the standards of the Frankish church. When the popes' letters are set against the charter evidence of ecclesiastical organisation and clerical behaviour in eastern Brittany, a gulf between canonical norm and everyday reality becomes immediately apparent. Whatever education and training some Breton clergy may have received, the practical work of local priests was not thereby affected. Even in the heartlands of the Carolingian empire, Carolingian ideals of reform may never have made appreciable impression on lay society; in Brittany even their impact on the clergy was restricted.[125] And, just as Breton bishops were at the mercy of princely power politics, so too at village level, the church remained intricately knitted into secular society.

In 774, Hadrian I gave Charlemagne a copy of the canon law collection in use in Rome, now known as the Dionysio-Hadriana. When the Frankish king laid the foundations of his programme of church reform in 789, he promulgated in the *Admonitio Generalis* selected canons of the Dionysio-Hadriana, thereby establishing the legal basis of the social transformation he hoped to engender.[126] Although the Dionysio-Hadriana was copied

[125] Compare J. L. Nelson, 'On the limits of the Carolingian renaissance', *Studies in Church History*, 14 (1977), 51–67 (reprinted in her *Politics and Ritual*, pp. 49–67).
[126] MGH Capit. I.53–62, no. 22.

extensively, it nevertheless had to compete with other, older canon law collections in use in parts of Francia, which it never entirely displaced.[127] One of the regions where it is not known to have circulated at all is Neustria, and there is no manuscript evidence that it was copied even at Tours itself.[128] In law as in learning, the Carolingian ideal of religious unity was tempered and constrained by traditional usages and regional habits.

A statement of the law of the church did nevertheless reach Brittany. At about the same time as, or shortly before, the synod of *Coitlouh*, all the Breton bishops together had written to Leo IV asking for clarification on a long list of subjects in what may have been the first formal communication between Breton churchmen and the papacy. Leo answered with a compendium of information of exemplary clarity and brevity, in which he set out the essence of canon law on the issues which the Bretons had raised.[129] This wide array of concerns included a desire to know to whom ecclesiastical status belonged and how a bishop should govern his diocese, what Rome's teaching was on the bringing of gifts to church councils, on divination and witchcraft, on marriage, on church property alienated to laymen, on the payment of tithes, on fasting, and, finally, on what constituted the corpus of canon law recognised in Rome. The topics covered by Leo's letter touch on many of the issues that were central to the Carolingian reforms: recognition of the clergy as a separate *ordo*, pastoral care, relations between clergy and laity, the management of church property, the conduct of the laity, and church law were all subjects of repeated legislation by Frankish kings and synods. The queries which prompted Leo's reply imply a Breton episcopate stimulated into action by a growing awareness of its own idiosyncrasy and of others' norms of ecclesiastical life. We have here a convenient agenda for enquiry into the state of pastoral care in ninth-century Brittany.

---

[127] On the significance of the Dionysio-Hadriana see McKitterick, *Frankish Church*, pp. 1–5. The continued use of older regional canon law collections is stressed by Kottje, 'Einheit und Vielfalt'; also R. McKitterick, 'Knowledge of canon law in the Frankish kingdoms before 789: the manuscript evidence', *Journal of Theological Studies*, n.s., 36 (1985), 97–117; H. Mordek, *Die Collectio Vetus Gallica: die älteste systematische Kanonessammlung des fränkischen Gallien*, Beiträge zur Geschichte und Quellenkunde des Mittelalters 1 (Berlin, 1975).

[128] Kottje, 'Einheit und Vielfalt', p. 337.

[129] Leo IV, ep. 16, MGH Epp. v.593–6. The value of this letter as a concise summary of the church's teaching is indicated by the heavy use which Gratian made of it: Ullmann, *Growth of Papal Government*, p. 176.

In his reply to the Breton bishops' final question Leo listed succinctly the canonical and decretal authorities used in the Dionysio-Hadriana. However, the actual text of the Dionysio-Hadriana is not known to have reached Brittany before the second half of the tenth century.[130] Throughout the Carolingian period, Brittany was one of those regions where older, and in this case non-Frankish, ecclesiastical law remained influential: the collections of British and Irish penitential tracts which circulated in Brittany in the ninth and tenth centuries have already been mentioned. Such texts were considered suspect by Frankish legislators, whose disapproval of Irish penitentials was nevertheless generally ineffectual.[131] As in other continental centres of heavy Irish influence such as Sankt Gallen, Frankish and papal influence did not displace local usages: in their legal basis, Breton churches retained their own identity.

Furthermore, we may suspect that in general, Leo IV's guidelines had minimal practical impact in Brittany. Where charters and other papal letters facilitate the study of ecclesiastical life in the later ninth and early tenth centuries, there certainly emerges a picture which is a far cry from the ideals which popes and Carolingian reformers strove to promote. Ignorance of canon law and a clergy scarcely distinguishable from the laity were probably endemic. A letter of John VIII to the bishop of Vannes in 875 offers a preliminary indication of this. The pope expressed concern that the bishop had even considered letting a priest guilty of homicide continue in his ministry, and had tried to persuade the pope to sanction this.[132]

If this is any indication of the ecclesiastical climate in Brittany, then it is little surprise that the issue addressed by the bishops' first question to Leo IV – to whom ecclesiastical rank pertained – was raised on various occasions. Bretons were evidently uncertain what constituted a valid ordination, for Salomon consulted Nicholas I about those priests initially ordained by Gislard whom

---

[130] Glossed in Old Breton, BN Lat. 3182 is a manuscript of the late tenth century which contains the Dionysio-Hadriana and the *Collectio Vetus Gallica* along with much canonical and penitential material of Irish origin.

[131] R. E. Reynolds, 'Unity and diversity in Carolingian canon law collections: the case of the *Collectio Hibernensis* and its derivatives', in *Carolingian Essays*, ed. U.-R. Blumenthal (Washington, DC, 1983), pp. 99–135; Kottje, 'Überlieferung und Rezeption der irischen Bussbücher'.

[132] John VIII, ep. 51, MGH Epp. VII.303–4.

Actard had reconsecrated, and some monks obtained a papal ruling that their ordination at the hands of their abbot was valid.[133]

As for the diocesan ministry itself, Leo had simply said that a bishop should govern with the help of his priests and clergy. There is, however, remarkably little evidence for how this was carried out. Certainly the bishops of Vannes had archdeacons to assist them, who sometimes appear as witnesses to property transactions and presumably also assisted their bishop in running the diocese, as they did in Frankish regions.[134] We know too that the intensification of Viking attacks in the later ninth century put at risk the ability of the bishop of Vannes to fulfil all his sacramental duties, for he granted the abbot of Redon permission to send his monks to another bishop for ordination, were it too dangerous for them to journey to Vannes.[135] Of day-to-day pastoral work we know nothing, except that in matters as serious as homicide episcopal jurisdiction might be invoked. In the case of a layman who had killed his three sons, the bishop of Alet negotiated an appropriate penance with the pope; John VIII's letter about the priest who had committed homicide presumes that the bishop of Vannes had ruled on the issue before the case caught papal attention.[136]

Of the organisation of the church at local level, rather more can be said, at least for the area covered by the Redon charters. The *plebs* was clearly the primary unit of religious organisation in Breton-speaking areas. Several *plebes* contained dependent chapels in addition to the main church of the *plebs*, sometimes as many as

---

[133] For the former, see Nicholas I, ep. 107, MGH Epp. VI.621. For the latter see John VIII, ep. 44, MGH Epp. VII.299–300. John VIII's letter does not survive in the extant portion of his register. Its superscription (*Magno archiepscopo*) and probably also the attribution to John VIII appear to be late eleventh-century tamperings to an authentic papal letter of uncertain date. Dol is known to have manufactured evidence of its archiepiscopal status during the pontificate of Gregory VII, and in the twelfth century, the church of Tours argued that the superscription of this particular letter was false. The letter's transmission is consistent with this. It survives in two places: (i) BL Add. 8873, a twelfth-century collection of papal letters known to contain falsified documents, which was compiled by canonists probably at Rome, and (ii) the seventeenth-century transcription of the (now lost) twelfth-century dossier from Tours pertaining to the dispute with Dol. P. Fournier and G. Le Bras, *Histoire des Collections Canoniques en Occident depuis les Fausses Décrétales jusqu'au Decret de Gratien*, 2 vols. (Paris, 1931–2), II.155–63; W. Ullmann, 'Nos si aliquid incompetenter...Some observations on the register fragments of Leo IV in the Collectio Britannica', *Ephemerides Iuris Canonici*, 9 (1953), 279–87; Lot, 'Festien', p. 31, n. 3.

[134] CR 247, 278.   [135] CR A46.

[136] Nicholas I, ep. 129, MGH Epp. VI.650; John VIII, ep. 51, MGH Epp. VII.303–4.

seven.[137] Also, a *plebs* characteristically had a staff of up to four priests, some of whom had a hereditary interest in the local priesthood; occasional references to deacons and local clergy in minor orders can also be found.[138]

Unlike many parts of ninth-century Francia, where disputes about parish boundaries and the formation of new parish units were both common, the network of rural churches and their priestly staffs in south-eastern Brittany appears to have been unchanging from pre-Carolingian times until at least the late tenth century.[139] The pressure put upon Frankish bishops to create new parishes came in part from landlords (ecclesiastical as well as lay) who wanted churches to serve their own estates and tenants. The result of this struggle for lordship over the church at the most local level was a parochial network which increasingly conformed to configurations of landowning.[140] In Brittany, on the other hand, only from the middle of the eleventh century did seigneurial pressures begin to modify the remarkably stable network of local pastoral care.[141] In Breton villages in the Carolingian period,

[137] Redon charters mention two adjacent churches within the *plebs* of Langon, the *ecclesia sancti Petri* and the *ecclesia sancti Veneris* (CR 124; Morice, *Preuves*, I.271–2); and at Bains an *antiqua ecclesia* at Espileuc in addition to the main church of the *plebs* (CR 2, 32, 199, 271). At the time of its donation to Saint-Maur-de-Glanfeuil, the huge *plebs* of Anast had seven *capellae* in addition to the *ecclesia sancti Petri* (Planiol, 'Donation d'Anowareth', pp. 233–4).

[138] Davies, 'Priests and rural communities', pp. 187–90 for details. Additional cases of men in minor orders are the *custos ecclesiae* at Guillac and the *hostiarii* at Ruffiac and Molac. CR 136, 144, 251.

[139] On the creation of new Frankish parishes and the delimitation of their boundaries see J.-F. Lemarignier, 'Quelques remarques sur l'organisation ecclésiastique de la Gaule du VIIᵉ à la fin du IXᵉ siècle principalement au nord de la Loire', *Settimane*, 13 (1966), 451–86; J. Semmler, 'Zehntgebot und Pfarrtermination in karolingischer Zeit', in *Aus Kirche und Reich: Studien zu Theologie, Politik und Recht im Mittelalter. Festschrift für Friedrich Kempf*, ed. H. Mordek (Sigmaringen, 1983), pp. 33–44. In Brittany there is no trace whatsoever of these processes, and the network of *plebes* traceable in the tenth century appears to be identical with that of the opening years of the ninth century.

[140] In general, see M. Chaume, 'Le mode de constitution et de délimitation des paroisses rurales aux temps mérovingiens et carolingiens', *Revue Mabillon*, 27 (1937), 61–73, and 28 (1928), 1–9; J.-F. Lemarignier, 'Encadrement religieux des campagnes et conjoncture politique dans les régions du royaume de France situées au nord de la Loire, de Charles le Chauve aux derniers carolingiens', *Settimane*, 28 (1980), 765–800, and for a careful regional case study, G. Fournier, *Le Peuplement rural en Basse Auvergne durant le haut Moyen Age* (Paris, 1962), pp. 401–75.

[141] Chédeville and Tonnerre, *Bretagne Féodale*, pp. 284–95; Planiol, *Institutions*, III.193–6; M. Duval, 'En Bretagne, recherche sur la formation des paroisses entre l'Ille et la Vilaine, XI–XVIᵉ siècle', in *109ᵉ Congrès National des Sociétés Savantes, Dijon 1984. Section philologique et historique* (Paris, 1985), pp. 93–110.

regulatory and judicial power structures did not interlock with seigneurial interests to form any coherent hierarchical ordering; the division of the countryside into *plebes* was independent of patterns of landowning and landlordship.[142]

Nevertheless, changes in the seigneurial matrix within which priests worked did begin to affect local Breton clergy in the course of the ninth century. The rapid growth of Redon's interests started to erode the close bond between priests and their communities. The abbey, in effect, bought out local priests. It encouraged them to donate their personal landed property and sometimes also land which they held for the benefit of the local *plebs* church, to be held from the monastery on precarial lease for the remainder of their active life, and gave them in return a place in the monastic community as old age and death approached.[143] Also, as rights of lordship over *plebes* were granted to Redon, these grants may well have brought with them unspecified rights over the churches within these *plebes*.[144]

To what extent the churches and chapels in Breton *plebes* were centres for the care of souls and pastoral activity is unclear. Such evidence for sacramental provision as there is almost all relates to Redon and other high status churches or clerics.[145] Certainly masses were said and psalms sung in *plebes* churches, but beyond that, there is no evidence for how they functioned.[146] Leo IV had told the Breton bishops that tithes were to be paid to baptismal churches, but there is no evidence that *plebs* churches were baptismal churches, and there is certainly no reference to tithes anywhere before the middle of the tenth century.[147] It is a fair guess that, had a tithing system been established, Redon would have sought to acquire rights to tithe as eagerly as many Frankish

---

[142] Compare above, pp. 30–1.   [143] Davies, *Small Worlds*, pp. 190–2.

[144] For the grant of a *plebs* to Redon bringing with it rights over the church of the *plebs*, see above, p. 134.

[145] Administration of extreme unction by a bishop: CR 235; masses and psalms for the dead at Redon: CR A44; names of the dead commemorated by the cathedral confraternity of Dol: William of Malmesbury, *Gesta Pontificum Anglorum*, v.249, ed. N. E. S. A. Hamilton, Rolls Series 52 (London, 1870), pp. 399–400.

[146] CR 143.

[147] There is one reference to tithes in a document of 944–52 for the Breton-speaking area of the Guérande peninsula, *Cartulaire de Landévennec*, 25, pp. 562–4. The earliest reference from the Redon archive is a charter of restitution of tithes from the very end of the tenth century, CR 357. Such grants are increasingly common in the eleventh century.

monasteries were doing in the ninth century.[148] Also, we do not know where villagers in the Redon area were buried any more than we know where they were baptised.[149] Members of the princely family and a few particularly powerful men were buried at Redon or its dependency at Plélan,[150] but amidst the wealth of topographical detail in the Redon charters, there is a conspicuous lack of reference to ordinary burials in or adjacent to the rural churches of the *plebes*, or for that matter anywhere else. Not until the eleventh century do Breton charters begin to mention cemeteries.[151]

Frankish kings from Pippin III onwards made the payment of tithes compulsory, and this legislation was a significant spur to the emergence of a network of territorially delimited parishes.[152] But in much of Europe, however, a full parochial network, as defined by rights to tithes, baptism, and burial, did not emerge until the eleventh century or even later.[153] In Italy, England, and parts of Germany, an older two-tier system of baptismal mother churches and dependent chapels prevailed into the eleventh or even twelfth

---

[148] Compare G. Constable, *Monastic Tithes from their Origins to the Twelfth Century* (Cambridge, 1964), pp. 57–63.

[149] No early medieval cemetery has been excavated in the area of the Redon charters. At Langon, both early medieval churches were on the site of a late Roman cemetery, but it is not reported when burial there ceased. Still standing, the *ecclesia Sancti Veneris* (now the chapel of Sainte-Agathe) incorporates part of a Gallo-Roman mausoleum. A. Grenier, *Manuel d'Archéologie Gallo-Romaine*, 3 vols. (Paris, 1931–58), III.530–2.

Two early medieval cemeteries which have been excavated in the north and west of Brittany suggest that burial did not take place in or around churches in the pre-Viking period. At Saint-Urnel on the south-westernmost coast, the cemetery remained in use from the sixth to the twelfth century. A chapel was built within it late in the tenth century, followed by a bell foundry in the eleventh. The site never became a parish church. P.-R. Giot and J.-L. Monnier, 'Le cimetière des anciens bretons de Saint-Urnel ou Saint-Saturnin en Plomeur (Finistère)', *Gallia*, 35 (1977), 141–71; P.-R. Giot and J. L. Monnier, 'Les oratoires des anciens bretons de Saint-Urnel ou Saint-Saturnin en Plomeur (Finistère)', *Archéologie Médiévale*, 8 (1978), 55–93. At the second site, the Ile Lavret in the estuary of the Trieux on the northern coast, an early medieval cemetery is adjacent to a late Roman domestic site which continued in use in the early Middle Ages. The island is traditionally associated with the hermitage of St Budoc but despite wishful thinking there is no good evidence that the site was an ecclesiastical one before the later Middle Ages. This too was never a parish church. P.-R. Giot, 'Saint Budoc on the Isle of Lavret, Brittany', in *The Early Church in Western Britain and Ireland*, ed. S. M. Pearce, British Archaeological Reports, British Series 102 (Oxford, 1982), pp. 197–210; Giot, '"Insula quae Laurea appellatur"'.

[150] CR 236, 241, 243, 260, A15.

[151] For example, CR 323, 326, 338, 364. These are typical eleventh-century restitutions of churches, their land, tithes, and cemeteries.

[152] Semmler, 'Zehntgebot and Pfarrtermination'.

[153] See the summary comments of Reynolds, *Kingdoms and Communities*, pp. 81–8.

century, and only broke down as large numbers of new urban or seigneurial churches were founded. Pastoral care in early medieval Wales may have been organised similarly.[154] Breton *plebes* would appear to have been a variant on this widespread, traditional organisation; all that is missing from the surviving evidence is any indication of whether the *plebes* churches were also the episcopal churches to which the baptismal chrism was taken.

Carolingian insistence on the payment of tithes was directed towards ensuring the livelihood of the parish clergy. The indigence of local priests was often the result of lay usurpation of ecclesiastical lands and revenues, and much legislation tried to limit priests' dependence on landlords.[155] By contrast, the financial situation of the Breton clergy was very much more secure, and their advantaged position reflects the fundamentally different place of priests and churches in local patterns of landowning. In the first instance, lay control and abuse of churches and church property was not the severe problem which it was for Frankish churchmen. Although small Breton monasteries were sometimes bought, sold, or donated, evidence for lay control of local non-monastic churches is rare, and such evidence as there is mostly comes from the Nantais rather than from Breton-speaking regions.[156] In the second place, priests numbered among the more notable landowners of the village communities of south-eastern Brittany, accumulating their own land by inheritance or purchase and through pledges that were never redeemed. Indeed, they were often the ones who had cash to spare to make loans to other villagers. Their relative prosperity went hand-in-hand with prominence in other aspects of village life: witnessing transactions, sometimes standing as surety, possibly presiding at gatherings in place of the machtiern, acting as the representatives of powerful

---

[154] H. Pryce, 'Pastoral care in early medieval Wales', to be published in *Pastoral Care*, ed. Blair and Sharpe. I am grateful to Huw Pryce for letting me see this article in advance of its publication.

[155] Amann, *Epoque Carolingienne*, pp. 91–2; W. Hartmann, 'Der rechtliche Zustand der Kirchen auf dem Lande: die Eigenkirche in der fränkischen Gesetzgebung des 7. bis 9. Jahrhunderts', *Settimane*, 28 (1980), 397–441.

[156] For transactions concerning *monasteriola* see CR 11, 97, A4, A26, A40, A45, and *Chronique de Nantes*, 25, p. 75. In the Nantais, Redon acquired by donation the church dedicated to St Mary in Grandchamp in 849, which had earlier been bought by the donor and his wife from a priest: CR 33, 42. Several churches in and near Nantes were given to Landévennec by Alan II in a charter of 944–52: *Cartulaire de Landévennec*, 25, pp. 562–4. The only reference to the purchase and subsequent donation of a local church west of the Vilaine is a charter of 954 referring to Le Saint in the diocese of Quimper, *Cartulaire de Landévennec*, 24, pp. 560–2.

laymen.[157] Whereas Frankish synods worried about the economic dependence of penurious clergy on landlords and legislated against the ordination of serfs, Breton priests enjoyed a prominent place amidst the landowners of the communities they served.

No texts elucidate relations between the priests of each *plebs* and their diocesan bishop. Presumably he ordained them, but their strong, even hereditary ties to their *plebes* and their relative affluence must have made it hard for a bishop to exercise the degree of supervision to which Frankish bishops aspired. If we knew where baptisms were performed we might have some idea of how the ecclesiastical hierarchy was structured in its lower, local, ranks. As it is, the local ecclesiastical organisation, such as we can reconstruct it, reflects none of the guidelines for episcopal supervision and financial organisation which Leo IV outlined. The place of priests in Breton village communities was both dissimilar from the conditions widespread in Francia and a sharp contrast to the norms of Carolingian ideals. Neither Carolingian conquest nor growing contact with the wider world affected ecclesiastical organisation. Leo IV's letter, together with other papal letters of pastoral guidance to Breton bishops, indicates that the upper echelons of the Breton ecclesiastical hierarchy were aware of and open to changing currents elsewhere on the continent. That awareness, however, was not translated into adoption of the canon law of the Romano-Frankish church, or into any restructuring of the close involvement of local priests with the life of the communities they served. At village level, churches remained intricately knitted into secular society, and mirrored the localism that rendered Carolingian Brittany distinctive.

Regino reminds us to pay attention to the distinctive features of ecclesiastical life in any early medieval province, and in commenting on the wide variety of ecclesiastical customs to be found within the Carolingian world, he perhaps had Brittany in mind.[158] Manifestations of Breton particularism were a refusal to accept the canon law of Rome in matters where jurisdictional authority and control of the church were at stake, non-parochial organisation of the relatively prosperous local clergy, and an

[157] Davies, 'Priests and rural communities', pp. 182–7 for details of all these points.
[158] Werner, 'Arbeitsweise', for the contacts at Angers which gave Regino intimate knowledge of Breton affairs.

intellectual life in which Carolingian and insular currents mingled. In Brittany we see what happened when high-minded official ideals of hierarchy and reform ran up against different conventions and traditions. The tension between centre and periphery is clear.

Implicit throughout this chapter has been another theme: that it is not possible to talk in any meaningful way about 'the Breton church' in the early Middle Ages. Cultural and political differences all ran deeper than the obvious linguistic divide between Breton and 'proto-Romance'. Support for the archiepiscopal endeavours of Dol, tastes in Latin learning, the functioning of saints' cults: all varied perceptibly within the Breton-speaking region. For the most part, Breton bishops were neither actively involved in the affairs of the archdiocese of Tours, nor did they share any collegiate identity as a distinct ecclesiastical province on their own. The only occasions when they are known to have come together were at princely behest. There is no evidence that a vigorous episcopal administration gave rigour and coherence to the clerical hierarchy in any individual diocese. Within the area which we may suppose to have been unified by Breton speech, ecclesiastical customs and learned culture suggest only an incoherent patchwork, in which the keynote was at all times intense localism. The lack of evidence for any self-conscious Breton political identity becomes more explicable when we realise that little cultural or religious cohesion underpinned the movement towards political unification. Salomon ruled a principality which was not unified in any of Regino's set of ethnic indicators, race, custom, language, or laws.

Chapter 7

THE END OF CAROLINGIAN BRITTANY

In the half century after Charles the Bald's death, profound changes transformed the political landscape of the West Frankish kingdom. By the time his grandson Charles the Simple was captured and imprisoned in 922, Charles the Bald's aggressive and powerful kingship had been reduced to the direct rule of the lands between the middle Seine and the Meuse, whilst further afield the king exercised a suzerainty that was generally recognised but carried virtually no powers of government or practical clout. In the intervening fifty years, kings not of the Carolingian dynasty had come to power, notably Odo son of Robert the Strong in West Francia (888–98) and Boso (Charles the Bald's brother-in-law) in Provence (879–87). Carolingian power was now neither uncontested nor widely effective.

This half-century was also one of persistent and often devastating Viking raids throughout atlantic Europe, of continuing tensions and conflicts within the Carolingian dynasty itself, and of the crystallisation of much of West Francia into aristocratic lordships controlled by the descendants of those to whom Charles the Bald had shown greatest generosity. All these processes were interlinked. A series of political crises brought about by the early death of young kings, royal determination to challenge East Frankish rulers for access to the ancient fiscal lands of Lotharingia, and the pressing need for vigorous local military leadership to combat the Vikings – all these gave West Frankish magnates the opportunity to consolidate and extend their own lands, to feud with their neighbours and increasingly to exercise the offices and powers of royal government in their own name.[1]

---

[1] Important, up-to-date surveys are K.-F. Werner, 'Westfranken-Frankreich unter den Spätkarolingern und frühen Kapetingern (888–1060)', in *Handbuch der europäischen Geschichte*, ed. T. Schieder (Stuttgart, 1976), pp. 731–83; J. Dunbabin, *France in the Making, 843–1180* (Oxford, 1985), pp. 1–123.

The territorial principalities of which medieval France was constituted originated in this way.

In such circumstances, Charles the Bald's successors can hardly be blamed for failing to exercise as vigorous an overlordship over the most peripheral regions of their kingdom as Charles himself had done. At the same time as direct royal control over the lands between the Seine and the Loire dwindled, Brittany stabilised in the form it would retain until the reign of Philip Augustus. The province passed from the Carolingian to the Capetian era as a compact territorial lordship stretching as far as the eastern boundaries of the counties of Rennes and Nantes, effectively independent of any royal hegemony, but instead arousing the attention of aggressive lords of Anjou and Normandy, and linked also to the sphere of influence of West Saxon (and subsequently Anglo-Norman) England. In the late ninth and early tenth centuries the changes in Breton political life which had been gathering apace during Charles the Bald's reign finally gelled, and Brittany's new identity as a single principality, both Frankish and Breton, was affirmed.

Although the outcome of the troubled years of the late ninth and early tenth centuries is clear, the changes themselves are less easy to document. As Carolingian horizons shrank, so the flow of information to major churches diminished, and chroniclers became more and more regional in outlook. As general assemblies ceased to meet, and as royal itineraries ventured ever more rarely south of the Seine, so the opportunities for Neustrian churches to procure royal diplomas were reduced. In Brittany itself, the number of private charters in the Carolingian section of Redon's archive from the years after 875 is only a small proportion of the earlier abundance. Knowledge of Viking raids in Brittany is patchy – and mostly derived from non-Breton or from very late sources. Only the sketchiest of political narratives can be reconstructed for the tenth century; as for charter evidence, not until the early eleventh century is it once again possible to use such material to reconstruct Breton social and economic life. A virtual lacuna in the documentation marks the end of Carolingian Brittany.

BRITTANY, NEUSTRIA, AND THE WANING OF CAROLINGIAN LORDSHIP

From a staunchly pro-Carolingian point of view in the late tenth century, no ambiguity attended the status of Brittany. In the eyes of Richer, writing at Reims in the 990s, Brittany was quite simply 'adjacent to and held in benefice from Gaul'.[2] In commenting thus, Richer evinced more nostalgia and wishful thinking than appreciation of the intricate reality of politics in western Francia at the turn of the millennium. Charles the Bald had been the last Carolingian to exercise any real influence or control over the Bretons, and Louis IV d'Outremer (936–52) was the last Carolingian to receive homage from a Breton duke. The next time homage was performed was in 1199. No French king before Philip Augustus equalled Charles the Bald's influence over Brittany.[3]

How did this relaxation of the bonds of overlordship come about? As far as the evidence permits us to see, it was as much as anything the dynastic difficulties and succession disputes of the Carolingians themselves which hindered them from taking a more active interest in Brittany. For the Bretons' part, their own internal difficulties after Salomon's death, coupled with increasing Viking onslaughts, meant an end to the former habits of raiding Neustria or intervening actively in the rivalries and wranglings of Frankish magnates. Preoccupation with defence and with internal crises characterised Bretons and Franks alike: the narrowing of horizons was mutual.

Nevertheless, it took a full generation or more for Neustria to achieve a new political configuration. During the reigns of Charles the Bald's immediate successors, Louis the Stammerer (877–9) and the latter's young sons Louis III (879–82) and Carloman (879–84), aristocratic rivalries whose roots lay in the later years of Charles the Bald's reign still sucked the Bretons into the forum of Neustrian unrest.[4] When Charles the Bald died suddenly in October 877, all the leading magnates of his kingdom were in revolt against him. The efforts of Louis the Stammerer to

---

[2] Richer, *Histoire de France*, I.4, ed. R. Latouche, 2 vols., Les Classiques de l'Histoire de France au Moyen Age 12, 17 (Paris, 1930–37), I.14.

[3] M. Jones, 'The Capetians and Brittany', *Historical Research*, 63 (1990), 1–16, esp. pp. 5–6.

[4] Werner, 'Gauzlin von Saint-Denis'; Airlie, 'Political behaviour', pp. 238–56, 267–74.

inaugurate his reign by casting aside those powerful and trusted few on whom his father had increasingly relied generated yet more mistrust.[5] Three of the small inner band of Charles the Bald's six close associates – Bernard, marquis of Gothia, Conrad, count of Paris, and Gauzlin, abbot of Saint-Denis – found themselves suddenly out of favour whereas Hugh the Abbot, Boso of Vienne and Bernard Hairypaws, count of the Auvergne, reaped the benefit. Hugh the Abbot was the man who had scooped up most of the Neustrian *honores* of Robert the Strong after the latter's death at Brissarthe.[6] Gauzlin, son of Rorigo of Le Mans, had long-standing family interests in Neustria, as did his nephew, Bernard of Gothia. In the spring of 878, a few months after Louis the Stammerer's coronation, open conflict broke out over the possession of certain Neustrian lands and *honores*. Hugh the Abbot used his influence with Louis to have the king march with his army against the Neustrian rebels, Gauzlin's brother's sons and Bernard of Gothia's brother. It seems that 'some of the Bretons' (perhaps either the faction of Judicael or that of Alan?) made common cause with the rebels, for when Gauzlin's brother Gauzfrid mediated between his sons and Louis the Stammerer, he also managed to persuade *pars de Brittonibus* to promise their fidelity to the West Frankish king.[7] Frankish lordship was recognised by the Bretons, as it had been in Charles the Bald's reign. But this was the last occasion on which the Bretons are known to have been drawn into the rivalries which set Neustrian magnates at loggerheads in their search to secure their *honores* and increase their access to royal patronage at each other's expense. Thereafter, the parameters of Neustrian politics gradually began to shift.

To deal with Neustrian unrest and with the Viking threat, Louis the Stammerer had been persuaded in 878 to move south of the Seine, as far as Tours, and the Bretons came to pledge their loyalty here.[8] In general, only ever when the West Frankish king was himself in Neustria did the opportunity exist for the renewal of Breton oaths of fidelity or the close supervision of the Neustrian aristocracy. Yet more and more, the West Frankish kings confined themselves to their Seine valley estates, or turned north-eastwards to defend their interests in Lotharingia. Except

[5] *AB*, a. 877, pp. 216, 218–19.
[6] *AB*, a. 866, 868, pp. 132, 141–2; Regino, *Chronicon*, a. 867, p. 93.
[7] *AB*, a. 878, p. 222.   [8] *AB*, a. 878, p. 222.

for Odo, none of Charles the Bald's successors had such a persistently wide-ranging itinerary as he.[9] Thus, when Neustria was not the focus of royal interests, the Bretons were left to their own devices, as were the Frankish landowners of the region.

After a reign of only eighteen months, Louis the Stammerer died in April 879, with the Breton dispute between Alan and Judicael still unresolved. The struggle for the West Frankish succession which centred around his two elder sons, Louis III and Carloman, was in effect a struggle between the two aristocratic factions which Louis the Stammerer had set at each other's throats. The invitation to intervene issued by Gauzlin and Conrad to the East Frankish king, Louis the Younger, ensured that the centre of political activity shifted from Neustria to western Lotharingia.[10] This time, the conflict seems to have passed the Bretons by. Although Louis III was confirmed in possession of the northern half of the West Frankish kingdom (including Neustria) by the partition effected at Amiens in March 880, the young king faced as immediate priorities Boso's claim to the crown for himself and the Vikings in the Somme valley. Only thereafter, in the spring of 882, could he turn to Neustria and the Bretons. Hincmar makes clear Louis' intention of receiving the Breton leaders, presumably with the aim of asserting his lordship over them : but the king died at Tours, apparently before the planned meeting with the Bretons had taken place.[11]

After Louis III's demise, the entire West Frankish kingdom was ruled by his brother Carloman until he too died in 884. Thereupon the West Frankish magnates offered the crown to the last surviving grandson of Louis the Pious, the emperor Charles the Fat. Across the English Channel, the compiler of the Anglo-Saxon chronicle noted the change of ruler and commented that Charles the Fat succeeded to the entire West Frankish kingdom as Charlemagne had had it, except for Brittany.[12] There is certainly no direct evidence that Charles the Fat ever had any contact with the Bretons during his visit to his western realm in 886.

---

[9] This is evident from *Recueil des Actes de Louis II le Bègue, Louis III et Carloman, Rois de France (877–884)*, ed. F. Grat, J. de Font-Réaulx, G. Tessier, and R.-H. Bautier (Paris, 1978), and *Recueil des Actes d'Eudes, Roi de France (888–898)*, ed. R.-H. Bautier (Paris, 1967), esp. pp. cliv–clvii.

[10] Discussed in detail by Werner, 'Gauzlin von Saint-Denis'.

[11] *AB*, a. 882, p. 246.

[12] *Two of the Anglo-Saxon Chronicles Parallel*, ed. J. Earle and C. Plummer, 2 vols. (Oxford, 1892–9), I.78, a. 885.

Nevertheless, circumstantial detail suggests that, despite an initial failure to secure Breton recognition of his rule, Charles the Fat may indeed have had contact with Alan I, and possibly even recognised him as a client ruler in the same way that Charles the Bald had recognised Erispoe and Salomon.

Like Salomon, Alan claimed to rule *more regio*, in the custom of a king, and he too made use in his charters of the regal language of Carolingian diplomas.[13] His occasional use of the title *rex* suggests that one or other of his West Frankish contemporaries – Charles the Fat, Odo, Charles the Simple – recognised him as a royal client.[14] From a diploma datable only to 897–900 which he issued in favour of Raino, bishop of Angers, it emerges that Alan had some contact with either Charles the Fat or Charles the Simple, for the list of those on behalf of whose salvation he made the grant is headed by *Karolus*.[15] The Charles in question is more likely to have been Charles the Fat than Charles the Simple (898–922) for two reasons.[16] In the first place, Charles the Fat is known (admittedly on the basis of the late and often unreliable evidence of the Chronicle of Nantes) to have been in contact with eastern Brittany. This chronicle reports that Landramn, bishop of Nantes, visited Charles the Fat who, on hearing of the devastated state to which the Vikings had reduced Nantes, granted the bishop a place of refuge in Angers.[17] Alan's own power in the county of Nantes was well established; for him to have been in direct communication with Charles the Fat is therefore not improbable. In the second place, Charles the Fat's familiarity with the techniques of establishing a dependent king, and his awareness of the political capital such an act might bring, has been pointed out earlier.[18] Charles the Simple, on the other hand, was not in any position to intervene in Neustrian affairs at all, let alone to negotiate with those on the distant frontiers of his kingdom.

Whilst encamped outside Paris in the autumn of 886, Charles the Fat issued a considerable number of diplomas for West Frankish beneficiaries. They show just how concerned he was to emphasise his position as heir of Charles the Bald and Louis the

---

[13] The phrase *more regio* occurs in one of his charters for the cathedral of Nantes. *Chronique de Nantes*, 25, p. 75. On the language of his charters, see above, p. 117.

[14] *Chronique de Nantes*, 25, pp. 74–7; *Cartulaire Noir*, 12, pp. 30–2.

[15] *Cartulaire Noir*, 12, pp. 30–2. For the date of this charter see Werner, 'Untersuchungen', 18 (1958), p. 273 n. 84.

[16] But for the contrary view, see Chédeville and Guillotel, *Bretagne*, pp. 368–72.

[17] *Chronique de Nantes*, 21, pp. 66–7. [18] See above, pp. 109–10.

Stammerer throughout the entire West Frankish kingdom. Churches as far afield as Burgundy and the Spanish march received confirmations of earlier royal or imperial grants of immunity and protection or of land.[19] However, the majority of Charles the Fat's West Frankish diplomas were issued for Neustrian beneficiaries, and they testify to his real effort to rule, not just to reign.[20] Concern with Brittany would have been a natural extension of responsibility for the rest of Neustria. A desire to establish himself as the worthy successor of Charles the Bald would have made a display of imperial hegemony over the Bretons an appropriate gesture. The probability is that Charles the Fat did indeed make Alan his client ruler.

During Charles the Fat's brief, and mostly absentee, rule of the West Frankish kingdom (885–7), Neustria ceased to be a major battleground of magnate factions. Hugh the Abbot lost much of the influence he had enjoyed during the reign of Carloman, and, indeed, died in May 886. His great Neustrian rival, Gauzlin, abbot of Saint-Denis, had predeceased him by less than one month.[21] In their place, Odo, count of Paris and son of Robert the Strong, became more and more prominent. Already the emperor's *fidelis*, Odo benefited from Hugh's death by grants of both his father's many Neustrian *honores* and also the military command of the land between the Seine and the Loire which Hugh had enjoyed.[22] When Odo was himself elected West Frankish king in 888, he passed his lands and offices on to his brother Robert.[23] Foremost amongst these were the counties of Angers, Tours, Blois, and Orléans, together with the lay abbacy of Saint-Martin of Tours. Thus it was that from 886 onwards, the land from the Seine to the Loire passed under firm and unrivalled Robertian domination.[24] No longer was Neustria the 'merry-go-round' on which the Carolingian aristocracy played.[25] Now it was the territory of a single, predominant family, a family whose offices and landed endowments were concentrated there.[26] Instead, the focus of

---

[19] MGH D.Ger. II.231–4, 238–40, nos. 145 (for Saint-Germain-d'Auxerre), 148 (for Gerona).

[20] MGH D.Ger. II.223–5, 227–30, 234–7, 240–1, nos. 139, 142, 143, 146, 149.

[21] Werner, 'Gauzlin von Saint-Denis', p. 458 n. 210.

[22] Regino, *Chronicon*, a. 887 (*recte* 886), p. 126; *Annales Vedastini*, a. 886, ed. B. von Simson, MGH SSRG (Hanover, 1909), p. 62; MGH D.Ger. II.229–30, no. 143.

[23] Dhondt, *Naissance*, pp. 101–2.   [24] Dhondt, *Naissance*, pp. 110–15.

[25] See above, p. 55.

[26] For lesser Neustrian aristocrats, see Werner, 'Untersuchungen', 19 (1959); Boussard, 'Destinées de la Neustrie'.

political conflict shifted decisively north-eastwards, to the Paris basin and the area where the West Frankish kingdom marched with Lotharingia.

Odo's family consolidated its grip on Neustria after his death. The support of his brother Robert was vital to Charles the Simple (898–922), for whose succession Odo had arranged before his own death.[27] Charles was all but excluded from any direct power in Neustria; royal power here was exercised through Robert.[28] Indeed, Charles the Simple added to Robert's influence by grants of possessions in the Paris basin and by recognising the entitlement of his young son Hugh to inherit all his father's *honores*. When Charles the Simple's rule was no longer acceptable to the West Frankish magnates, who revolted against him and imprisoned him, it was Robert whom they chose as king in his place in 922.

Robertian Neustria epitomises one of the great shifts which overtook Frankish politics in the closing years of the ninth century and the early tenth century. Unlike the empire-wide concerns of the 'Widonid' family in the reigns of Charlemagne and Louis the Pious, or the interplay of the Neustrian and Aquitainian interests of the descendants of Rorigo of Le Mans in the days of Charles the Bald, there had emerged by the reign of Charles the Simple a clear pattern of regional aristocratic power blocs. In similar fashion, other great aristocratic families consolidated their power elsewhere: the descendants of Charles the Bald's son-in-law Baldwin in Flanders; the heirs of Herbert of Vermandois (descended from Louis the Pious' nephew Bernard of Italy) to the north of the Paris basin; William the Pious, son of Bernard Hairypaws, in Aquitaine; Richard the Justiciar (brother of Boso) and his son Hugh the Black in Burgundy.[29]

As the gap between Carolingian and Robertian power and status narrowed, so Robert of Neustria and his descendants became more and more preoccupied with properties and politics in the Paris region. They abandoned western Neustria and the Loire valley to the attention of their vassals, appointed as counts

---

[27] On the reign of Charles the Simple, see Werner, 'Westfranken-Frankreich', pp. 738–41.

[28] The counties under Robertian control are detailed by Dhondt, *Naissance*, pp. 112–14. Charles did, however, make one known journey into Neustria, for he issued a diploma at Collège, north of Angers, on 21 June 914. The purpose of the visit cannot be established. *Recueil des Actes de Charles III le Simple, Roi de France (893–923)*, ed. F. Lot and P. Lauer (Paris, 1949), no. 79, pp. 176–7.

[29] The most up-to-date survey is Dunbabin, *France in the Making*.

and viscounts. It was symptomatic of this that Alan I and his successors were in contact not with Robert himself but with the bishops and viscounts who represented his power in the lower Loire valley and western Neustria. The Frankish lands of eastern Brittany tempted Robert's men, and we may surmise conflict and rivalry with the Bretons. Indeed, until Brittany was incorporated into the Angevin empire by Henry II in 1166, the county of Nantes remained a focus of tensions between the Breton dukes and the counts of Anjou.

It seems that Alan I continued to hold that part of western Anjou which Charles the Bald had given to Salomon in 863; as has been noted he had within his gift the lay abbacy of Saint-Serge at Angers, which he gave to Bishop Raino. Brother of Adalard, archbishop of Tours (875–91), and related by marriage to the viscounts of Angers, Raino was an influential figure in the politics of the lower Loire valley. To Alan, he was a 'dear friend', *dilectus amicus nobis*.[30] Also during Raino's episcopate, Landramn, bishop of Nantes was given refuge in Angers.[31] After Alan's death, however, his successors lost control of Nantes. By 914, Fulk the Red, a vassal of Robert of Neustria and his viscount in Angers, was installed as count of Nantes, in all probability with the support and encouragement of his lord. Fulk possibly claimed Nantes through his wife Roscilla, descended from a Tourangelle branch of the family of Wido and Lambert that had been so prominent in the lower Loire valley in the early ninth century.[32] In seizing Nantes, Fulk was also able to recover the western part of the county of Anjou, which thereafter was once more part of the lands of the counts of Anjou.[33] He may also have installed his own relative as bishop of the city.[34]

To the north of the county of Nantes, Breton control of the lands granted in benefice by Charles the Bald also weakened. Alan I certainly controlled the full extent of territory which Salomon had done, for he had lands in the Cotentin at his disposal, and as late as 890, the river Vire in the eastern Cotentin was regarded as the frontier between Franks and Bretons.[35] His successors,

---

[30] *Cartulaire Noir*, 12, pp. 30–2, and above, n. 14; Werner, 'Untersuchungen', 18 (1958), pp. 272–3. [31] *Chronique de Nantes*, 21, pp. 66–7.
[32] Werner, 'Untersuchungen', 18 (1958), pp. 268–71.
[33] O. Guillot, *Le Comte d'Anjou et son entourage au XIe siècle*, 2 vols. (Paris, 1972), I.136–7.
[34] Werner, 'Untersuchungen', 18 (1958), p. 268.
[35] *Chronique de Nantes*, 22, pp. 68–72; Regino, *Chronicon*, a. 890, pp. 134–5; *Two Anglo-Saxon Chronicles*, a. 890, I.82.

however, were unable to defend this region from Viking attack and settlement. In 933, King Rodulf conceded it to William Longsword, leader of the inchoate Viking principality of the lower Seine valley.[36] To the south, a family of mixed Frankish and Breton origin, in which the name Berengar was current, acquired control of the county of Rennes after Alan I's death.[37] The Berengar who ruled Rennes in the early tenth century accepted the lordship of Robert of Neustria, whose service he entered at some point during Robert's brief reign (922–3).[38] When the same Berengar negotiated an end to hostilities with William Longsword in 931, a precedent was set for the late tenth and eleventh centuries: as counts of Rennes, his descendants acknowledged the hegemony of the dukes of Normandy from 992 onwards.[39]

At the same time as Neustrian aristocrats clawed their way back into eastern Brittany, Breton-speaking Brittany was coming into the sphere of influence of the powerful West Saxon kings. Asser claims that Bretons numbered amongst those who submitted themselves to Alfred's lordship, and that the recipients of West Saxon alms included Breton monasteries.[40] Certainly Alfred's heir, Edward the Elder, was in contact with the Bretons, for he joined the confraternity of the cathedral of Dol.[41] Behind the prayers for the safety of the English kings offered by the Breton archiepiscopal clergy may lie an effort by the West Saxon kings to extend their overlordship over the Bretons, just as they were doing over the Welsh.[42] It is highly significant that Breton tradition remembered the Matuedoe, count of Poher, had fled from the Vikings to Athelstan's court, that Athelstan had stood

---

[36] *Les Annales de Flodoard*, ed. P. Lauer, Collection de Textes pour servir à l'Etude et à l'Enseignement de l'Histoire 39 (Paris, 1905), a. 933, p. 55. But for what this grant meant in practice, see C. Potts, 'Normandy or Brittany? A conflict of interests at Mont Saint Michel (966–1035)', *Anglo-Norman Studies*, 12 (1989), 135–56.

[37] Above, p. 125.

[38] H. Guillotel, 'L'exode du clergé breton devant les invasions scandinaves', *MSHAB*, 59 (1982), 269–315, at pp. 300, 315.

[39] Hugh of Fleury, *Modernorum Regum Francorum Actus*, 4, MGH SS IX.382; Guillotel, 'Premier siècle'; J. Le Patourel, *The Norman Empire* (Oxford, 1976), pp. 14–16, 74–6, 215–16.

[40] *Asser's Life of King Alfred*, ed. W. H. Stevenson with introduction by D. Whitelock (Oxford, 1959), chaps. 76, 102, pp. 59–60, 89.

[41] This is revealed in the letter by Radbod, prior of Dol to Athelstan, cited by William of Malmesbury, *Gesta Pontificum Anglorum*, v.249, pp. 399–400.

[42] H. R. Loyn, 'Wales and England in the tenth century: the context of the Athelstan charters', *Welsh History Review*, 10 (1981), 283–301.

godfather to Matuedoe's infant son Alan II, and that it was with his godfather's assistance that Alan launched his drive to clear the Vikings out of Brittany in 936.[43] All the conventions of hegemonic lordship are represented here. A close, if short-lived, political bond between Wessex and Brittany helps explain why there are signs that a sizeable Breton community may have been established right in the heart of the West Saxon kingdom, at Winchester and possibly also at Wareham, when Viking devastations made Brittany too unsafe a place for many of its monastic communities.[44] The large number of Breton manuscripts which have been in England since the tenth century testify to the welcome extended to Breton exiles by the English.[45]

West Saxon claims to overlordship over the Bretons, if indeed such there were, cannot have lasted for more than a generation. When Alan II left England to reconquer Brittany, another refugee at the English court, Athelstan's nephew Louis IV (the son of Charles the Simple), also set out to regain his inheritance – the West Frankish throne.[46] Alan and Louis (known as Louis d'Outremer) must have grown up together as exiles in Athelstan's court. It is therefore little surprise to read than in 942 Alan was amongst those who recognised Louis IV's lordship.[47] But this

---

[43] *Chronique de Nantes*, 27, pp. 82–3.

[44] At Winchester, an influx of Breton refugees has been posited to explain the 'veritable devotional *furore* in Bretonism' in late tenth-century Winchester liturgical documents. F. A. Gasquet and E. Bishop, *The Bosworth Psalter* (London, 1908), p. 56. See also L. Gougaud, 'Mentions anglaises des saints bretons et de leurs reliques', *Annales de Bretagne*, 34 (1919–21), 273–7.

At Wareham, inscribed stones in insular script bearing Brittonic names survive on the site of the Anglo-Saxon church. These are more plausibly interpreted as early tenth-century Breton funerary stones than as relics of a British community surviving in the heart of Wessex into Alfredian times, particularly since Wareham is the Anglo-Saxon sea port at the northern end of the crossing from Alet via the Channel Islands. E. McClure, 'The Wareham Inscriptions', *English Historical Review*, 22 (1907), 728–30, and for further bibliography on the controversy these stones have occasioned, S. R. I. Foot, *Anglo-Saxon Minsters AD 597–975* (Woodbridge, forthcoming). I am grateful to Sarah Foot for giving me access to her work on Wareham in advance of publication.

[45] These include: the Bradfer-Lawrence gospels (Fitzwilliam Museum, Cambridge); the Leofric gospels (Oxford, Bodleian Auct. D.2.16); the Bodmin gospels (BL Add. 9381); the Canterbury gospels (BL Royal 1.A.xviii); several other gospel books (BL Add. 40000, Cotton Otho B.ix; Oxford, St John's College 194); St Dunstan's Classbook (Oxford, Bodleian Auct. F.4.32); a canon collection (Oxford, Bodleian Hatton 42).

[46] Flodoard, *Annales*, a. 936, p. 63; cf. the discussion of the complications raised by other accounts of the circumstances of Alan's return from exile by Guillotel, 'Premier siècle', pp. 69–73.

[47] Richer, *Histoire*, II.28, ed. Latouche, I.168; cf. Flodoard, *Annales*, a. 942, p. 84.

renewal of contact between the Bretons and the Carolingian dynasty was a backward-looking gesture without consequence. Other than confirming a privilege of Charles the Bald for Nantes cathedral, Louis IV had no practical concern for Breton affairs.[48] Alan's homage marked the end of an old era, not the beginning of a new one.

By 936, the mould of ninth-century politics had been broken definitively. Louis IV was unable to dislodge the magnates who dominated so much of his kingdom, unable too to press home his claims to Lotharingia.[49] His own political agenda left no room for any real concern for the Bretons. And in most of central Neustria and the Paris basin Hugh the Great (son of Robert of Neustria) was in effective control; even for him Brittany was too peripheral to bother with. By the time that Alan II is reputed to have hacked his way through the brambles that had overgrown the city of Nantes, effective Carolingian hegemony over outlying areas was a thing of the past.[50] By the middle of the tenth century, the politics of western Francia were characterised by limited horizons, by the fragmentation of royal authority, by the multiplication of frontiers and of arenas of conflict. Within this very different world, Alan's successors fought off the challenges from Anjou, Blois, and Normandy, and finally managed to establish that the counties of Rennes and Nantes, though not the Cotentin peninsula or western Anjou, were part of Brittany.

EPILOGUE

The success of Robert of Neustria's vassals in extending their influence into Frankish Brittany coincided with the decade when Viking assaults on Brittany were at their peak. Throughout the entire ninth century, all north-western Europe had been subject to Viking raids, sporadic at first but increasingly insistent and

---

[48] Brunterc'h, 'Puissance temporelle', p. 31.

[49] On the reign of Louis IV, see Werner, 'Westfranken-Frankreich', pp. 745–9; J.-F. Lemarignier, 'Les fidèles du roi de France (936–987)', *Recueil des Travaux offert à M. Clovis Brunel*, 2 vols. (Paris, 1955), II.138–62.

[50] Alan's re-entry into Nantes is vividly described in *Chronique de Nantes* 30, pp. 91–2: 'Alanus...intravit urbem Namneticam, a pluribus annis desertam...mucrone suo cum omnibus suis Britannis viam faciens, veprium spinarumque resecando densitatem.' No excavations have yet been undertaken to test the literary picture of the fate of Nantes, but it is worth noting that archaeological investigation at Tours has made considerable modifications to the account of that city's Carolingian history as derived from written sources. H. Galinié, 'Archéologie et topographie historique de Tours – IVe–XIe siècle', *Zeitschrift für Archäologie des Mittelalters*, 6 (1978), 33–56.

devastating from the 840s onwards. Astride the sea lanes from both the English Channel and the Irish Sea to the Bay of Biscay, Brittany was inevitably affected. Although we know few details of Viking activity in the peninsula, a few main points are clear. In the first place, Nominoe, Erispoe, and Salomon are all on record as active campaigners against the Vikings.[51] Secondly, in Brittany as in Francia, the Vikings seized the opportunity presented by internal wranglings and dissensions to throw in their lot with one or other faction. For example, both Robert the Strong and Salomon hired Viking help in 862; in 874, Vikings joined Pascweten in his struggle against Wrhwant, and shortly thereafter, whilst Alan and Judicael were unable to resolve their differences, they overran all of western Brittany.[52] Thirdly, Breton tactics for dealing with the Vikings were much as Frankish ones. On occasion, the Vikings were paid to go away;[53] there is also much evidence that by the late ninth century, the Bretons were building defensive fortifications, refurbishing old Roman city walls and reoccupying Iron Age earthworks, as were the Franks and the West Saxons.[54] Fourthly, in Brittany as elsewhere in West Francia at times of greatest danger, saints' relics were moved long distances for safe-keeping, and the timing of these translations is a sensitive indicator for pinpointing the location and incidence of the worst devastation.[55]

[51] Nominoe's campaigns are noted in *AB*, a. 844, 847, pp. 47–8, 54. For Erispoe, see *GSR*, III.9, pp. 213–19. For Salomon, see CR 242; *AB*, a. 873, pp. 192–3; Regino, *Chronicon*, a. 873, p. 106. A full discussion of all these campaigns and of the literary evidence for them is provided by S. C. Coupland, 'Charles the Bald and the defence of the West Frankish kingdom against the Viking invasions, 840–877' (PhD, Cambridge, 1987).

[52] *AB*, a. 862, p. 89; Regino, *Chronicon*, a. 874, 890, pp. 107–8, 135.

[53] *AB*, a. 847, p. 54; Regino, *Chronicon*, a. 874, p. 108.

[54] Regino describes how Salomon spent the winter of 868 building fortifications against the Vikings, *Chronicon*, a. 874, p. 108. Whereas the residences of Salomon and his predecessors were all described as *aula* or *lis*, two of Alan I's were *castella*: at Plessé and Rieux (CR 266, A51, A52, A54; *Chronique de Nantes*, 25, p. 74; *Cartulaire Noir*, 12, pp. 30–2). Alan was also associated with the rebuilding of the Roman walls of Nantes, *Chronique de Nantes*, 26, p. 78. Archaeological evidence for late ninth- to early tenth-century earthworks, and for the reuse of pre-Roman defences is presented by J.-Y. Hamel-Simon, L. Langouët, F. Nourry-Denayer, and D. Mouton, 'Fouille d'un retranchement d'Alain Barbetorte datable de 939: Le Camp des Haies à Trans (Ille-et-Vilaine)', *Les Dossiers du Centre Régional Archéologique d'Alet*, 7 (1979), 47–74, and by J.-P. Nicolardot, 'Chronique des fouilles médiévales: Plédran (Côtes-du-Nord)', *Archéologie Médiévale*, 15 (1985), 281. Summary notes of unpublished excavations are provided by Chédeville and Tonnerre, *La Bretagne Féodale*, pp. 182–3.

[55] Guillotel, 'L'exode du clergé breton'. The only unusual aspect of the removal of relics from Brittany is the apparent lack of concern to return them to their homes as soon

In Brittany, this was the decade *c.* 910 to *c.* 920. When Flodoard commenced writing his Annals in 919, he commented that plundering and slave-raiding were widespread in Brittany as he wrote:[56] twice within the next decade, parts or all of Brittany were abandoned to the Vikings by the Franks struggling to limit the ravages of the Loire-based fleets.[57] By *c.* 920, most of Brittany had been overrun. At about this time Matuedoe, count of Poher, fled to Wessex, a highly unusual move for a secular leader. Stripped of their relics and unattended by their clergy, Breton churches appear to have stood unoccupied for a matter of years, perhaps even of decades.[58] Any resistance to the Norsemen was organised locally:[59] until Alan II's return in 936 no central leadership co-ordinated defence or won general recognition.[60]

Yet this hiatus was of little lasting significance, and although the collapse seems total, it is perhaps a historiographical mirage. There is no evidence that the Vikings ever colonised Brittany.[61] Monasteries retained much of their land.[62] Alan II immediately

---

as was at all possible. Cf. P. Gasnault, 'Le tombeau de Saint Martin et les invasions normandes dans l'histoire et dans la légende', *Revue d'Histoire de l'Eglise de France*, 47 (1961), 51–66.   [56] Flodoard, *Annales*, a. 919, p. 1.

[57] Flodoard, *Annales*, a. 921, 927, pp. 6, 38.

[58] This is certainly true for Landévennec. The monastery was destroyed in 913/14, whereupon the monks fled via Château-du-Loir to Montreuil-sur-Mer. They returned from there as soon as Alan II arrived from England. It is not known when other monastic communities returned to Brittany.

[59] Flodoard, *Annales*, a. 931, pp. 50–2; Hugh of Fleury, *Modernorum Regum Francorum Actus*, 4, p. 382.

[60] For details of Alan's campaigns to clear the Vikings out of Brittany and claim the ducal title for himself, see Guillotel, 'Premier siècle'.

[61] There are very few Scandinavian place-names in Brittany indeed. They cluster around Dol and Mont-Saint-Michel and are outliers of the Scandinavian settlements in the Cotentin peninsula. F. de Beaurepaire, 'Toponymie et évolution du peuplement sur le pourtour de la baie du Mont-Saint-Michel', in *Millénaire Monastique du Mont Saint-Michel*, 4 vols. (Paris, 1966–71), II, *Vie montoise et rayonnement intellectuel du Mont Saint-Michel*, ed. R. Foreville, pp. 49–72. Also L. Musset, 'Observations sur les noms d'hommes normands en Bretagne et d'ailleurs', *Bulletin de la Société des Antiquaires de Normandie*, 57 (1963–4), 612–16.

[62] The evidence for this is indirect. At Landévennec, the monks' frantic effort to reconstitute their cartulary in the middle of the tenth century hints at a need to defend their title to lands held before their flight into exile. W. Davies, 'Les chartes du cartulaire de Landévennec', in *Landévennec et le Monachisme Breton*, ed. Simon, pp. 85–95, esp. p. 94. As for Redon, it seems to have retained much of its ninth-century endowment throughout the Middle Ages. The monastery's eleventh and twelfth-century acquisitions were concentred in areas where the monks had not owned land in the Carolingian period, and yet in the late Middle Ages they still owned extensive properties in precisely those places so well represented in ninth-century charters but virtually ignored in the later ones. A. Guillotin de Corson, *Pouillé Historique de*

revived Breton claims to Nantes and Rennes. Under his rule, the development of ducal and ecclesiastical government proceeded apace.[63] By Alan II's death in 952, the disruption was largely a thing of the past. Only the occasional raid launched by the Viking colony of the Seine valley indicated that Brittany was still within the Norsemen's field of operation.

The last recorded Viking raids on Brittany took place in 1014–15.[64] By this date, much of central and northern France was beginning to experience a rise in population, rapid economic growth, and considerable geographical mobility amongst the middle and upper ranks of society. Also, it was from the early eleventh century onwards that old hierarchies of officialdom and public power either broke down altogether, or became far less distinguishable from private relationships than ever had been the case in the Carolingian period. One token of this was the intertwining of tenurial relations with the obligations of service and loyalty to a lord, symbolised by the conjunction of fief and vassalage. Another was the proliferation of castles. Banal lordships, in which the power to command, coerce, and punish was legitimated by inheritance and by custom (*consuetudo*) affected power relations at all levels of society. These lordships represented 'legitimized and organized pillage, tempered only by the resistance of village communities'.[65] Changes in family structure amongst the landowning sector of the population also contributed to this evolution. Evident in many regions was a shift from loosely defined kin-groups to lineages in which primogeniture was practised, and which defined themselves toponymically by reference to their main residence and seat of power. A redistribution of landed resources accompanied the redistribution of power amongst the governing elite; vulnerable ecclesiastical lands and income often suffered from the depredations of the

l'Archevêché de Rennes, 6 vols. (Rennes, 1880–6), II.177, 187 (commenting on the *aveu* of 1580). Also Davies, *Small Worlds*, p. 23 n. 39.

[63] Guillotel, 'Premier siècle'; Chédeville and Tonnerre, *La Bretagne Féodale*, pp. 25–32. The continuing development of ducal government in Alan's reign is suggested by the first Breton references to *vicecomites* in his charters. *Cartulaire de Landévennec*, 25, 40, pp. 562–4, 569.

[64] R. Couffon, 'A quelles dates Dol et Guérande ont-elles étés ravagées par Olaf Haraldson?', *MSHAB*, 29 (1949), 25–33.

[65] G. Duby, *The Early Growth of the European Economy: Warriors and Peasants from the Seventh to the Twelfth Century* (London, 1974), p. 176. See also Duby's now classic definition of banal lordship ('seigneurie banale') in his *La Société aux XIe et XIIe siècles dans la Région Mâconnaise* (2nd edn, Paris, 1971), pp. 173–90.

secular aristocracy. Gradually too the military retinues of powerful secular and ecclesiastical lords emerged as a distinct social group, the knights, with their own status, ethic, and code of conduct.[66]

No part of eleventh-century France was left untouched by economic growth and the fundamental transformation of power relations.[67] Naturally, the timing and extent of these changes varied greatly from one province to another. In some places, princely power emerged strengthened, in others, it collapsed almost completely. As much as ever, Christendom remained a mosaic of local, regional societies, each distinctive in its own way. It does seem, however, that in central and northern France the pace of change was quickest, and the ensuing social dislocation greatest, in the second and third quarters of the century. In Normandy, the Chartrain, and Anjou, the decades from *c.* 1020 to *c.* 1080 saw unprecedented changes in the disposition of power and wealth.[68]

In Brittany, precisely these years are characterised by a resumption of relatively plentiful charter evidence, in sharp contrast to the dearth of documents from the preceding century. New endowments of old monasteries such as Redon, Landévennec, and Mont-Saint-Michel, and of new foundations such as Quimperlé or Saint-George at Rennes, prompted a renewed spate of charter-writing. This rush of generosity to the church parallels similar benefactions throughout much of France, and betokens changes in the allocation of resources in Brittany, much as elsewhere. Although the extent to which Brittany was touched by the transformation of the old order has never been fully investigated, it is nevertheless clear that many other profound changes were sweeping the province in the eleventh century.[69]

---

[66] But for suggestive comments on the Carolingian origins of knighthood, see J. L. Nelson, 'Ninth-century knighthood: the evidence of Nithard', in *Studies in Medieval History Presented to R. Allen Brown*, ed. C. Harper-Bill, C. J. Holdsworth, and J. L. Nelson (Woodbridge, 1989), pp. 255–66.

[67] For a guide to the voluminous literature on the eleventh century written with full reference to regional diversities, see R. Fossier, *Enfance de l'Europe, X^e–XIIe siècles*, 2 vols. Nouvelle Clio 17 (Paris, 1982).

[68] Guillot, *Comte d'Anjou*; A. Chédeville, *Chartres et ses Campagnes, XIe–XIIIe siècles* (Paris, 1973); D. Bates, *Normandy before 1066* (London, 1982).

[69] No one has devoted a monograph to eleventh- and twelfth-century Brittany. The new survey by Chédeville and Tonnerre, *La Bretagne Féodale*, offers a brief outline of these centuries in the light of developments known to have been taking place elsewhere in France.

LIST OF MANUSCRIPTS CITED

ANGERS

Bibliothèque Municipale

476

477

817

BERN

Burgerbibliothek

160

167

277

CAMBRIDGE

Corpus Christi College

192

279

Fitzwilliam Museum

Bradfer-Lawrence gospels

COPENHAGEN

Kongelige Bibliotek

Thott 239

GOTHA

Landesbibliothek MBR 1.147 + New York, Pierpont Morgan Library G
28 + Herdringen, Archiv der Grafen von Fürstenburg, frag. s.n. + Hanover,
Kestner-Museum, Culemann Kat. 1.45 (366) + Paderborn, Bibliothek der
Erzbischöflichen philosophisch-theologischen Akademie, frag. 10 + Weimar,
Staatsarchiv Hardenburg-Sammlung 12a, 14a

LEIDEN

Universiteits-Bibliotheek

Voss. Lat. F.24

Voss. Lat. F.96A

LONDON

British Library

Additional 8873

Additional 9381

Additional 40000

Cotton Otho B.IX

Cotton Otho E.XIII

Egerton 609
Harley 2719
Harley 3941
Royal 1.A.xviii

LUXEMBURG
Bibliothèque Royale Grand-Ducale
89

MERSEBURG
Domstiftbibliothek
I.204

MUNICH
Bayerische Staatsbibliothek
Clm 18961

NEW YORK
Public Library
115

ORLEANS
Bibliothèque Municipale
73
221
302

OXFORD
Bodleian Library
Auct. D.2.16
Auct. F.4.32
Hatton 42
St John's College
194

PARIS
Bibliothèque Nationale
Lat. 2051
Lat. 3182
Lat. 4839
Lat. 10289
Lat. 10290
Lat. 11411
Lat. 12021
Lat. 13029
Lat. 13386
Nouv. Acq. Lat. 1587
Nouv. Acq. Lat. 1616
Nouv. Acq. Lat. 1983

REIMS
Bibliothèque Municipale
414

SAINT-OMER
Bibliothèque Municipale
666

List of manuscripts cited

SANKT GALLEN
Stiftsbibliothek
  759
VATICAN
Biblioteca Apostolica
  Lat. 1480
  Lat. 1974
  Reg. Lat. 49
  Reg. Lat. 81
  Reg. Lat. 296
  Reg. Lat. 691
VENICE
Biblioteca Marciana
  Zanetti 349
WÜRZBURG
Universitätsbibliothek
  M.p.th.f.67

BIBLIOGRAPHY

PRIMARY SOURCES

Abelard, Peter, *Historia Calamitatum*, ed. J. Monfrin, 4th edn, Paris, 1978.

Acta Frederici Episcopi et Martiris Ultrajecti in Belgio, AASS Jul. IV.460–71.

Actus Pontificum Cenomannis in Urbe Degentium, ed. G. Buson and A. Ledru, Archives Historiques du Maine 2, Le Mans, 1901.

Adrevald, *Miracula Sancti Benedicti*, MGH SS XV.i, 474–97.

Alcuin, *Epistolae*, MGH Epp. IV.

Amalarius of Metz, *De Ecclesiasticis Officiis*, PL CV.986–1242.

Annales de Saint-Bertin, ed. F. Grat, J. Viellard, and S. Clémencet, Paris, 1964.

Annales Engolismenses, MGH SS XVI.485–7.

Annales Fuldenses, ed. F. Kurze, MGH SSRG, Hanover, 1891.

Annales Mettenses Priores, ed. B. de Simson, MGH SSRG, Hanover, 1905.

Annales Ordinis Sancti Benedicti, ed. J. Mabillon, 6 vols., Paris, 1703–39.

Annales Regni Francorum, ed. F. Kurze, MGH SSRG, Hanover, 1895.

Annales Vedastini, ed. B. von Simson, MGH SSRG, Hanover, 1909.

Annales Xantenses, ed. B. von Simson, MGH SSRG, Hanover, 1909.

Armes Prydein. The Prophecy of Britain, ed. I. Williams; English version by R. Bromwich, Medieval and Modern Welsh Series 6, Dublin, 1972.

Asser's Life of King Alfred, ed. W. H. Stevenson with introduction by D. Whitelock, Oxford, 1959.

'Astronomer', *Vita Hludowici Imperatoris*, MGH SS II.604–48.

Audradus Modicus, *Liber Revelationum*, ed. L. Traube, '*O Roma Nobilis*. Philologische Untersuchungen aus dem Mittelalter', *Abhandlungen der philosophisch-philologischen Classe der königlichen bayerischen Akademie der Wissenschaften*, 19 (1892), 297–394.

Beyer, H., *Urkundenbuch zur Geschichte der, jetzt die preussischen Regierungsbezirke Coblenz und Trier bildenden mittelrheinischen Territorien. I (bis zum 1169)*, Koblenz, 1860.

Bieler, L., *The Irish Penitentials*, Scriptores Latini Hiberniae 5, Dublin, 1975.

Bili, *Vita Machutis, Vie de Saint-Malo, Evêque d'Alet*, ed. G. Le Duc, Dossiers du Centre Régional Archéologique d'Alet B, n.p., 1979.

Canterbury Professions, ed. M. Richter, Canterbury and York Society 67, Torquay, 1973.

Cartulaire de l'Abbaye de Landévennec, ed. R. Le Men and E. Ernault, Documents Inédits sur l'Histoire de France, Mélanges 5, Paris, 1886, pp. 533–600.

Bibliography

Cartulaire de l'Abbaye de Redon en Bretagne, ed. A. de Courson, Documents Inédits sur l'Histoire de France, Paris, 1863.

Cartulaire Noir de la Cathédrale d'Angers, ed. C. Urseau, Paris, 1908.

Chronicon Aquitanicum, MGH SS II.252–3.

Chronicon Fontanellense, Les Premières Annales de Fontenelle, ed. J. Laporte, Société de l'Histoire de Normandie, Mélanges, 15th ser., Rouen, 1951, pp. 63–91.

Chronicon Moissacense, MGH SS I.280–313.

La Chronique de Nantes, ed. R. Merlet, Collection de Textes pour servir à l'Etude et à l'Enseignement de l'Histoire 19, Paris, 1896.

Concilia Galliae A. 314–A. 505, ed. C. Munier, Corpus Christianorum Series Latina 148, Turnholt, 1963.

Concilia Galliae A. 511–A. 695, ed. C. Munier, Corpus Christianorum Series Latina 148a, Turnholt, 1963.

Donatus, *Vita Ermenlandi Abbatis Antrensis*, MGH SSRM v.674–710.

Egil of Sens, *Eulogium Historicum*, AASS OSB IV.ii, 237–43.

Einhard, *Vita Karoli Magni*, ed. O. Holder-Egger, MGH SSRG, Hanover, 1911.

Ermoldus Nigellus, *Carmen in Honorem Hludowici Pii*, MGH Poet. II.5–79.

Fawtier, R., 'Une rédaction inédite de la vie de saint Guénolé', *Mélanges d'Archéologie et d'Histoire de l'Ecole Française de Rome*, 32 (1912), 27–44.

Flodoard, *Historia Remensis Ecclesiae*, MGH SS XIII.405–599.

Flodoard, *Les Annales de Flodoard*, ed. P. Lauer, Collection de Textes pour servir à l'Etude et à l'Enseignement de l'Histoire 39, Paris, 1905.

Formulae Andecavenses, MGH Form. pp. 4–31.

Formulae Imperiales e Curia Ludovici Pii, MGH Form. p. 285–328.

Fredegar, *The Fourth Book of the Chronicle of Fredegar with its Continuations*, ed. J. M. Wallace-Hadrill, London, 1960.

Gesta Aldrici Episcopi Cenomannensis, MGH SS XV.i, 304–27.

Gregory of Tours, *Libri Historiarum Decem*, ed. B. Krusch and W. Levison, MGH SSRM I.i, 2nd edn, 1951.

Hincmar of Reims, *Opera*, PL CXXV–CXXVI.

The Hisperica Famina: I, the A-text, ed. M. Herren, Toronto, 1974.

Historia Translationis Corporum Sanctorum Ragnoberti et Zenonis, AASS Mai. III.618–25.

Historia Translationis Sancti Launomari Abbatis Corbionensis in Oppidum Blesas, AASS OSB IV.ii, 245–59.

Hugh of Flavigny, *Chronicon*, MGH SS VIII.280–503.

Hugh of Fleury, *Modernorum Regum Francorum Actus*, MGH SS IX.376–95.

Itinerarium Bernardi, monachi franci, ed. T. Tobler, *Descriptiones Terrae Sanctae ex saeculo VIII, IX, XII et XV*, Leipzig, 1874, pp. 85–99.

Jordanes, *Getica*, MGH AA v.53–138.

Legislatio Aquisgranensis, ed. J. Semmler, *Corpus Consuetudinum Monasticarum*, I, ed. K. Hallinger, Siegburg, 1963, pp. 433–99.

Lupus of Ferrières, *Correspondance*, ed. L. Levillian, 2 vols., Les Classiques de l'Histoire de France au Moyen Age 10, 16, 2nd edn, Paris, 1964.

McNally, R. E., 'Dies dominica: two Hiberno-Latin texts', *Mediaeval Studies*, 22 (1960), 355–61.

Marius of Avenches, *Chronica*, MGH AA XI.225–39.

Bibliography

Martyrologium Hieronymianum, AASS Nov. II.i, 1–156.

'Miracles de Saint Magloire et fondation du monastère de Léhon', ed. A. de La Borderie, *Mémoires de la Société Archéologique et Historique des Côtes-du-Nord*, 2nd ser., 4 (1891), 224–411.

Miracula Sancti Albini Episcopi Andegavensis, AASS Mar. I.60–3.

Miracula Sancti Maglorii, Catalogus Codicum Hagiographicorum Latinorum in Bibliotheca Nationali Parisiensi, 4 vols., Brussels, 1889–93, III.308–16.

Miracula Sancti Wandregiseli, MGH SS xv.i, 406–9.

The Monks of Redon: Gesta Sanctorum Rotonensium and Vita Conwoionis, ed. C. Brett, Studies in Celtic History 10, Woodbridge, 1989.

Morice, H., *Mémoires pour servir de Preuves à l'Histoire Ecclésiastique et Civile de Bretagne*, 3 vols., Paris, 1742–6.

Nithard, *Histoire des Fils de Louis le Pieux*, ed. P. Lauer, Les Classiques de l'Histoire de France au Moyen Age 7, Paris, 1926.

Notitia Dignitatum, ed. O. Seeck, Berlin, 1876.

Odo of Glanfeuil, *Historia Translationis Sancti Mauri*, MGH SS xv.i, 462–72.

Orderic Vitalis, *The Ecclesiastical History of Orderic Vitalis*, ed. M. Chibnall, 6 vols., Oxford, 1969–80.

Otto of Freising, *Gesta Frederici Imperatoris*, MGH SS xx.338–493.

Paschasius Radbert, *Vita Walae*, MGH SS II.533–69.

Passio Sancti Ragneberti Martyris, MGH SSRM v.209–11.

Quentin, H., 'Lettre de Nicholas I pour le concile de Soissons et formules ecclésiastiques de la province de Tours dans un manuscrit de Nicholas Le Fèvre', *Le Moyen Age*, 17 (1904), 97–114.

Ralph Glaber, *Rodolfus Glaber: The Five Books of the Histories*, ed. J. France, Oxford, 1989.

Recueil des Actes de Charles II le Chauve, ed. G. Tessier, 3 vols., Paris, 1943–55.

Recueil des Actes de Charles III le Simple, Roi de France (893–923), ed. F. Lot and P. Lauer, Paris, 1949.

Recueil des Actes d'Eudes, Roi de France (888–898), ed. R.-H. Bautier, Paris, 1967.

Recueil des Actes de Louis II le Bègue, Louis III et Carloman, Rois de France (877–884), ed. F. Grat, J. de Font-Réaulx, G. Tessier, and R.-H. Bautier, Paris, 1978.

Recueil des Historiens des Gaules et de la France, ed. M. Bouquet, 24 vols., Paris, 1738–1904.

Regino of Prüm, *Chronicon*, ed. F. Kurze, MGH SSRG, Hanover, 1890.

Richer, *Histoire de France*, ed. R. Latouche, 2 vols., Les Classiques de l'Histoire de France du Moyen Age 12, 17, Paris, 1930–7.

Sacrorum Conciliorum Nova et Amplissima Collectio, ed. J.-D. Mansi, 31 vols., Florence, 1759–98.

Sidonius Apollinaris, *Epistulae*, MGH AA VIII.

The Text of the Book of Llan Dâv, ed. J. G. Evans and J. Rhys, Oxford, 1893.

Thegan, *Vita Hludowici Imperatoris*, MGH SS II.590–604.

Two of the Anglo-Saxon Chronicles Parallel, ed. J. Earle and C. Plummer, 2 vols., Oxford, 1892–9.

Venantius Fortunatus, *Carmina*, MGH AA IV.i.

    Vita Sancti Albini, MGH AA IV.ii, 27–33.

Bibliography

Vita Sancti Paterni, MGH AA iv.ii, 33–7.

'Vie antique et inédite de S. Turiau', ed. F. Duine, *Bulletin de la Société Archéologique d'Ille-et-Vilaine*, 41 (1912), 1–47.

Vita Ansberti, MGH SSRM v.613–41.

Vita Antiquissima Sancti Martini Vertavensis, AASS Oct. x.802–5.

Vita Eligii Episcopi Noviomagensis, MGH SSRM iv.643–742.

Vita et Miracula Leutfredi Abbatis Madriacensis, MGH SSRM vii.i, 7–18.

Vita Maglorii Episcopi, AASS Oct. x.782–91.

Vita Melanii Episcopi Redonici, MGH SSRM iii.370–6.

Vita Sancti Guenaili, AASS Nov. i.669–79.

Vita Sancti Marculphi Abbatis, AASS Mai. i.71–5.

Wasserschleben, H., *Die irische Kanonensammlung*, 2nd edn, Leipzig, 1885.

William of Malmesbury, *Gesta Pontificum Anglorum*, ed. N. E. S. A. Hamilton, Rolls Series 52, London, 1870.

William of Poitiers, *Histoire de Guillaume le Conquérant*, ed. R. Foreville, Les Classiques de l'Histoire de France au Moyen Age 23, Paris, 1952.

Wrdisten, '*Vita S. Winwaloei primi abbatis landevenecensis auctore Wurdestino*', ed. C. de Smedt, *Analecta Bollandiana*, 7 (1888), 167–264.

Wrmonoc, '*Vie de Saint Paul de Léon en Bretagne*', ed. C. Cuissard, *Revue Celtique*, 5 (1881–2), 413–60.

SECONDARY WORKS

Alexander, J. J. G., and Wormald, F., *An Early Breton Gospel Book*, The Roxburghe Club, Cambridge, 1977.

Alföldi, A., 'The moral barrier on Rhine and Danube', in *Congress of Roman Frontier Studies, 1949*, ed. E. Birley, Durham, 1952, pp. 1–16.

Althoffer, B., *Les Scabins*, Nancy, 1938.

Amann, E., *L'Epoque Carolingienne*, Histoire de l'Eglise depuis les Origines jusqu'à Nos Jours, gen. eds. A. Fliche and V. Martin, 6, Paris, 1947.

Angenendt, A., *Kaiserherrschaft und Königstaufe: Kaiser, Könige und Päpste als geistliche Patrone in der abendländischen Missiongeschichte*, Arbeiten zur Frühmittelalterforschung 15, Berlin, 1984.

'Taufe und Politik im frühen Mittelalter', *Frühmittelalterliche Studien*, 7 (1973), 143–68.

Atsma, H., ed., *La Neustrie. Les Pays au Nord de la Loire, 650 à 850*, 2 vols., Beihefte der Francia 16, Sigmaringen, 1989.

Aupest-Conduché, D., 'Quelques réflexions sur les débuts du Christianisme dans les diocèses de Rennes, Vannes et Nantes', *Annales de Bretagne*, 79 (1972), 135–47.

Auzias, L., *L'Aquitaine Carolingienne*, Bibliothèque Méridionale, 2nd ser., 28, Toulouse, 1937.

Barbier, J., 'Aspects du fisc en Neustrie (VIe–IXe siècles). Résultats d'une recherche en cours', in *La Neustrie*, ed. Atsma, i.129–42.

Barley, M. W., and Hanson, R. P. C., eds., *Christianity in Britain, 300–700*, Leicester, 1968.

Bibliography

Bates, D., *Normandy before 1066*, London, 1982.

Beaurepaire, F. de, 'Toponymie et évolution du peuplement sur le pourtour de la baie du Mont-Saint-Michel', in *Millénaire Monastique du Mont-Saint-Michel*, 4 vols., Paris, 1966–71, II, *Vie montoise et rayonnement intellectuel du Mont-Saint-Michel*, ed. R. Foreville, pp. 49–72.

Bigot, A., *Essai sur les Monnaies du Royaume et Duché de Bretagne*, Paris, 1857.

Bischoff, B., 'Annales Rotonenses (um 919)', in B. Bischoff, *Analecta Novissima. Texte des vierten bis sechzehnten Jahrhunderts*, Quellen und Untersuchungen zur lateinischen Philologie des Mittelalters 7, Stuttgart, 1984, pp. 103–5.

'Die Bibliothek im Dienste der Schule', *Settimane*, 19 (1972), 385–415.

Latin Palaeography: Antiquity and the Middle Ages, trans. D. Ganz and D. Ó Cróinín, Cambridge, 1990.

Blair, J., and Sharpe, R., eds., *Pastoral Care before the Parish*, Leicester, forthcoming.

Bouchard, C. B., 'The origins of the French nobility: a reassessment', *American Historical Review*, 86 (1981), 501–32.

Boussard, J., 'Les destinées de la Neustrie du IXe au XIe siècle', *Cahiers de Civilisation Médiévale*, 11 (1968), 15–28.

'L'ouest du royaume franc aux VIIe et VIIIe siècles', *Journal des Savants* (1973), 3–27.

Bowen, E. G., *Saints, Seaways and Settlements in the Celtic Lands*, Cardiff, 1969.

Braunfels, K., ed., *Karl der Grosse: Lebenswerk und Nachleben*, 4 vols., Düsseldorf, 1965.

Brett, C., 'Breton Latin literature as evidence for literature in the vernacular, AD 800–1300', *Cambridge Medieval Celtic Studies*, 18 (1989), 1–25.

Brühl, C., *Fodrum, Gistum, Servitium Regis*, 2 vols., Kölner Historische Abhandlungen 14, Cologne, 1968.

Brunner, K., 'Die fränkische Fürstentitel im neunten und zehnten Jahrhundert', in *Intitulatio II*, ed. H. Wolfram, Mitteilungen des Instituts für österreichische Geschichtsforschung Ergänzungsband 24, Vienna, 1973, pp. 179–340.

Oppositionelle Gruppen im Karolingerreich, Veröffentlichungen des Instituts für österreichische Geschichtsforschung 25, Vienna, 1979.

Brunterc'h, J.-P., 'Le duché du Maine et la marche de Bretagne', in *La Neustrie*, ed. Atsma, I.29–127.

'Géographie historique et hagiographie: la vie de Saint Mervé', *Mélanges de l'Ecole Française de Rome. Moyen Age, Temps Modernes*, 95 (1983), 7–63.

'Puissance temporelle et pouvoir diocésain des évêques de Nantes entre 936 et 1049', *MSHAB*, 61 (1984), 29–82.

Buchner, R., *Deutschlands Geschichtsquellen im Mittelalter. Vorzeit und Karolinger. Beiheft: Die Rechtsquellen*, Weimar, 1953.

Bullough, D. A., 'The educational tradition in England from Alfred to Aelfric: teaching *utriusque linguae*', *Settimane*, 19 (1972), 453–94.

'*Europae pater*: Charlemagne and his achievement in the light of modern scholarship', *English Historical Review*, 85 (1970), 59–105.

Burns, J. H., ed., *The Cambridge History of Medieval Political Thought c. 350–c. 1450*, Cambridge, 1988.

Bibliography

Burns, R. I., 'The significance of the frontier in the Middle Ages', in *Medieval Frontier Societies*, ed. R. Bartlett and A. MacKay, Oxford, 1989, pp. 307–30.

Champaud, C., 'L'exploitation ancienne de cassitérite d'Abbaretz-Nozay', *Annales de Bretagne*, 64 (1957), 46–96.

Chaume, M., 'Le mode de constitution et de délimitation des paroisses rurales aux temps mérovingiens et carolingiens', *Revue Mabillon*, 27 (1937), 61–73, and 28 (1928), 1–9.

Les Origines du Duché de Bourgogne, 2 vols. in 4, Dijon, 1925–37.

Chédeville, A., *Chartres et ses Campagnes, XI*e*–XIII*e* siècles*, Paris, 1973.

Chédeville, A., and Guillotel, H., *La Bretagne des Saints et des Rois, V*e*–X*e* siècle*, Rennes, 1984.

Chédeville, A., and Tonnerre, N.-Y., *La Bretagne Féodale, XI*e*–XIII*e* siècle*, Rennes, 1987.

Cheyette, F. L., *Lordship and Community in Medieval Europe*, New York, 1968.

Classen, P., 'Die Verträge von Verdun und von Coulaines, 843, als politische Grundlagen des westfränkischen Reiches', *Historische Zeitschrift*, 196 (1963), 1–35.

Collins, R., *The Basques*, Oxford, 1986.

'The Basques in Aquitaine and Navarre: problems of frontier government', in *War and Government in the Middle Ages. Essays in Honour of J. O. Prestwich*, ed. J. Gillingham and J. C. Holt, Woodbridge, 1984, pp. 3–17.

Congar, Y. M.-J., *L'Ecclésiologie du Haut Moyen Age*, Paris, 1968.

Constable, G., *Monastic Tithes from their Origins to the Twelfth Century*, Cambridge, 1964.

Contreni, J. J., 'The Carolingian renaissance', in *Renaissances before the Renaissance: Cultural Revivals of Late Antiquity and the Middle Ages*, ed. W. Treadgold, Stanford, 1984, pp. 59–74.

'Going to school in Carolingian Europe', in *Aspects of Carolingian Learning*, ed. R. E. Sullivan (forthcoming).

Couffon, R., 'A quelles dates Dol et Guérande ont-elles étés ravagées par Olaf Haraldson?', *MSHAB*, 29 (1949), 25–33.

Cunliffe, B., 'Britain, the Veneti and beyond', *Oxford Journal of Archaeology*, 1 (1982), 39–68.

Greeks, Romans and Barbarians: Spheres of Interaction, London, 1988.

David, P., *Etudes Historiques sur la Galice et le Portugal du VI*e* au XII*e* siècle*, Lisbon, 1947.

Davies, R. R., *Conquest, Coexistence and Change. Wales 1063–1415*, Oxford, 1987.

Davies, W., 'Les chartes du Cartulaire de Landévennec', in *Landévennec et le Monachisme Breton*, ed. Simon, pp. 85–95.

'The composition of the Redon cartulary', *Francia*, 17.i (1990), 69–90.

'Disputes, their conduct and their settlement in the village communities of eastern Brittany in the ninth century', *History and Anthropology*, 1 (1985), 289–312.

'Forgery in the cartulaire de Redon', in *Fälschungen im Mittelalter*, MGH Schriften 33, 6 vols., Munich, 1988–9, IV.265–74.

'The Latin charter-tradition in western Britain, Brittany and Ireland in the early medieval period', in *Ireland and Europe in the Early Middle Ages*, ed. D.

Bibliography

Whitelock, R. McKitterick, and D. N. Dumville, Cambridge, 1982, pp. 258–80.

'On the distribution of political power in Brittany in the mid-ninth century', in *Charles the Bald*, pp. 98–114.

'People and places in dispute in ninth-century Brittany', in *The Settlement of Disputes in Early Medieval Europe*, ed. W. Davies and P. Fouracre, Cambridge, 1986, pp. 65–84.

'Priests and rural communities in east Brittany in the ninth century', *EC*, 20 (1983), 177–97.

Small Worlds: The Village Community in Early Medieval Brittany, London, 1988.

'Suretyship in the *Cartulaire de Redon*', in *Lawyers and Laymen*, ed. T. M. Charles-Edwards, M. E. Owen, and D. B. Walters, Cardiff, 1986, pp. 72–91.

Davies, W. H., 'The Church in Wales', in *Christianity in Britain, 300–700*, ed. Barley and Hanson, pp. 131–50.

Deshman, R., 'Antiquity and empire in the throne of Charles the Bald' (forthcoming in the Festschrift for K. Weitzmann).

'*Christus Rex et magi reges*: kingship and Christology in Ottonian and Anglo-Saxon art', *Frühmittelalterliche Studien*, 10 (1976), 375–405.

Deuffic, J.-L., 'La production manuscrite des scriptoria bretons (VIIIe–XIe siècles)', in *Landévennec et le Monachisme Breton*, ed. Simon, pp. 289–321.

Devisse, J., *Hincmar, Archevêque de Reims 845–882*, 3 vols., Geneva, 1975–6.

Devroey, J.-P., 'Un monastère dans l'économie d'échanges: les services de transport à l'abbaye Saint-Germain-des-Prés au IXe siècle', *Annales: Economies, Sociétés, Civilisations*, 39 (1984), 570–98.

'Les services de transport à l'abbaye de Prüm au IXe siècle', *Revue du Nord*, 61 (1979), 543–69.

Dhondt, J., *Etudes sur la Naissance des Principautés Territoriales en France, IXe au Xe siècle*, Bruges, 1948.

Dierkens, A., *Abbayes et Chapitres entre Sambre et Meuse (VIIe–XIe siècles). Contribution à l'Histoire Religieuse des Campagnes du haut Moyen Age*, Beihefte der Francia 14, Sigmaringen, 1985.

'La christianisation des campagnes de l'empire de Louis le Pieux: l'exemple du diocèse de Liège sous l'épiscopat de Walcaud (c. 809–c. 831)', in *Charlemagne's Heir*, pp. 309–29.

Drinkwater, J., 'The Bagaudae in fifth-century Gaul', in *Fifth-Century Gaul: A Crisis of Identity?* (forthcoming).

Duby, G., *The Early Growth of the European Economy: Warriors and Peasants from the Seventh to the Twelfth Century*, London, 1974.

La Société aux XIe et XIIe siècles dans la Région Mâconnaise, 2nd edn, Paris, 1971.

Duchesne, L., *Fastes Episcopaux de l'Ancienne Gaule*, 3 vols., Paris, 1894–1915.

'Lovocat et Catihern', *Revue de Bretagne et de Vendée*, 57 (1885), 5–21.

'La vie de Saint Malo: étude critique', *Revue Critique*, 11 (1890), 1–22.

Dumas-Dubourg, F. *Le Trésor de Fécamp et le Monnayage en France Occidentale pendant le second moitié du Xe siècle*, Paris, 1971.

Dumville, D. N., 'On the dating of the early Breton lawcodes', *EC*, 21 (1984), 207–21.

Bibliography

'Some British aspects of the earliest Irish Christianity', in *Irland und Europa: die Kirche im Frühmittelalter*, ed. P. Ní Chatháin and M. Richter, Stuttgart, 1984, pp. 16–24.

'Sub-Roman Britain: history and legend', *History*, n.s., 62 (1977), 173–92.

Dunbabin, J., *France in the Making, 843–1180*, Oxford, 1985.

Duplessy, J., *Les Trésors Monétaires Médiévaux et Modernes Découverts en France, I, 751–1223*, Paris, 1985.

Duval, M., 'En Bretagne, recherche sur la formation des paroisses entre l'Ille et la Vilaine, XI–XVIe siècle', in *109e Congrès National des Sociétés Savantes, Dijon 1984. Section philologique et historique*, Paris, 1985, pp. 93–110.

Ebling, H., *Prosopographie der Amtsträger des Merowingerreiches von Chlothar II (613) bis Karl Martell (741)*, Beihefte der Francia 2, Munich, 1974.

Ernst, R., 'Karolingische Nordostpolitik zur Zeit Ludwigs des Frommen', in *Östliches Europa: Spiegel der Geschichte. Festschrift für Manfred Hellmann*, ed. C. Goehrke, E. Oberländer, and D. Wojtecki, Quellen und Studien zur Geschichte des östlichen Europa 9, Wiesbaden, 1977, pp. 81–107.

Estey, F. N., 'The *scabini* and the local courts', *Speculum*, 26 (1951), 119–29.

Ewig, E., 'Descriptio Franciae', in *Karl der Grosse*, I.143–77 (reprinted in Ewig, *Spätantikes und fränkisches Gallien*, I.274–322).

'Die fränkischen Teilungen und Teilreiche (511–613)', *Akademie der Wissenschaften und der Literatur Mainz. Abhandlungen der geistes- und sozialwissenschaftlichen Klasse*, 9 (1953), 651–715 (reprinted in Ewig, *Spätantikes und fränkisches Gallien*, I.114–71).

'Saint Chrodegang et la réforme de l'église franque', in *Saint Chrodegang. Communications presentés au Colloque tenu à Metz à l'occasion du XIIe centenaire de sa mort*, Metz, 1967, pp. 25–53 (reprinted in Ewig, *Spätantikes und fränkisches Gallien*, II.232–59).

Spätantikes und fränkisches Gallien. Gesammelte Schriften (1952–1973), ed. H. Atsma, 2 vols., Beihefte der Francia 3, Munich, 1976–9.

'Überlegungen zu den merowingischen und karolingischen Teilungen', *Settimane*, 27 (1979), 225–53.

'Volkstum und Volksbewusstsein im Frankenreich des 7. Jahrhunderts', *Settimane*, 5 (1958), 587–648 (reprinted in Ewig, *Spätantikes und fränkisches Gallien*, I.231–73).

Fahy, D., 'When did the Britons become Bretons? A note on the foundation of Brittany', *Welsh History Review*, 2 (1964–5), 111–24.

Falc'hun, F., *L'Histoire de la Langue Bretonne d'après la Géographie Linguistique*, 2 vols., 2nd edn, Paris, 1963.

Fischer, B., 'Bibeltext und Bibelreform unter Karl dem Grossen', in *Karl der Grosse*, II.156–216.

'Zur Überlieferung des lateinischen Textes der Evangelien', *Cahiers de la Revue Théologique de Louvain*, 19 (1987), 51–104.

Flatrès, P., 'Les anciennes structures rurales de Bretagne d'après le cartulaire de Redon', *Etudes Rurales*, 41 (1971), 87–93.

Fleuriot, L., *Dictionnaire des Gloses en Vieux Breton*, Paris, 1964.

'Un fragment en latin des très anciennes lois bretonnes armoricaines du VIe siècle', *Annales de Bretagne*, 78 (1971), 601–60.

'Gloses inédites en vieux-breton', *EC*, 16 (1979), 197–210.

Bibliography

'Nouvelles gloses vieilles-bretonnes à Amalarius', *EC*, 11 (1964–7), 415–64.

'Old Breton genealogies and early British traditions', *Bulletin of the Board of Celtic Studies*, 26 (1974), 1–6.

Les Origines de la Bretagne, Paris, 1982.

'Recherches sur les enclaves romanes anciennes en territoire bretonnant', *EC*, 8 (1958), 164–78.

Fontaine, J., 'De la pluralité à l'unité dans le "latin carolingien"', *Settimane*, 27 (1979), 765–805.

Foot, S. R. I., *Anglo-Saxon Minsters AD 597–975*, Woodbridge, forthcoming.

Fossier, R., *Enfance de l'Europe, X^e–XIIe siècles*, 2 vols., Nouvelle Clio 17, Paris, 1982.

Fournier, G., *Le Peuplement rural en Basse Auvergne durant le haut Moyen Age*, Paris, 1962.

Fournier, P., and Le Bras, G., *Histoire des Collections Canoniques en Occident depuis les Fausses Décrétales jusqu'au Decret de Gratien*, 2 vols., Paris, 1931–2.

Freed, J. B., 'Reflections on the medieval German nobility', *American Historical Review*, 91 (1986), 553–75.

Fried, J., 'Der karolingische Herrschaftsverband im 9. Jh. zwischen "Kirche" und "Könighaus"', *Historische Zeitschrift*, 235 (1982), 1–43.

'Laienadel und Papst in der Frühzeit der französischen und deutschen Geschichte', in *Aspekte der Nationenbildung im Mittelalter. Ergebnisse der Marburger Rundgespräche 1972–75*, ed. H. Beumann and W. Schröder, Sigmaringen, 1978, pp. 367–406.

Fuhrmann, H., *Einfluss und Verbreitung der pseudoisidorischen Fälschungen*, 3 vols., MGH Schriften 24, Stuttgart, 1972–4.

Galinié, H., 'Archéologie et topographie historique de Tours – IVe–XIe siècle', *Zeitschrift für Archäologie des Mittelalters*, 6 (1978), 33–56.

Galliou, P., *L'Armorique Romaine*, Braspars, 1984.

Galliou, P., Fulford, M., and Clément, M., 'La diffusion de la céramique "à l'éponge" dans le nord-ouest de l'empire romain', *Gallia*, 38 (1980), 265–78.

Ganshof, F. L., *Frankish Institutions under Charlemagne*, New York, 1968.

'The treaties of the Carolingians', *Medieval and Renaissance Studies*, 3 (1967), 23–52.

Gasnault, P., 'Les actes privés de l'abbaye de Saint-Martin de Tours du VIIIe au XIIe siècle', *Bibliothèque de l'Ecole des Chartes*, 112 (1954), 24–66.

'Le tombeau de Saint Martin et les invasions normandes dans l'histoire et dans la légende', *Revue d'Histoire de l'Eglise de France*, 47 (1961), 51–66.

Gasquet, F. A., and Bishop, E., *The Bosworth Psalter*, London, 1908.

Geary, P., *Aristocracy in Provence. The Rhône Basin at the Dawn of the Carolingian Age*, Monographien zur Geschichte des Mittelalters 31, Stuttgart, 1985.

'Germanic tradition and royal ideology in the ninth century: the "Visio Karoli Magni"', *Frühmittelalterliche Studien*, 21 (1987), 274–94.

Geberding, R. A., *The Rise of the Carolingians and the 'Liber Historiae Francorum'*, Oxford, 1987.

Gibson, M. T., and Nelson, J. L., eds., *Charles the Bald: Court and Kingdom*, 2nd revised edn., Aldershot, 1990.

Bibliography

Giot, P.-R., '"Insula quae Laurea appellatur". Fouilles archéologiques sur l'île Lavret', in *Landévennec et le Monachisme Breton*, ed. Simon, pp. 219–37.

'Saint Budoc on the Isle of Lavret, Brittany', in *The Early Church in Western Britain and Ireland*, ed. S. M. Pearce, British Archaeological Reports, British Series 102, Oxford, 1982, pp. 197–210.

Giot, P. R., L'Helgouach, J., and Briard, J., *Brittany*, Ancient Peoples and Places 13, London, 1960.

Giot, P.-R., and Monnier, J.-L., 'Le cimetière des anciens bretons de Saint-Urnel ou Saint-Saturnin en Plomeur (Finistère)', *Gallia*, 35 (1977), 141–71.

'Les oratoires des anciens bretons de Saint-Urnel ou Saint-Saturnin en Plomeur (Finistère)', *Archéologie Médiévale*, 8 (1978), 55–93.

Giry, A., 'Sur la date de deux diplômes de l'église de Nantes', *Annales de Bretagne*, 13 (1898), 485–508.

Godman, P., 'Louis "the Pious" and his poets', *Frühmittelalterliche Studien*, 19 (1985), 239–89.

Godman, P., and Collins, R., eds., *Charlemagne's Heir: New Perspectives on the Reign of Louis the Pious (814–840)*, Oxford, 1990.

Goetz, H.-W., '*Dux*' und '*Ducatus*'. *Begriffs- und verfassungsgeschichtliche Untersuchungen zur Entstehung des sogenannten 'jüngeren' Stammesherzogtums an der Wende vom neunten zum zehnten Jahrhundert*, Bochum, 1977.

Gougaud, L., 'Mentions anglaises des saints bretons et de leurs reliques', *Annales de Bretagne*, 34 (1919–21), 273–7.

'Les relations de l'abbaye de Fleury-sur-Loire avec la Bretagne et les îles britanniques, X^e–XIe siècle', *MSHAB*, 4 (1923), 3–30.

Graus, F., 'Rex-Dux Moraviae', *Sbornik prací filosofické faculty brnenske university, Rada historicke*, 7 (1960), 181–90 (with German summary).

Grenier, A., *Manuel d'Archéologie Gallo-Romaine*, 3 vols., Paris, 1931–58.

Grierson, P., and Blackburn, M., *Medieval European Coinage with a Catalogue of the Coins in the Fitzwilliam Museum, Cambridge. I. The Early Middle Ages (5th–10th centuries)*, Cambridge, 1986.

Grosjean, P., '*Confusa caligo*: remarques sur les *hisperica famina*', *Celtica*, 3 (1956), 35–85.

Guillot, O., *Le Comte d'Anjou et son Entourage au XIe siècle*, 2 vols., Paris, 1972.

Guillotel, H., 'L'action de Charles le Chauve vis-à-vis de la Bretagne de 843 à 851', *MSHAB*, 53 (1975–6), 5–32.

'Les cartulaires de l'abbaye de Redon', *MSHAB*, 63 (1986), 27–48.

'Les évêques d'Alet du IXe au milieu du XIIe siècle', *Annales de la Société d'Histoire et d'Archéologie de l'Arrondissement de Saint-Malo* (1979), 251–66.

'L'exode du clergé breton devant les invasions scandinaves', *MSHAB*, 59 (1982), 269–315.

'Les origines du ressort de l'évêché de Dol', *MSHAB*, 54 (1977), 31–68.

'Le premier siècle du pouvoir ducal breton (936–1040)', in *103e Congrès National des Sociétés Savantes, Nancy–Metz, 1978. Section Philologique et Historique jusqu'à 1610. Principautés et Territoires et Etudes d'Histoire lorraine*, Paris, 1979, pp. 63–84.

Guillotin de Corson, A., *Pouillé Historique de l'Archevêché de Rennes*, 6 vols., Rennes, 1880–6.

Bibliography

Halphen, L., *Charlemagne et l'Empire Carolingien*, Paris, 1947.

Hamel-Simon, J.-Y., Langouët, L., Nourry-Denayer, F., and Mouton, D., 'Fouille d'un retranchement d'Alain Barbetorte datable de 939: Le Camp des Haies à Trans (Ille-et-Vilaine)', *Les Dossiers du Centre Régional Archéologique d'Alet*, 7 (1979), 47–74.

Hamp, E. P., 'Morphological correspondences in Cornish and Breton', *The Journal of Celtic Studies*, 2 (1953–8), 5–24.

Hannig, J., 'Pauperiores vassi de infra palatio? Zur Entstehung der karolingischen Königsbotenorganisation', *Mitteilungen des Instituts für österreichische Geschichtsforschung*, 91 (1983), 309–74.

'Zentrale Kontrolle und regionale Machtbalance. Beobachtungen zum System der karolingischen Königsboten am Beispiel des Mittelrheingebietes', *Archiv für Kulturgeschichte*, 66 (1984), 1–46.

Hartmann, W., 'Der rechtliche Zustand der Kirchen auf dem Lande: die Eigenkirche in der fränkischen Gesetzgebung des 7. bis 9. Jahrhunderts', *Settimane*, 28 (1980), 397–441.

Die Synoden der Karolingerzeit im Frankenreich und in Italien, Paderborn, 1989.

Haselbach, I., *Aufstieg und Herrschaft der Karlinger in der Darstellung der sogennanten Annales Mettenses Priores*, Historische Studien 412, Lübeck, 1970.

Head, T., *Hagiography and the Cult of Saints: The Diocese of Orléans, 800–1200*, Cambridge, 1990.

Hedeager, L., 'Empire, frontier and the barbarian hinterland: Rome and northern Europe from AD 1–400', in *Centre and Periphery in the Ancient World*, ed. M. Rowlands, M. Larsen, and K. Kristiansen, Cambridge, 1987, pp. 125–40.

Heinzelmann, M., *Bischofsherrschaft in Gallien: Zur Kontinuität römischer Führungsschichten vom 4. zum 7. Jahrhundert. Soziale, prosopographische und bildungsgeschichtliche Aspekte*, Beihefte der Francia 5, Munich, 1976.

Hodges, R., Moreland, J., and Patterson, H., 'San Vincenzo al Volturno, the kingdom of Benevento and the Carolingians', in *Papers in Italian Archaeology*, ed. C. Malone and S. Stoddart, 4 vols., British Archaeological Reports, International Series 243–6, Oxford, 1985, IV.261–85.

Hoffmann, H., *Untersuchungen zur karolingischen Annalistik*, Bonn, 1958.

Hogan, R. M., 'The *Rainaldi* of Angers: "New Men" or descendants of Carolingian *nobiles*?', *Medieval Prosopography*, 2 (1981), 35–62.

Holtz, L., and Lambert, P.-Y., 'La tradition ancienne du *Liber in partibus Donati* de Smaragde de Saint-Mihiel', *Revue d'Histoire des Textes*, 16 (1986), 171–211.

Ineichen-Eder, C. E., 'Theologisches und philosophisches Lehrmaterial aus dem Alkuin-Kreise', *DA*, 34 (1978), 192–201.

Jackson, K. H., *Language and History in Early Britain*, Edinburgh, 1953.

James, E., *The Franks*, Oxford, 1988.

'Ireland and western Gaul in the Merovingian period', in *Ireland in Early Medieval Europe*, ed. D. Whitelock, R. McKitterick, and D. Dumville, Cambridge, 1982, pp. 362–86.

The Merovingian Archaeology of South-West Gaul, 2 vols., British Archaeological Reports S-25, Oxford, 1977.

The Origins of France: From Clovis to the Capetians, 500–1000, London, 1982.

Bibliography

Jeulin, P., 'L'hommage de la Bretagne en droit et dans les faits', *Annales de Bretagne*, 41 (1934), 380–473.

Jones, M., 'The Capetians and Brittany', *Historical Research*, 63 (1990), 1–16.

Jones, W. R., 'The image of the barbarian in medieval Europe', *Comparative Studies in Society and History*, 13 (1971), 376–407.

Kaiser, R., *Bischofsherrschaft zwischen Königtum und Fürstenmacht*, Pariser Historische Studien 17, Bonn, 1981.

'Royauté et pouvoir épiscopal au nord de la Gaule (VIIe–IXe siècles)', in *La Neustrie*, ed. Atsma, 1.143–60.

Kenney, J. F., *The Sources for the Early History of Ireland: Ecclesiastical. An Introduction and Guide*, New York, 1929.

Keranflec'h-Kernezne, C. de, 'Castel Cran, IXe siècle', *Bulletin Archéologique de l'Association Bretonne*, 12 (1891), 111–44.

Kerhervé, J., 'Aux origines d'un sentiment national. Les chroniqueurs bretons de la fin du Moyen Age', *Bulletin de la Société Archéologique du Finistère*, 108 (1980), 165–206.

Kerlouégan, F., 'Approche stylistique du latin de la *Vita Pauli Aureliani*', in *Landévennec et le Monachisme Breton*, ed. Simon, pp. 207–17.

'Une citation de la *Consolatio Philosphiae* (III, mètre 9) de Boèce dans la *vita Pauli* d'Uurmonoc', *EC*, 24 (1987), 309–14.

'Les citations d'auteurs latins chrétiens dans les vies des saints bretons carolingiennes', *EC*, 19 (1982), 215–57.

'Les citations d'auteurs latins profanes dans les vies des saints bretons carolingiennes', *EC*, 18 (1981), 181–95.

'Une mode stylistique dans la prose latine des pays celtiques', *EC*, 13 (1972–3), 275–97.

'Les vies des saints bretons les plus anciennes dans leurs rapports avec les îles britanniques', in *Insular Latin Studies*, ed. M. Herren, Papers in Mediaeval Studies 1, Toronto, 1981, pp. 195–213.

Kienast, W., *Der Herzogtitel in Frankreich und Deutschland 9. bis 12. Jahrhundert*, Munich, 1968.

Studien über die französischen Volksstämme des Frühmittelalters, Pariser Historische Studien 7, Stuttgart, 1968.

Klebel, E., 'Herzogtümer und Marken bis 900', *DA*, 2 (1938), 1–53.

Kottje, R., 'Einheit und Vielfalt des kirchlichen Lebens in der Karolingerzeit', *Zeitschrift für Kirchengeschichte*, 76 (1965), 323–42.

'Überlieferung und Rezeption der irischen Bussbücher auf dem Kontinent', in *Die Iren und Europa im früheren Mittelalter*, ed. H. Löwe, 2 vols., Stuttgart, 1982, I.511–24.

La Borderie, A. de, *Histoire de la Bretagne*, 6 vols., Rennes, 1896–1904.

Ladner, G. B., 'On Roman attitudes towards barbarians in late antiquity', *Viator*, 7 (1976), 1–26.

Lafaurie, J., *Catalogue des Deniers Mérovingiens de la Trouvaille de Bais (Ille-et-Vilaine) rédigé par Maurice Prou et Etienne Bougenot. Edition de 1907 avec de nouveaux commentaries et attributions par Jean Lafaurie*, Paris, 1981.

'Deux trésors monétaires carolingiens: Saumeray (Eure-et-Loire), Rennes (Ille-et-Vilaine)', *Revue Numismatique*, 6th ser., 7 (1965), 262–305.

Bibliography

'Monnaies mérovingiennes de Nantes du VIe siècle', *Bulletin de la Société Française de Numismatique*, 28 (1973), 391–4.

Lambert, P.-Y., 'Les commentaires celtiques à Bède le Vénérable', *EC*, 20 (1983), 119–43, and 21 (1984), 185–206.

'Les gloses celtiques aux commentaires de Virgile', *EC*, 23 (1986), 81–128.

'Les gloses grammaticales brittoniques', *EC*, 24 (1987), 285–308.

'Les gloses du manuscrit B. N. Latin 10290', *EC*, 19 (1982), 173–213.

Landévennec: aux Origines de la Bretagne, Daoulas, 1985 (exhibition catalogue).

Langouët, L., 'Les fortifications des terre et les mottes castrales', in *Artistes, Artisans et Production Artistique en Bretagne au Moyen Age*, ed. X. Barral i Altet, G. de Carne, and A. Chédeville *et al.*, Rennes, 1983, pp. 187–92.

'L'origine gallo-romaine de l'évêché d'Alet à la lumière des fouilles récentes', *Bulletin de la Société d'Histoire et d'Archéologie de l'Arrondissement de Saint-Malo* (1974), 95–107.

Lapidge, M., 'Gildas' education and the Latin culture of sub-Roman Britain', in *Gildas: New Approaches*, ed. Lapidge and Dumville, pp. 27–50.

'Latin learning in dark age Wales: some prolegomena', in *Proceedings of the Seventh International Congress of Celtic Studies, Oxford 1983*, ed. D. E. Evans, J. G. Griffith, and E. M. Jope, Oxford, 1986, pp. 91–107.

Lapidge, M., and Dumville, D., *Gildas: New Approaches*, Studies in Celtic History 5, Woodbridge, 1984.

Lapidge, M., and Sharpe, R., *A Bibliography of Celtic-Latin Literature, 400–1200*, Dublin, 1985.

Le Maître, P., 'Evêques et moines dans le Maine: IVe–VIIIe siècles', *Revue d'Histoire de l'Eglise de France*, 62 (1976), 91–101.

'L'oeuvre d'Aldric du Mans et sa signification', *Francia*, 8 (1980), 43–64.

Le Patourel, J., *The Norman Empire*, Oxford, 1976.

Leguay, J.-P., and Martin, H., *Fastes et Malheurs de la Bretagne Ducale, 1213–1532*, Rennes, 1982.

Lemarignier, J.-F., 'Encadrement religieux des campagnes et conjoncture politique dans les régions du royaume de France situées au nord de la Loire, de Charles le Chauve aux derniers carolingiens', *Settimane*, 28 (1980), 765–800.

'Les fidèles du roi de France (936–987)' in *Recueil des Travaux offert à M. Clovis Brunel*, 2 vols., Paris, 1955, II.138–62.

'Quelques remarques sur l'organisation ecclésiastique de la Gaule de VIIe à la fin du IXe siècle principalement au nord de la Loire', *Settimane*, 13 (1966), 451–86.

Lesne, E., *La Hiérarchie Episcopale. Provinces, Metropolitains, Primats en Gaule et Germanie depuis la Réforme de Saint Boniface jusqu'à la Mort d'Hincmar*, Mémoires et Travaux des Facultés Catholiques de Lille 1, Lille, 1905.

Levillain, L., 'La marche de Bretagne, ses marquis et ses comtes', *Annales de Bretagne*, 58 (1951), 89–117.

Lewis, A. R., 'The dukes in the *Regnum Francorum*, AD 550–751', *Speculum*, 51 (1976), 381–410.

Leyser, K. J., *Rule and Conflict in an Early Medieval Society: Ottonian Saxony*, London, 1979.

Bibliography

Lindsay, W. M., 'Breton scriptoria: their Latin abbreviation symbols', *Zentralblatt für Bibliothekswesen*, 29 (1912), 264–72.

Lot, F., 'La conquête du pays d'entre Seine-et-Loire par les Francs: la ligue armoricaine et les destinées du duché du Maine', *Revue Historique*, 155 (1930), 241–53.

'Un faiseur d'étymologies bretonnes au IXe siècle', in *Mélanges Bretons et Celtiques offerts à J. Loth*, Rennes, 1927, pp. 381–5.

Mélanges d'Histoire Bretonne, Paris, 1907.

'Vivien et Larchamp', *Romania*, 35 (1906), 258–77.

Lot, F., and Halphen, L., *Le Règne de Charles le Chauve (840–877). Première partie (840–851)*, Bibliothèque de l'Ecole des Hautes Etudes 175, Paris, 1909.

Loth, J., *L'Emigration Bretonne du 5e au 7e siècle de notre ère*, Rennes, 1883.

Les Noms des Saints Bretons, Paris, 1910.

Löwe, H., 'Geschichtsschreibung der ausgehenden Karolingerzeit', *DA*, 23 (1967), 1–30.

Loyn, H. R., 'Wales and England in the tenth century: the context of the Athelstan charters', *Welsh History Review*, 10 (1981), 283–301.

Lynch, J. H. *Godparents and Kinship in Early Medieval Europe*, Princeton, 1986.

'*Spirituale vinculum*: the vocabulary of spiritual kinship in early medieval Europe', in *Religion, Culture and Society in Early Medieval Europe. Studies in Honor of Richard E. Sullivan*, ed. T. F. X. Noble and J. J. Contreni, Studies in Medieval Culture 23, Kalamazoo, 1987, pp. 181–204.

Mabille, E., 'Les invasions normandes dans la Loire et les pérégrinations du corps de Saint Martin. Pièces justificatives', *Bibliothèque de l'Ecole des Chartes*, 30 (1869), 423–60.

McCammon, A. L. T., *Currencies of the Anglo-Norman Isles*, London, 1984.

McClure, E., 'The Wareham inscriptions', *English Historical Review*, 22 (1907), 728–30.

McGurk, P., 'The gospel book in Celtic lands before AD 850: contents and arrangement', in *Irland und die Christenheit: Bibelstudien und Mission*, ed. P. Ní Chatháin and M. Richter, Stuttgart, 1987, pp. 165–89.

McKitterick, R., 'Carolingian book production: some problems', *The Library*, 6th ser., 12 (1990), 1–33.

The Frankish Church and the Carolingian Reforms, 789–895, London, 1977.

The Frankish Kingdoms under the Carolingians, 751–987, London, 1983.

'Knowledge of canon law in the Frankish kingdoms before 789: the manuscript evidence', *Journal of Theological Studies*, n.s., 36 (1985), 97–117.

Manitius, M., 'Regino und Justin', *Neues Archiv der Gesellschaft für ältere deutsche Geschichtskunde*, 25 (1899), 192–201.

Martindale, J., 'Charles the Bald and the government of the kingdom of Aquitaine', in *Charles the Bald*, pp. 115–38.

'The French aristocracy in the early Middle Ages. A Reappraisal', *Past and Present*, 75 (1977), 5–45.

'The kingdom of Aquitaine and the "Dissolution of the Carolingian fisc"', *Francia*, 11 (1983), 131–91.

Merlet, R., 'Origine de la famille des Bérenger, comtes de Rennes', in *Mélanges F. Lot*, Paris, 1925, pp. 549–61.

Bibliography

Metcalf, D. M., 'A sketch of the currency in the time of Charles the Bald', in *Charles the Bald*, pp. 65–97.

Metcalf, D. M., and Northover, J. P., 'Carolingian and Viking coins from the Cuerdale hoard: an interpretation and comparison of their metal contents', *The Numismatic Chronicle*, 148 (1988), 97–116.

Metz, W., 'Miszellen zur Geschichte der Widonen und der Salier, vornehmlich in Deutschland', *Historisches Jahrbuch*, 85 (1965), 1–27.

Mitterauer, M., *Karolingische Markgrafen im Sudosten. Fränkische Reichsaristokratie und bayerischer Stammesadel im österreichischen Raum*, Archiv für österreichische Geschichte 123, Vienna, 1963.

Mohr, W., 'Die Krise des kirchlichen Einheitsprogram im Jahre 858', *Archivum Latinitatis Medii Aevi*, 25 (1955), 189–213.

Mordek, H., *Die Collectio Vetus Gallica: die älteste systematische Kanonessammlung des fränkischen Gallien*, Beiträge zur Geschichte und Quellenkunde des Mittelalters 1, Berlin, 1975.

Morey, C. R., Rand, E. K., and Kraeling, C. H., 'The gospel-book of Landévennec (the Harkness gospels) in the New York Public Library', *Art Studies*, 8 (1931), 225–86.

Mostert, M., *The Library of Fleury: A Provisional List of Manuscripts*, Hilversum, 1989.

Musset, L., 'Observations sur les noms d'hommes normands en Bretagne et d'ailleurs', *Bulletin de la Société des Antiquaires de Normandie*, 57 (1963–4), 612–16.

'Saint-Samson-sur-Risle', in *Annuaire des Cinq Départements de la Normandie, Congrès de Pont-Audemer*, Caen, 1961, pp. 11–18.

Nelson, J. L., 'The Annals of St Bertin', in *Charles the Bald*, pp. 23–40.

'Charles the Bald and the Church in town and countryside', *Studies in Church History*, 16 (1979), 103–18 (reprinted in *Politics and Ritual*, pp. 75–90).

'The Church's military service in the ninth century: a contemporary comparative view?', *Studies in Church History*, 20 (1983), 15–30 (reprinted in *Politics and Ritual*, pp. 117–32).

'Dispute settlement in Carolingian West Francia', in *The Settlement of Disputes in Early Medieval Europe*, ed. W. Davies and P. Fouracre, Cambridge, 1986, pp. 45–64.

'Kingship and empire', in *Cambridge History of Medieval Political Thought*, ed. Burns, pp. 211–51.

'The last years of Louis the Pious', in *Charlemagne's Heir*, pp. 147–59.

'Ninth-century knighthood: the evidence of Nithard', in *Studies in Medieval History Presented to R. Allen Brown*, ed. C. Harper-Bill, C. J. Holdsworth, and J. L. Nelson, Woodbridge, 1989, pp. 255–66.

'On the limits of the Carolingian renaissance', *Studies in Church History*, 14 (1977), 51–67 (reprinted in *Politics and Ritual*, pp. 49–67).

Politics and Ritual in Early Medieval Europe, London, 1986.

'Public *Histories* and private history in the work of Nithard', *Speculum*, 60 (1985), 251–93 (reprinted in *Politics and Ritual*, pp. 195–237).

'The reign of Charles the Bald: a survey', in *Charles the Bald*, pp. 1–22.

'Translating images of authority: the Christian Roman emperors in the Carolingian world', in *Images of Authority. Essays in Honour of Joyce*

Bibliography

Reynolds, ed. M. M. Mackenzie and C. Roueché, Cambridge, 1989, pp. 196–205.

Nicolardot, J.-P., 'Chronique des fouilles médiévales: Plédran (Côtes-du-Nord)', *Archéologie Médiévale*, 15 (1985), 281.

Noble, T. F. X., 'Louis the Pious and the frontiers of the Frankish realm', in *Charlemagne's Heir*, pp. 333–47.

'The monastic ideal as the model for reform: the case of Louis the Pious', *Revue Bénédictine*, 86 (1976), 235–50.

'The revolt of King Bernard of Italy in 817: its causes and consequences', *Studi Medievali*, 3rd ser., 15 (1974), 315–26.

Oexle, O. G., 'Bischof Ebroin von Poitiers und seine Verwandten', *Frühmittelalterliche Studien*, 3 (1969), 138–210.

Oheix, A., 'L'histoire de Cornouaille d'après un livre récent', *Bulletin de la Société Archéologique du Finistère*, 39 (1912), 3–24.

Olson, B. L., and Padel, O. J., 'A tenth-century list of Cornish parochial saints', *Cambridge Medieval Celtic Studies*, 12 (1986), 33–71.

Padel, O. J., 'Cornish names of parish churches', *Cornish Studies*, 4–5 (1976–7), 15–27.

Cornish Place-Name Elements, English Place-Name Society 56–7, Nottingham, 1985.

'Cornish *plu*, "parish"', *Cornish Studies*, 2 (1974), 75–8.

Pape, L., *La Civitas des Osismes à l'Epoque Gallo-Romaine*, Paris, 1978.

Penndorf, U., *Das Problem der 'Reichseinheitsidee' nach der Teilung von Verdun (843)*, Münchener Beiträge zur Mediävistik und Renaissance-Forschung 20, Munich, 1974.

Pietri, L., *La Ville de Tours du IVe au VIe siècle: Naissance d'une Cité Chrétienne*, Collection de l'Ecole Française de Rome 69, Rome, 1983.

Pietri, L., and Biarne, J., *Topographie Chrétienne des Cités de la Gaule des origines au milieu du VIIIe siècle. V: Province Ecclésiastique de Tours (Lugdunensis Tertia)*, Paris, 1987.

Planiol, M., 'La donation d'Anowareth', *Annales de Bretagne*, 9 (1893–4), 216–37.

Histoire des Institutions de la Bretagne, 5 vols., Mayenne, 1981–4.

Pocquet du Haut-Jussé, B.-A., *Les Papes et les Ducs de Bretagne*, 2 vols., Bibliothèque de l'Ecole Française d'Athènes et de Rome 133, Paris, 1928.

Poncelet, A., 'Une source de la vie de S. Malo par Bili', *Analecta Bollandiana*, 24 (1905), 483–6.

Potts, C., 'Normandy or Brittany? A conflict of interests at Mont Saint Michel (966–1035), *Anglo-Norman Studies*, 12 (1989), 135–56.

Prou, M., *Catalogue des Monnaies Françaises à la Bibliothèque Nationale. Les Monnaies Carolingiennes*, Paris, 1896.

Les Monnaies Mérovingiennes de la Bibliothèque Nationale, Paris, 1892.

Pryce, H., 'Pastoral care in early medieval Wales', in *Pastoral Care before the Parish*, ed. Blair and Sharpe (forthcoming).

Raison de Cleuziou, J., 'De quelques sources de la vie de Saint Guénolé', *Bulletin et Mémoires de la Société d'Emulation des Côtes-du-Nord*, 88 (1960), 29–35.

'Landévennec et les destinées de la Cornouaille', *Bulletin et Mémoires de la Société d'Emulation des Côtes-du-Nord*, 93 (1965), 7–26.

Bibliography

Reindel, K., 'Bayern im Karolingerreich', in *Karl der Grosse*, 1.220–46.

Reuter, T., 'The end of Carolingian military expansion', in *Charlemagne's Heir*, pp. 391–405.

'Plunder and tribute in the Carolingian empire', *Transactions of the Royal Historical Society*, 5th ser., 35 (1985), 75–94.

Reynolds, R. E., 'Unity and diversity in Carolingian canon law collections: the case of the *Collectio Hibernensis* and its derivatives', in *Carolingian Essays*, ed. U.-R. Blumenthal, Washington, DC, 1983, pp. 99–135.

Reynolds, S., *Kingdoms and Communities in Western Europe, 900–1300*, Oxford, 1984.

'Medieval *Origines Gentium* and the community of the realm', *History*, 68 (1983), 375–90.

Riché, P., *Les Ecoles et l'Enseignement dans l'Occident Chrétien de la fin du Ve siècle au milieu du XIe siècle*, Paris, 1979.

'Les hagiographes bretons et la renaissance carolingienne', in *Bulletin Philologique et Historique du Comité des Travaux Historiques et Scientifiques*, *année 1966*, Paris, 1968, pp. 651–9.

Robinson, I. S., 'Church and papacy', in *Cambridge History of Medieval Political Thought*, ed. Burns, pp. 252–305.

Rouche, M., *L'Aquitaine des Wisigothes aux Arabes (418–781)*, Paris, 1979.

Sahlins, P., *Boundaries: The Making of France and Spain in the Pyrenees*, Berkeley, 1989.

Scheibelreiter, G., *Der Bischof in der Merowingischer Zeit*, Veröffentlichungen des Instituts für österreichische Geschichtsforschung 27, Vienna, 1983.

Schieffer, T., 'Die Krise des karolingische Imperiums', in *Aus Mittelalter und Neuzeit: Festschrift für G. Kallen*, ed. J. Engel and H. M. Klinkenburg, Bonn, 1957, pp. 1–15.

Schmitz, P., 'L'influence de Saint Benoît dans l'histoire de l'orde de Saint-Benoît', *Settimane*, 4 (1957), 401–15.

Schneider, R., *Brüdergemeine und Schwurfreundschaft. Die Auflösungsprozess des Karlingerreiches im Spiegel der caritas-Terminologie der karlingischen Teilkönige des 9. Jahrhunderts*, Historische Studien 388, Lübeck, 1964.

Schott, C., 'Der Stand der Leges-Forschung', *Frühmittelalterliche Studien*, 13 (1979), 29–55.

Semmler, J., 'Die Beschlüsse des Aachener Konzils im Jahre 816', *Zeitschrift für Kirchengeschichte*, 74 (1963), 15–82.

'Episcopi potestas und karolingische Klosterpolitik', *Vorträge und Forschungen*, 20 (1974), 305–95.

'Mönche und Kanoniker im Frankenreiche Pippins III. und Karls des Grossen', in *Untersuchungen zu Kloster und Stift*, Veröffentlichungen des Max-Planck-Instituts für Geschichte 68, Göttingen, 1980, pp. 78–111.

'Pippin III. und die fränkischen Klöster', *Francia*, 3 (1975), 88–146.

'Reichsidee und kirchliche Gesetzgebung', *Zeitschrift für Kirchengeschichte*, 71 (1960), 37–65.

'Traditio und Königsschutz. Studien zur Geschichte der königlichen Monasteria', *Zeitschrift der Savigny-Stiftung für Rechtsgeschichte. Kanonistische Abteilung*, 45 (1959), 1–33.

Bibliography

'Zentgebot und Pfarrtermination in karolingischer Zeit', in *Aus Kirche und Reich. Studien zu Theologie, Politik und Recht im Mittelalter. Festschrift für Friedrich Kempf*, ed. H. Mordek, Sigmaringen, 1983, pp. 33–44.

Sharpe, R., 'Gildas as a father of the church', in *Gildas: New Approaches*, ed. Lapidge and Dumville, pp. 191–205.

Sheringham, J. T., 'Les machtierns. Quelques témoignages gallois et corniques', *MSHAB*, 58 (1981), 61–72.

Simon, M., ed., *Landévennec et le Monachisme Breton dans le Haut Moyen Age*, Landévennec, 1986.

Smith, J. M. H., 'The "archbishopric" of Dol and the ecclesiastical politics of ninth-century Brittany', *Studies in Church History*, 18 (1982), 59–70.

'Culte impérial et politique frontalière dans la vallée de la Vilaine: le témoignage des diplômes carolingiens dans le cartulaire de Redon', in *Landévennec et le Monachisme Breton*, ed. Simon, pp. 129–39.

'Oral and written: saints, miracles and relics in Brittany, c. 850–1250', *Speculum*, 65 (1990), 309–43.

'The sack of Vannes by Pippin III', *Cambridge Medieval Celtic Studies*, 11 (1986), 17–27.

Stafford, P., 'Sons and mothers: family politics in the early Middle Ages', in *Medieval Women*, ed. D. Baker, Oxford, 1978, pp. 79–100.

Stroheker, K. F., *Der senatorische Adel im spätantiken Gallien*, Tübingen, 1948.

Tanguy, B., 'L'hagio-onomastique bretonne: problématique et methodologie', in *107e Congrès National des Sociétés Savantes, Brest, 1982. Philologie et Histoire jusqu'à 1610. II: Questions d'Histoire de Bretagne*, Paris, 1984, pp. 323–40.

'La limite linguistique dans la péninsule armoricaine à l'époque de l'émigration bretonne (IVe–Ve siècle) d'après les données toponymiques', *Annales de Bretagne et des Pays de l'Ouest*, 87 (1980), 429–62.

'Les paroisses primitives en plou- et leurs saints éponymes', *Bulletin de la Société Archéologique du Finistère*, 109 (1981), 121–55.

Tessier, G., 'A propos de quelques actes toulousains du IXe siècle', in *Recueil de Travaux Offerts à M. Clovis Brunel*, 2 vols., Paris, 1955, II.566–80.

Thomas, C., *A Provisional List of Imported Pottery in Post-Roman Britain and Ireland*, Institute of Cornish Studies Special Report 7, Redruth, 1981.

Thompson, E. A., 'Britonia', in *Christianity in Britain, 300–700*, ed. Barley and Hanson, pp. 201–5.

'Procopius on Brittia and Britannia', *The Classical Quarterly*, 30 (1980), 498–507.

Tonnerre, N.-Y., 'Les pays de la basse Vilaine au haut moyen âge', *MSHAB*, 63 (1986), 29–72.

Ullmann, W., *The Growth of Papal Government in the Middle Ages*, 3rd edn, London, 1970.

'*Nos si aliquid incompetenter* ... Some observations on the register fragments of Leo IV in the Collectio Britannica', *Ephemerides Iuris Canonici*, 9 (1953), 279–87.

Van Caenegem, R., 'Government, law and society', in *Cambridge History of Medieval Political Thought*, ed. Burns, pp. 174–210.

Van Dam, R., *Leadership and Community in Late Antique Gaul*, Berkeley, 1985.

Bibliography

Van Rey, M., 'Die Münzprägung Karls des Kahlen und die westfränkische Königslandschaft', in *Die Stadt in der europäischen Geschichte. Festschrift Edith Ennen*, ed. W. Besch, K. Fehn, D. Höroldt, F. Irsigler, and M. Zender, Bonn, 1972, pp. 153–84.

Vezin, J., 'Les scriptoria de Neustrie 650–850', in *La Neustrie*, ed. Atsma, II.307–18.

Wallace-Hadrill, J. M., *The Frankish Church*, Oxford, 1983.

Wattenbach, W., and Levison, W., *Deutschlands Geschichtsquellen im Mittelalter. Vorzeit und Karolinger. V Die Karolinger vom Vertrag von Verdun bis zum Herrschaftsantritt der Herrscher aus dem sächsischen Hause. Das westfränkische Reich*, re-ed. H. Löwe, Weimar, 1973.

Weidemann, M., 'Bischofsherrschaft und Königtum in Neustrien von 7. bis 9. Jahrhundert am Beispiel des Bistum Le Mans', in *La Neustrie*, ed. Atsma, I.161–93.

Werner, K.-F., 'Bedeutende Adelsfamilien im Reich Karls des Grossen', in *Karl der Grosse*, I.83–142.

'Gauzlin von Saint-Denis und die westfränkische Reichsteilung von Amiens (März 880)', *DA*, 35 (1979), 395–462.

'La genèse des duchés en France et en Allemagne', *Settimane*, 27 (1979), 175–207.

'*Hludovicus Augustus*: gouverner l'empire chrétien – idées et réalités', in *Charlemagne's Heir*, pp. 3–123.

'Kingdom and principality in twelfth-century France', in *The Medieval Nobility*, ed. T. Reuter, Amsterdam, 1979, pp. 243–90.

'*Missus – marchio – comes*. Entre l'administration centrale et l'administration locale de l'empire carolingien', in *Histoire Comparée de l'Administration (IVe–XVIIIe siècles)*, ed. W. Paravicini and K.-F. Werner, Beihefte der Francia 9, Munich, 1980, pp. 191–239.

'Untersuchungen zur Frühzeit des französichen Fürstentums', *Die Welt als Geschichte*, 18 (1958), 256–89, 19 (1959), 146–93, 20 (1960), 87–119.

'Westfranken-Frankreich unter den Spätkarolingern und frühen Kapetingern (888–1060)', in *Handbuch der europäischen Geschichte*, ed. T. Schieder, Stuttgart, 1976, pp. 731–83.

'Zur Arbeitsweise des Regino vom Prüm', *Die Welt als Geschichte*, 19 (1959), 96–116.

Whittaker, C. R., 'Trade and frontiers of the Roman empire', in *Trade and Famine in Classical Antiquity*, ed. P. Garnsey and C. R. Whittaker, Proceedings of the Cambridge Philological Society Supplement 8, Cambridge, 1983, pp. 110–27.

Wickham, C., *Early Medieval Italy. Central Power and Local Society, 400–1000*, London, 1981.

Wilmart, A., *Analecta Reginensa: Extraits des Manuscrits Latins de la Reine Christine Conservés au Vatican*, Studi e Testi 59, Vatican City, 1933.

Wolff, P., 'L'Aquitaine et ses marges', in *Karl der Grosse*, I.269–306.

Wood, I. N., *The Merovingian North Sea*, Alingsås, 1983.

Wright, N., 'Knowledge of Christian Latin poets and historians in early medieval Brittany', *EC*, 23 (1986), 163–85.

Bibliography

'Some further Vergilian borrowings in Breton hagiography of the Carolingian period', *EC*, 20 (1983), 161–75.

Yates, W. N., 'The "Age of Saints" in Carmarthenshire: a study of church dedications', *The Carmarthenshire Antiquary*, 9 (1973), 53–81.

UNPUBLISHED THESES

Airlie, S. R., 'The political behaviour of the secular magnates in Francia, 829–879', DPhil, Oxford, 1985.

Brunterc'h, J.-P., 'L'extension du ressort politique et religieux du Nantais au sud de la Loire: essai sur les origines de la dislocation du *pagus* d'Herbauge (IXe s.–987)', thesis, Université de Paris IV, 1981, with published summary in *Positions des Thèses de l'Ecole des Chartes*, Paris, 1981, pp. 39–49.

Coupland, S. C., 'Charles the Bald and the defence of the West Frankish kingdom against the Viking invasions, 840–877', PhD, Cambridge, 1987.

INDEX

Index

Lambert, count of Nantes 818–34, 53, 66, 77–8, 79, 80, 81
Lambert, count of Nantes in 840s, 53, 92, 94, 95, 96, 97, 98, 99, 101, 132
land
  belonging to churches, 56–7, 131
  familial transactions, 38–9
  resources of Breton rulers, 129–31
  taxes and obligations on, in Brittany, 133–4
  tenure: in Guérande, 37; in Nantais, 38–40; in Vannetais, 25–6
  transactions concerning, 26, 36, 75
  women and, 38–9
Landévennec, 72
  literary culture at, 173–5
Landramn, bishop of Nantes, 53, 192, 195
Landramn I, archbishop of Tours, 53
Landramn II, archbishop of Tours, 53
Latin language, in Brittany, 166, 173–4
lawsuits, 75–6
Le Mans, 45, 46, 47
  bishopric of, 46, 80, 152
  counts of, 81n
  duchy of, 45, 46, 48, 50–1, 84, 103
Léhon, 130
  see also Saint-Magloire
Leo III, pope, 153
Leo IV, pope, 149, 154, 178
Letavii, 13
Liosmonoc, 170
Lothar I, 78, 80, 88, 90, 97, 99
  foments unrest, 93–4
  and Neustria, 91–2
  and Nominoe, 93, 97
Louis III, 191
Louis IV d'Outremer, 189, 197, 198
Louis the German, 60, 78, 80, 88, 90, 97, 100
  and West Frankish revolts, 102, 103
Louis the Pious, 60
  baptismal sponsor of Harald, 109
  campaigns against Bretons, 65–6, 78
  diplomas for Breton churches, 71–2
  Frankish revolts against, 77–9, 80–1
  grants land in Breton march, 57
  historiography of reign, 63, 64
  and imperial frontiers, 64–5
  monastic legislation, 71–2
  in Neustria, 48
  overlordship over Bretons, 68, 70–1
Louis the Stammerer, 51, 114
  betrothed to Erispoe's daughter, 102, 110

in revolt of 858, 103, 104, 105
  reign of, 189–91
Louis the Younger, 102, 191
Lovocat and Catihern, British priests, 12
Lupus of Ferrières, 96, 111

machtiern, definition of, 28
machtierns, 30–1, 125–6
Macliau, ruler of Vannes, 21
Mahen, bishop of Alet, 156
maiores, 30
Mansuetus, 11–12
manuscripts, Breton, 164–5, 167–73
  in England, 197; in Norman monasteries, 163
  script of, 14, 167, 169
  see List of Manuscripts for individual citations
marches
  of Louis the Pious' empire, 61
  Breton march, 45–6, 58; ecclesiastical lands in, 56–7
Matfrid, count of Orléans, 78, 79, 80, 81
Matuedoe, 124, 135, 196–7, 200
mining, 37
missi, 74
  of Breton rulers, 123, 125–6
Monte Cassino, 70
Morman, 65, 66, 68, 73, 74, 119

Nantes
  bishopric, 15, 155, 156; diplomas for, 110, 111, 198; ecclesiastical reform in, 152; individual bishops, *see* Actard, Agatheus, Amito, Felix, Landramn, Pascharius
  county: Breton raids into, 19; economy, 36–43; fiscal resources in, 139–40; grant to Salomon confirmed, 107; granted to Erispoe, 100; individual counts, *see* Amalric, Lambert, Rainald, Richowin; lost by Bretons, 195; support for Lothar I in, 96; under Breton rule, 138–42; under Carolingian rule, 47; under Merovingian rule, 44
  trade at, 41–2, 139
Neustria, 34, 44, 84, 91, 100
  aristocracy in, 50–1, 77–81
  breakdown of royal power in, 96, 98
  Carolingian rule in, 47–9
  ecclesiastical lands in, 56–7
  minting of coins in, 143
  passes under Robertian control, 193–4

Index

Nicholas I, pope, 107, 124, 149, 155, 157–8, 159–60, 179
Nominoe
  appointment by and relations with Louis the Pious, 80, 82–4, 86–7
  campaigns against Vikings, 199
  charters of, 117
  claims to authority throughout Brittany, 119
  death, 99
  deposes Breton bishops, 155–7
  grants *plebes* to Redon, 135
  lands of, 129–30
  patronage of Redon, 82, 93
  relations with Charles the Bald: oath of loyalty to, 93; peace with Charles the Bald, 97; rebels and raids Neustria, 88, 89, 95, 97, 98, 133
  titles for, 97
  Vannes, possibly count of, 82n
Nonius Marcellus, *De Proprietate Sermonum*, 172
Normandy, 45, 144, 202

Odo, count of Orléans, 78, 79
Odo, king, 187, 190–1, 193
Old Breton, 13–14
  glosses in manuscripts, 168, 172
  see also Breton language
Ordinatio Imperii, 60, 63, 77, 91
Orosius, *Historia contra paganos*, 171
Osismii, *civitas* of, 15
overlordship, symbols and rituals of, 67–9, 108–14

Pascharius, bishop of Nantes, 47
Pascweten, count of Vannes 107, 112, 121, 122, 124
  lands of, 130
pastoral care, in Brittany, 182–4
pasturage of horses, 136–7
pastus caballorum et canum, see pasturage of horses
pays de Retz
  grant to Erispoe, 101
  grant to Salomon confirmed, 107
pilgrims, to and from Brittany, 163, 164
Pippin II, of Herstal, 47
Pippin III, 47, 48, 58
Pippin I of Aquitaine, 60, 78, 80
Pippin II of Aquitaine, 91, 95, 96, 97, 101, 102
plebs, plebes
  definition of, 27

ecclesiastical life in, 180–1, 182–4
  rights over, 31, 134–5
popes, *see* Hadrian I, Hadrian II, John VIII, Leo III, Leo IV, Nicholas I
Priscian, Grammar, *Periegesis*, 172
Prüm, monastery of, 56, 57, 131, 136, 144
pseudo-Isidorian decretals, *see* False Decretals

Quierzy, capitulary of, 139
Quimper, bishopric of, 15, 156

Radulf of Thuringia, 114
Raginarius, bishop of Vannes, 76
Rainald, count of Nantes, 54, 80, 92, 94, 132
Raino, bishop of Angers, 195
ran (unit of land), 25, 26
Redon
  cartulary of, 23, 24–5
  donations from Breton rulers, 129–30
  foundation of, 23–4, 76, 82
  granted protection by Charles the Bald, 98
  landholdings, 24, 144
  plebes granted to, 134–5
  rights to transport services, 137
regalia, royal apparel, 109, 111, 112, 114
Reims, archbishopric of, 56, 57
Rennes
  bishopric, 15; ecclesiastical reform in, 152; individual bishops, *see* Agatheus, Victurius, Wernar
  county: Breton raids into, 19; counts acknowledge Norman hegemony, 196; grant to Salomon confirmed, 107; granted to Erispoe, 100; support for Lothar in, 96; under Breton rule, 139–43; under Carolingian rule, 47; under Merovingian rule, 44
  trade at, 42
rent, 133
Rethwalatr, bishop of Alet, 156
Richowin, count of Nantes, 84, 92
Riotimus, 12
Riwallon, brother of Salomon, 123, 124
Riwalt, 28
Robert of Neustria, 193, 194
  vassals of, 194–5
Robert the Strong, 54–5, 101, 103, 104, 105, 106, 199

Index

Rodulf, king, 196
Roiantdreh, 131, 134, 135
Roland, *praefectus* of Breton march, 58
Rome, 164
Rorigo, 54, 70–1, 76, 80, 84
Rorigo, family of, 53–4, 98, 104
Rouen, 47
Rudalt, count of Vannes, 124, 128
Rule of St Benedict, 72, 77

St Peter, Breton veneration for, 164
Saint-Aubin, 48, 53, 105
Saint-Brieuc, bishopric, 15
Saint-Denis, 56, 57
Saint-Magloire, 132
  see also Léhon
Saint-Maixent, 29
Saint-Martin, Tours, 48, 163
Saint-Maur, 54, 135
Saint-Médard, 57, 58
Saint-Méen, 70, 71–2
Saint-Philibert, 111
Saint-Pol-de-Léon, bishopric, 15, 156
  lands of, 22
Saint-Samson-sur-Risle, 162
Saint-Wandrille, 56, 57
saints' lives, Breton, 131, 165, 173–6
Salocon, bishop of Dol, 155–6
Salomon, 87, 88, 100, 103, 106, 122
  aid to Frankish rebels, 105
  assists Charles the Bald against Vikings, 107
  campaigns against Vikings in Brittany, 199
  charters of, 117
  compaternity with Charles the Bald, 112
  death, 120
  fidelis of Charles the Bald, 101
  given regalia, 112
  government of, 116–46, *passim*
  grants *plebes* to Redon, 135, 140
  kills Erispoe, 103, 112
  lands of, 130
  and Louis the German, 103–4
  makes peace with Charles the Bald, 105, 107, 112
  requests pallium for see of Dol, 158–9
  titulature, 118; styled *rex*, 112, 114–15
salt panning, 37
San Vincenzo, 70
Savonnières, synod of, 105, 155
Saxons, 18, 61
  settlement in Gaul, 11

scabini, 75, 76
Scandinavians, 2, 143
  see also Danes
Sedulius, *Carmen Paschale*, 171
simony, allegations against Breton bishops, 154–5
Slavs, 2, 61, 65, 68, 73, 86, 94, 143
Smaragdus, *Liber in partibus Donati*, 169, 172
Soissons, synod of, 161
spiritual kinship, 108
Susannus, bishop of Vannes, 155

'territorial principalities', 87
  emergence of Brittany as a territorial principality, 144–6, 186, 188, 205–6
Tertry, battle of, 47
Theuderic, son of Bodic, 21
tithes, 182–3
Tours, metropolitan see of, 17, 151
  jurisdiction over Brittany asserted, 153
  jurisdiction over Brittany rejected, 157–8
  links with Brittany, 163
trade routes, 10, 12, 41, 42
transport services, 136–7
Tréguier, bishopric, 15

Vannes
  bishopric, 15, 155, 180
  county, 18, 74–7, 84; counts of, 125
Verdun, treaty of, 90
Victurius, bishop of Rennes, 40
Vikings, 97, 106
  attack on Nantes, 94
  invasions of Brittany, 176, 198–201
Vilaine, river, as boundary, 18, 35, 144
Virgil, 171, 174, 176
viticulture, 36–7

warfare
  Breton military service, 131–2
  Breton warbands, 29–30
  plunder taken, 132–3
  tactics, 19–20
Warnar, brother of Lambert, 53, 98, 99, 101
Waroch, ruler of Vannes, 18–19, 21
Wernar, bishop of Rennes, 53
Wido, commander of the Breton march, 52, 53, 67–8
Wido, count of Le Mans, 81
  his kinsmen, 92

236

Index

Cambridge studies in medieval life and thought
Fourth series

Title in the series

★ *Also published as a paperback*